HEALING
ISRAEL/PALESTINE

HEALING
ISRAEL/PALESTINE

A PATH TO PEACE AND RECONCILIATION

RABBI MICHAEL LERNER

TIKKUN BOOKS
תיקון

Healing Israel/Palestine: A Path to Peace and Reconciliation
by Rabbi Michael Lerner

Published by
TIKKUN BOOKS
2107 Van Ness Ave., Suite 302
San Francisco, CA 94109 USA
415-575-1200   Fax: 415-575-1432
www.tikkun.org   magazine@tikkun.org

Printed in the United States of America

Library of Congress Cataloging-in-Publication Data:
  Lerner, Michael
  Healing Israel/Palestine: A Path to Peace and Reconciliation

Library of Congress Catalogue Number: 2002116399

ISBN: 0-935933-99-9

Cover: *Shema Yisrael* by Samuel Bak. Courtesy of Pucker Gallery.
www.puckergallery.com

TABLE OF CONTENTS

INTRODUCTION xiii

Chapter One:
PEOPLES OF THE LAND 1
THE ANCIENT WORLD 1
CHRISTIAN OPPRESSION OF THE JEWS 6
JEWISH RESPONSES TO MODERN
EUROPEAN ANTI-SEMITISM 11
THE PALESTINIANS 13

Chapter Two:
ZIONISM COMES TO THE LAND 19
WERE THE ZIONISTS AN EXTENSION OF
WESTERN COLONIALISM? 21
DEALING WITH THE BRITISH 25
CLASH OVER THE LAND 28
WHO HAS A RIGHT TO THE LAND? 31
THE ECONOMIC CLASH 35

Chapter Three:

THE EMERGENCE OF A JEWISH STATE 41
THE HOLOCAUST 46

Chapter Four:

AFTER THE 1948 WAR 61
PALESTINIAN REFUGEES 61
STRUGGLE WITH THE ARAB STATES 1949–2002 71
ARAB STATES 76

Chapter Five:

DIFFICULTIES SUSTAINING PEACE 87
AFTER RABIN 100
BARAK'S "GENEROUS OFFER" 108
ARIEL SHARON 118

Chapter Six:

STRATEGIES FOR HEALING AND TRANSFORMATION 129
THE TIKKUN INITIATIVE FOR MIDDLE EAST PEACE 134

Chapter Seven:

ANSWERS TO THE HARD QUESTIONS 139

Appendix:

RESOURCES FOR PEACE 185

RECOMMENDED READING 185

GETTING INVOLVED:
THE TIKKUN COMMUNITY 186

OTHER ORGANIZATIONS DOING
PEACE AND JUSTICE WORK 190

ISRAELI HUMAN RIGHTS GROUPS
AND ADVOCATES OF PEACE 191

U.S. BASED MIDDLE EAST PEACE ORGANIZATIONS .. 197

Acknowledgments

I wish to thank Jo Ellen Green Kaiser for her editing of an earlier draft of this manuscript, David Van Ness for layout and design, and to Deborah Kory, Liat Weingart, and Eric Zassenhaus for help in various stages of the editing and production of this book.

Publication of this book was made possible by support from the Max and Anna Levinson Foundation, The Catlin Foundation, the Ford Foundation, and by Trish and George Vradenburg.

This book is dedicated to
my granddaughter Ellie Lyla Lerner.

Let her generation continue
the work of *tikkun*.

MODERN
ISRAEL

LEBANON

GOLAN
HEIGHTS
OCCUPIED
AND
ANNEXED
BY ISRAEL

SYRIA

Akko (Acre)   Zefat

Haifa   Tiberias

MEDITERRANEAN
SEA

Nazareth
Afula

Sea of
Galilee
(Lake
Tiberias)

Jordan

Netanya
Petah Tiqwa

Nablus

WEST
BANK

Nahr az Zarqa

Tel Aviv–Jaffa
Ramla   Lod
Rehovot

Ramallah

Jerusalem

GAZA
STRIP

Ashdod

Bethlehem
(Bayt Lahm)

Ashqelon   Hebron
(Al Khalil)

Khan Yunis
Rafah   Gaza

DEAD
SEA

Beersheba

JORDAN

Nizzana

Sinai   NEGEV

Arabah

Paran

EGYPT

Elat

0   50 mi

0   80km

Gulf of Aqaba

INTRODUCTION

Jews did not return to their ancient homeland to oppress the Palestinian people, and Palestinians did not resist the creation of a Jewish state out of hatred of the Jews. In the long history of propaganda battles between Zionists and Palestinians, each side has at times told the story to make it seem as if the other side was consistently doing bad things for bad reasons. In fact, both sides have made and continue to make terrible mistakes. Yet it is also true that both sides can make a reasonable case for their choices, given the perceptions they had of their own situation and of those who opposed them. As long as each side clings to its own story, and is unable to acknowledge what is plausible in the story of the other side, peace will remain a distant hope.

In this book, I offer the Tikkun Community's more balanced perspective of this story—a perspective that seeks to highlight the way that decent human beings on both sides could end up perceiving each other as irreconcilable enemies, and how, within their own frameworks, they became blind to the legitimate needs of the other side and the ways that each side contributed to the current mess.

The first step in the process of healing is to tell the story of how we got where we are in a way that avoids demonization. We need to learn how two groups of human beings, each containing the usual range of people—from loving to hateful, rational to demented, idealistic to self-centered—could end up feeling so angry at each other.

Here's the short version: From 1880 to 1950 the Jewish people jumped from the burning buildings of Europe. We jumped not because we wished to, but because of a legacy of hate that culminated in our being the victims of genocide. And we landed on the backs of Palestinians. The Palestinians and the Arab people of the Middle East were in the midst of a struggle to free themselves from colonial powers, and were afraid of the Zionist dream of the creation of a Jewish state right on top of their own fledgling Palestinian society. They viewed the Jews who came to Palestine not as desperate refugees but as Europeans introducing European cultural assumptions, economic and political arrangements, and thereby extending the dynamics of European domination. So the Arabs in general, and those who lived in Palestine in particular, were unwilling to give Jews a safe place to land.

The Palestinians used acts of violence and the influence of Arab states with the British to deny Jews a refuge. Their insensitivity to the Jewish people and our needs helped create a dynamic in which Jews actually became what the Palestinians had feared: a group that would cause Palestinians to become refugees. Years later, Jews responded in kind when we refused to provide Palestinians with a way to return to *their* homes when it was *we* who had power.

As Jews established our state in our ancient homeland, we hurt many Palestinians and evicted many from their homes. When the Palestinian people cried out, we could not hear their pain—because we believed that the genocide we had barely survived proved that our pain was so much greater. Israelis defended themselves against knowing how much violence they had done to the Palestinian people by telling themselves that the Jewish people have never done anything to the Palestinian people even vaguely comparable to the genocide that was done to us in Europe.

But from the standpoint of the Palestinian people, the pain they suffered at our hands was very real. Yet, because we are still so traumatized by our own pain, we Jews still have difficulty acknowledging that we have caused any pain to the Palestinians, just as Palestinians continue to be unable to acknowledge the pain they caused to the Jewish people when it was we who were the powerless and the homeless. That denial on both sides has made it impossible for each of us to talk honestly to each other, or to find a path to heal the wounds. Neither of us can acknowledge the pain we caused each other, and instead, we continue to inflict new pains that intensify the old. For decades Israel has ruled over the Palestinian people, and as Palestinians responded to that Occupation with armed struggle and acts of terror against Israeli civilians, Israelis have increasingly used methods to secure the Occupation that violate international standards of human rights and make a mockery of the highest values of the Jewish tradition. Both sides act in ways that are cruel and insensitive to the other. This book is written as a contribution to those who wish to break this cycle of pain, mutual indifference, and cruelty.

There is never any one "right way" or "objective approach" to tell an historical story. There is no way to avoid one's own bias and interests. The Tikkun Community's goal is to build a peaceful reconciliation between Israel and Palestine, so we tell the story in a way that emphasizes that both sides have co-created the current mess (helped along by world powers, whose particular interests have frequently led them to intensify rather than ameliorate the Arab-Israeli struggle).

For those who have grown up within the dominant Zionist narrative which is told and retold in the schools and media of the West, the way I tell the story may seem weighted on the side of the Palestinians, because the very act of telling their perspective seems radical and foreign to most people in the West. On the other hand, those who are familiar with the Palestinian experience will likely feel that the way I tell the story is inadequate—a story told by a Jew who doesn't fully understand or know the psychodynamics and realities of Palestinian and Arab history and society. (I hope to find a nationally-known Palestinian historian, theologian, or social change activist who could work with me to write a version of this story that would do fuller justice to the dynamics of Palestinian history. Such a person would have to be as willing to critique Palestinian society as I have been to critique Israeli and Jewish society.) I acknowledge the validity of these critiques. I can understand why both sides would feel uncomfortable with my attempt to tell the story in ways that give the other side's narrative more validity than they have ever considered giving it in the past. And they will be right to point to the limits of my perspective, inevitably shaped as it is by my own background and assumptions.

I am Jewish and the rabbi of Beyt Tikkun synagogue in San Francisco. I grew up in a Zionist household. My father was national vice president of the Zionist Organization of America. As a result, I was able to hear the Zionist account from the inside. David Ben Gurion, Abba Eban, Golda Meir, and Abba Hillel Silver visited our home, and their perceptions of the world shaped the discourse in my family. My parents believed that their own role as political forces inside the Democratic Party (my father was a judge, my mother a political advisor to a U.S. Senator and to several governors) made it possible for them to do more for Israel than they could by making aliyah (moving to Israel).

Israel was not a huge issue in public consciousness during my years at the Jewish Theological Seminary in New York, nor was it a central issue in Jewish thought. I shared with my mentor Abraham Joshua Heschel a clear commitment to Israel's well being, but also an understanding that the central issue on the Jewish agenda must move from "security" and "defense" to spiritual grounding and a relationship to serving God and healing the world.

I waited until I was twenty-two to spend my first extended stay on a kibbutz—and I loved it. Yet I was stunned by the lack of a strong commitment to the socialist ideals that had originally motivated that kibbutz—the ideals of equality and social justice that were supposedly going to be instantiated in the life of the kibbutz and which would, the early kibbutzniks believed, shape the larger Israeli society. It was only when I began to ask about the origins of the kibbutz in the struggle against the Palestinian Arabs that I stumbled upon a terrible truth: the land on which I was working had been owned by Arabs who had been displaced by the Zionist enterprise. In the course of that struggle, many people picked nationalist loyalties over internationalist commitments, which played a powerful role in undermining the larger socialist commitments that had led the founders of this kibbutz to start the enterprise in the first place.

Still, I loved the kibbutz and loved the people I met on it. When the 1967 (Six Days) war happened, I cheered Israel's victories and defended it against some of my friends in the anti-Vietnam war movement who were hostile toward Zionism. I had no hesitation in identifying with the State of Israel.

The next year, in response to the challenges to Israel from lefties on the campus where I was doing my Ph.D. and organizing against the war in Vietnam, I started an organization called Committee for Peace in the Middle East, together with my co-chair Mario Savio. We spoke then for a position that both validated the Zionist enterprise and also validated the claims of Palestinians for their own national self-determination. Even then the response of the Jewish world was outrage at our daring to criticize Israeli policies and the American Jewish institutions that supported it. The Jewish world reacted with fury and outrage at anyone who articulated criticism of Israeli policy toward Palestinians, and it has gotten steadily more repressive toward dissenters. The next year the American Jewish Congress fired the editor of *Judaism* magazine, Stephen Schwartzchild, for the "sin" of having reprinted a section of our founding statement of the Committee for Peace in the Middle East.

As I am writing, this spirit of denial of free speech has gone much further so that today most people refuse to even vaguely criticize Israeli policy unless they are willing to face loss of jobs or promotions, isolation in many parts of the Jewish world, and outright slander and abuse. There are few Jewish families in the United States in which some member has not been accused of being a "self-hating Jew" because she or he raised some questions about Israeli policy. As a rabbi, I find that one of my most difficult tasks is to bring people back into the Jewish world who have come to believe that their own independent moral judgments are so unwelcome that they had to leave their Jewishness altogether in order to maintain their own ethical and spiritual integrity.

Since then, my study of the history of the Israel/Palestine conflict has led me to a deeper understanding of some of the pathologies and evils that have been perpetuated by people on both sides. That understanding has re-enforced my view that both sides have legitimate claims, both sides have legitimate grievances against the other, and both sides have made terrible errors.

In my study of the history of past societies and their conflicts and also in my work as a rabbi and psychotherapist working with couples, families, and individuals, I've seen that most struggles are co-created by the people involved; it is very rare that one party to a struggle is "right" and the other "wrong." In fact, most people who engage in discourse about the Middle East know this. In the rest of their lives they are far more sophisticated, and they look for economic, social, and psychological factors to explain the realities that they encounter. But when it comes to the Middle East, their prejudices require that they suspend their own intellectual and psychological sophistication and use their smarts to weave tales that "prove" that their side is right and the other is wrong. They justify this failure of nerve by saying, "The

different, the people there are unlike other people, so
y what you know to this reality." And what they are really
e people I disagree with there are evil and you are naïve
not ᴡ   ᴇ that."

I have not discovered a bad guy and a good guy in this situation, any
more than I found a good and bad guy in my therapy office. Reality is
much more complex. In fact, overcoming this narrow way of thinking
is one of the necessary preconditions for building lasting peace and
safety for the people of that region.

It is the contention of this book that people on both sides have
caused unnecessary suffering and done terribly evil things, but that
"evil" is not a very useful category to explain why things have happened—if you stick with "evil," you soon end up in despair. And this
book is meant to be a contribution to activism aimed at healing and
transformation, not despair and resignation. Of course, activism cannot be based on naïve optimism—because it will quickly "burn out"
when the world doesn't change overnight. But neither can it be based
on the cynical logic of those who see every fact in light of their deep
belief in Evil as a central aspect of human reality.

We are publishing this book at a time when there are many reasons
for people to despair. But we are committed to the view that *tikkun* (the
Hebrew word for healing and transformation) is always possible, though
rarely in any simple or easy way. A major contribution to that healing
can occur when people begin to tell the story of the Middle East in ways
that validate the truth on both sides, validate the pain and suffering that
both sides have had to endure, and affirm the fundamental decency of
people on both sides of this struggle. I am both pro-Israel and pro-
Palestine, and this book will show you how that can be possible.

Peace can be achieved in the Middle East. The scary news is this: it
depends on ordinary people like you and me to make it happen. One
reason I've written this book is to give you some tools which may help
you be more effective when you talk to others. Please use this book as a
basis for a small study group to read and discuss the issues raised here,
and as a jumping off point for future readings, study, and action. Please
get it into the hands of others, and encourage them to read it as well.
You'll find that many people have never heard a balanced perspective,
never really tried to think themselves into the mind of those with
whom they disagree, and that even if they still disagree after reading

this book, they may have less anger and less willingness to totally dismiss the other side as "evil."

This is *not* meant to be a new work of scholarship, but rather a way to understand the contemporary reality in order to have the tools to change that reality. It is not a book of history, but a framework through which one can understand the history. I don't use footnotes because I don't want to interrupt the flow of the argument to "prove" my historical reading. I make no claims to have unearthed new historical facts. I'm not an academic seeking to use this to prove my credentials. Rather, this book is heavily dependent on the works of many other historians and Middle East scholars, social theorists, political activists, psychologists, poets, novelists and philosophers. In some places I've nearly just summarized the writing of these scholars. I encourage you to read a set of books that are listed at the end and will provide some of the empirical basis for my reading. Don't be surprised if you find sentences that are almost straight out of their work. What is original here is the attempt to provide a way of thinking about the facts that tells both sides in a compassionate way—and that is something that you won't find too often in any of the history books.

I rely particularly on the work of Benny Morris and Samih K. Farsoun, whose writings are sometimes taken into this text without direct attribution. Yet my perspective is also influenced by the writings of or the personal conversations (and sometimes intense arguments) I had with Shulamit Aloni, Yehuda Amichai, Hanan Ashrawi, Shlomo Avineri, Uri Avnery, Mubarak Awad, Aaron Back, Uzi Baram, Mordechai Bar-On, Zygmunt Bauman, Yossi Beilin, David Biale, Azmi Bishara, Tsvi Blanchard, Cherie Brown, Avrum Burg, Yael Dayan, Abba Eban, Bassem Eid, Akiva Eldar, Sidra DeKoven Ezrahi, Yoram Ezrahi, Yaakov Fogelman, Yitzhak Frankenthal, Tom Friedman, Mordecai Gafni, Galia Golan, Yosef Gorny, Yitz Greenberg, David Grossman, Bonna Devora Haberman, Moshe Halbertal, David Hartman, Geoffrey Hartman, Naomi Hazan, Yoram Hazony, Hanan Hever, Arthur Hertzberg, Anat Hoffman, Faisal Husseini, Rashid Khalidi, Baruch Kimmerling, Michael Kleiner, Daoud Kuttab, Irwin Kula, Daniel Landes, Yishayahu Leibowitz, Akiba Lerner, Debora Kohn Lerner, Joseph Lerner, Mark Levine, Ian Lustick, Tzvi Marx, Uri Milstein, David Newman, Micha Odenheimer, Adi Ofir, Wendy Orange, Amos Oz, Ilan Pappe, Pinchas Peli, Shimon Peres, Letty Cottin Pogrebin, Yehoshua

Porath, Yitzhak Rabin, Avi Ravitsky, Amnon Raz, Michael Rosenak, Mordecai Rotenberg, Edward Said, David Saperstein, Yossi Sarid, Uri Savir, Ze'ev Schiff, Jonathan Schorsch, Jerome M. Segal, Tom Segev, Gershon Shafir, Alice Shalvi, Anita Shapira, Stanley Sheinbaum, Avi Shlaim, Uri Simon, Ze'ev Sternhell, Ehud Sprinzak, Shabtai Teveth, Eric Yoffie, Yossi Yonah, David Vital, Michael Walzer, Arthur Waskow, Avi Weiss, A.B. Yehoshua, Oren Yiftachel, and Idith Zertal.

I would be surprised if any of these thinkers really agree with me, and I suspect some (like Morris) would probably be upset that I had used their research to come to different conclusions than they had arrived at. Needless to say these historians and thinkers bear no responsibility for any of my conclusions.

More than any of the reading and thinking I have done, I have learned the most about Israel/Palestine from the thirty-two months I've spent there since 1984—in conversations with Palestinians in the West Bank and Gaza, in interviews with Israeli government leaders (some of which have appeared in TIKKUN Magazine), in the endless meetings of various Israeli peace organizations, in my time visiting West Bank settlements, in study sessions at the Hartman Institute in Jerusalem, and in time I spent studying in yeshivot, davening at Kehilat Yedidya and many other orthodox synagogues in Jerusalem and Tel Aviv, and in the many pleasant but sometimes upsetting Shabbat afternoons spent in the homes of Orthodox Jews and labor Zionist secularists talking about what had happened and what could yet be.

From all my reading and studying and talking, I have learned that there are many perspectives on the same facts, and that many of them make sense. In all humility I offer up the deepest truths that I have been able to learn from the combination of books, study, conversations, first-hand experience, and my training as a psychologist, philosopher and rabbi. I offer my perspective not as "the truth" but as a truth, rooted in the worldview of the prophets of Israel and their teachings as transmitted to me personally by Abraham Joshua Heschel, Zalman Schachter Shalomi, Joachim Prinz, and Emanuel Levinas, and, in secularized form, by the writings of Erich Fromm, Wilhelm Reich, Herbert Marcuse, and Martin Buber.

I am, like everyone else on the planet, a flawed and limited human being. I speak the deepest truths I can access, and I've been blessed with incredible teachers and the opportunity to meet and learn from many wise people. I urge you not to rely on my perspective, but to use your own intelligence, creativity, moral sensitivity, and connection to God or Spirit or whatever transcendent connection you have—and then apply that to the reality of building peace and reconciliation between Israel and Palestine. Go and learn—and then go and make *tikkun*.

One place to start is to join the Tikkun Community. You can do that by going to www.tikkun.org and reading the *Core Vision*, and, if it excites you, joining the organization. However, I want to make clear from the start that this book is directed at a wide audience of people who wish to prepare themselves for discussions and debates about the Middle East, and that it should be used by people in a wide variety of organizational frameworks. My hope is that it will be used in classes and study groups, in synagogues, churches and mosques, in policy circles and in universities, in youth groups and in college dorms, in social change movements and in private non-profits, and in a wide array of social change organizations. There are many groups doing valuable work on the Middle East in addition to the Tikkun Community, and I've listed some of them in the back of this book. There are also study groups in various synagogues and churches which could benefit from this analysis.

The Tikkun Community grew from TIKKUN magazine, which started in 1986 as the voice of liberal and progressive Jews. TIKKUN has since evolved to become the center for those of all religious and spiritual traditions who seek to integrate spiritual depth with social change. The Tikkun Community similarly reaches out to all those who attend to the development of their spiritual lives, whether Jews, Christians, Muslims, Buddhists, Hindus, from other spiritual traditions, or even those who do not believe in God but do believe in a life of spirit.

"*Tikkun*" is a Hebrew word that means "healing" or "transformation." We see our task in the Tikkun Community as the spiritual healing of the planet, a healing which requires both a fundamental transformation of our economic and political lives as well as the development of strong inner lives in each of us (for a deeper explanation of the connection between conventional political change and spiritual healing, you might want to look at my book *Spirit Matters: Global Healing and the Wisdom of the Soul*).

The Tikkun Community seeks a world based on love and caring, generosity and open-heartedness, compassion and celebration of the grandeur of the universe. We are a group of people who have made a commitment to stay connected and support each other as we work, both in our own lives and in our communal efforts, to build a world that fully embodies our highest ideals. We are beginning this work by focusing on a few areas that we know we can change for the better. If you want to know more about the full scope of our project, or would like to join us, you can visit our website at www.tikkun.org, email us at magazine@tikkun.org, or call us at 415-575-1200. Meanwhile, what you are holding in your hands now represents one of the first foci of our attention, the Israel/Palestine struggle—but our larger agenda is also to fight for a New Bottom Line of love and generosity in every part of our world.

—Rabbi Michael Lerner
December 2002

Chapter One:

Peoples of the Land

The Ancient World

From our earliest recorded history, the Jewish people have been the objects of both respect and hatred, admiration and fear. Non-Jewish intellectuals have sometimes praised the Jews for having an advanced concept of God and highly developed legal and moral codes. Jews have often been denigrated, however, by those most closely aligned to the ruling elites. This was particularly true in the ancient world.

It is no wonder that rulers of the ancient world felt threatened by the Jewish people and thus hoped to provoke anger between the Jews and others in their kingdom or empire. Just look at the way Jews have told their own story.

Although the origins of the Jewish people are clouded in historical debate, the Jews emerged into history with a conception of themselves as having been enslaved in Egypt, and as having subsequently broken out of slavery and created a free and self-governing existence for themselves in the area they called Judea and Israel. At a moment in the ancient world when slavery was becoming more and more prominent, the Jews told of the ways they had broken out of slavery.

Elites in the ancient world tended to rule through a combination of brute force and the imposition of various ideologies based on the central theme that existing class distinctions are sanctified by an unchanging natural and sacred order. Whether in the form of ancient myths about the gods who ruled nature, or in the far more sophisticated form proposed by Plato in *The Republic*, elite ideology taught that society was destined to remain divided by class, either by virtue of some inherent feature of each class itself (the ontological nature of human beings) or by will of the gods.

The Jewish story was a living testimony that these myths and ideologies were untrue. Jews had managed to break out of the most degrading position on the class ladder—slavery—and had gone on to run their own society successfully. Most ancient people traced their descent to heroes of the past. Here was a people who identified instead with the most oppressed! If their story was concocted, even more were they to be distrusted—a people who consciously chose to tell this kind of revolutionary story, who insisted that the world could change, that slaves could become rulers!!

The account of this liberation struggle was the main focus of the Torah. In fact, the Torah mandates that one day of the week be set aside as a Sabbath (Shabbat) "in commemoration of the exodus from Egypt." On this day (Saturday), no one can make Jews work; instead, Jews are enjoined to read one section of the liberation story. The very idea that the oppressed could set a limit on their oppression, and that the oppressors would have to kill them before they would work on that day, was itself a revolutionary reform—the first real victory in the class struggle against the oppressors and an enduring, weekly reminder that oppression could be overcome.

Even Judaism's essential concept of God is revolutionary. God described her/himself to Moses as *ehyeh asher ehyeh,* which means "I shall be whom I shall be"—that is, the God of the universe is the Force of what can be. The primary force that rules the universe is the principle of possibility and freedom. Unlike the gods of nature, it is the force of possibility for healing and transformation that rules the universe in the Jewish cosmology, and that ensures the possibility that everything can be changed (including the entire social order of oppression).

This, of course, isn't the only message of the Torah. The Torah is a record of how human beings hear God's voice, and sometimes the voice they hear is not the God of possibility but an angry, vengeful God.

(I detail the struggle between these two voices in my book *Jewish Renewal: A Path to Healing and Transformation*)

One voice validates a despairing view of human beings—in which anger and hatred prevail, rule-breakers are cruelly punished, the Children of Israel will always dwell alone and are directed to conquer the Land of Israel and exterminate all of its inhabitants. The other voice validates a hopeful vision of a world which can be transformed into an embodiment of justice, love, and communal welfare. It calls for radical redistribution of the land every fifty years (the Jubilee), for a Sabbatical Year every seventh year when the land is to lie fallow and debts are eliminated, for a society based on generosity (loaning for interest is forbidden), and for all members of the society to fight against oppression and to "love the Other" (the stranger).

Both voices are there, both identified as the voice of God, and sometimes both are subtly intermixed, because both voices are inside most of us—a voice of hope which leads toward trust and caring for others, and a voice of despair which leads toward rigid boundaries, doing to others what we suspect they might want to do to us, and protecting ourselves from a world we believe to be essentially filled with evil and hatred.

Which of these voices gets to predominate (and hence how we hear God) at any one time in the history of the Jews, or in the history of any other people, depends on how much hope people are feeling at the time. The less hope, the more people gravitate to accounts of the world based on the belief in evil and the certainty that selfishness and ego and the tendency to pass on cruelty will predominate. The more hope, the more people gravitate to accounts of the world that highlight our capacity to break the repetition compulsion (the tendency to act out on others what was done to us) and to focus on the possibilities for transformation in even the most discouraging of circumstances.

There will never be some neutral time, because any set of circumstances, contemporary or historical, can be read from within either of these two frameworks. It is a matter of belief—and those who see the world primarily through the framework of hope are seeing the world through the lens that Jews call God.

I start from this point, from a Judaism that is based in a liberation struggle and embraces the revolutionary belief in God as the Force for transformation and healing. This does not mean, however, that I want to romanticize the realities of Jewish society or Judaism. Alongside the revolutionary ethos, and sometimes even within the very same people who expressed this revolutionary yearning, there remained deep ethical distortions.

How the Jews actually established a Jewish society in the land of Israel is typical of the ethical dilemmas Jewish history raises. According to the Torah account, the Jews ended forty years of wandering in the desert by conquering the land of Canaan and killing the people there. Many contemporary anthropologists tell a different story, (e.g. Norman Gottwald's *The Tribes of Israel* or his more recent *The Politics of Israel*). On their account, there never was a conquest of the land of Israel by outside (presumably Jewish) tribes. Rather, the tribes of Israel were composed of people who had escaped the domination of Egyptian-ruled city-states in the lowlands. They were united by a "Moses group," a tribe of Levites who came from the desert with a tale of once having been slaves and now having been freed. That group united the tribes into a joint struggle against the city-states, and together they were able to create one of the most democratic, decentralized regimes in human history.

It was only with the emergence of a Philistine threat that these decentralized tribes were forced to unite for "national defense," and to allow for a set of kings who could lead them in joint battle against the invaders. But the rule of Saul, David, and Solomon introduced a counter-revolution, subordinating the tribes to a dominating central authority, challenging the revolutionary ideology (because the new Jewish regime embodied the same patterns of class rule and power over others that the tribes had originally rebelled against), and finally splitting of the Jews into a Northern Kingdom of Israel and a Southern Kingdom of Judea.

There is no way to know which of these accounts will ever be firmly established, or if new hypotheses will emerge (at the moment, some people are arguing that there is no solid evidence for the existence of a Jewish presence in the land before the Exile period around 400 BCE). What we know as hard fact is that by some 2300 years ago a group we now call the Jews created religious and cultural institutions in some part of the area we now call Israel/Palestine. We know that some in this group were willing to claim as their own the version of history which celebrates Jewish conquest of Canaan and the annihilation of the residents there, a version you can read in the Book of Joshua. We also know that a group of rabbis and teachers emerged who preached a religion of love and justice and read Torah as a story that portrayed the Jewish people as having been part of a revolutionary transformation from slavery to freedom, a transformation which became the object of hatred and ridicule by others. Both the voice of despair and the voice of hope were already present 2300 years ago.

The sexism and xenophobia built into Torah-based religious practices, the willingness to claim as their own stories of conquering and annihilating the residents of Canaan, the compromises that allowed slavery to persist—all these were part of the reality of ancient Israel. To me it is no surprise that Jews copied some of the most oppressive practices of the societies which surrounded them and in which they had developed as a people. Or that the Torah has some elements of cruelty and proposed genocide of "the Other" that are as insensitive as the blood-lust of other religious traditions that surrounded them in the ancient Near East. What is surprising is not the degree of similarity but the degree of difference, the level of transcendence that one also finds in Torah along with the other voice of cruelty, the voice that calls for a world of love and justice and support for the most oppressed and its explicit challenge to oppressive norms. It was because Jews differed from other people—it was precisely because their dominant story taught them that God made it both wrong and unnecessary to accept reality and subordinate themselves to the logic of imperial regimes or to a world based on injustice and lack of love—that they were a threat to ruling elites. In turn, ruling elites often believed that if they could instill a hatred of Jews in their own peoples before they heard the Jewish message, they might be inoculated to the subversive potential of an encounter with Jews. No wonder, then, that they set out to create hatred between their own peoples and the Jews.

I am not suggesting that Jews were a self-conscious revolutionary vanguard plotting to overthrow empires, an ancient-world version of Che Guevara, Trotsky, or Mao. For the most part, Jews did not consciously say to themselves that their very existence as Jews was aimed at threatening existing systems of domination around the world (although the biblical language of Jews as a chosen people and the prophetic language urging Jews to become a "light unto the nations" contained this element of a world-transforming vanguard). Nor did ruling elites explicitly or consciously articulate their opposition to the Jews in this kind of nineteenth-century language. Yet, as the biblical scroll of Esther makes clear, even in the ancient world Jews understood that their refusal to act in a subordinate way infuriated ruling elites and provoked anti-Semitic attacks.

This confrontational attitude and refusal to play along as an obedient client state eventually led to the Hashmonean rebellion against Greek rule in 165 B.C.E and to a whole series of later rebellions against Roman rule. These uprisings, in turn, led Rome to brutally repress Judaism, forbid the study of Torah, rename the country "Palestine," and eventually destroy the Temple in Jerusalem in 70 C.E. But it was only the massive and militarily futile uprising of Bar Kochba and Rabbi Akiba from 132-135 C.E. that finally provoked the Romans to realize that the Jewish spirit of freedom must be suppressed if the Roman Empire was to survive. Roman imperialism momentarily triumphed, hundreds of thousands of Jews were murdered, and tens of thousands taken as slaves to Rome. Some remained in the land under Roman rule, while many others moved to Babylonia and to other parts of the then known world.

CHRISTIAN OPPRESSION OF THE JEWS

Though many early Christians also practiced Judaism, there were many converts to Christianity who felt antagonism to the Jews. In those early centuries after Jesus' death, many Christians competed with Jews for converts in the Roman empire, and they had great difficulty explaining why the very people who had known this Jewish man from Samaria had either been unimpressed or had at least failed to see him as either "messiah" or "son of God." The elaborate stories of miracles and resurrection made a bigger impression on non-Jews than on most Jews. One way Christians could account for their failure to convince many Jews was to say that the Jews had at one point been chosen, but had lost that status and become outcasts because they had rejected Jesus. They interpreted the Roman's success in destroying the Temple and exiling the Jews as a sign that God had rejected Judaism, which would now be superseded by Christianity. The Jews deserved punishment and denigration, these Christians argued, because they had rejected the messiah.

In the very early years after Jesus' death, this kind of teaching had only limited impact. The Christians were themselves being persecuted, so it did not work well to claim that one could read God's intentions or the objective worth of one's religion by how well they were received by the ruling elites of Roman society. But once the church assumed state power in the fourth century, Christian triumphalism was widely accepted and led to an intensification of the persecution of the Jews. Jewish proselytism was outlawed in 329, and soon thereafter began the demonization of Jews. As Edward Flannery describes it in his classic work, *The Anguish of the Jews: 23 Centuries of Anti-Semitism*, at the close of the third century (before the triumph of Christianity in the Roman world), the Jew "was no more than a special type of unbeliever; at the end of the fourth, [the Jew was] a semi-satanic figure, cursed by God, and marked off by the State." It was this institutionalization of hatred against Jews that would evolve eventually into the possibility and then actuality of the systematic genocide we call the Holocaust.

A full-scale attack on Jews as "inveterate murderers, destroyers" and "lustful, rapacious, greedy, perfidious bandits" whose synagogues were "the house of the devil" and filled with prostitution (the words of St. John Chrysostom, ca. 344-407) helped generate a popular culture of hatred toward Jews that would grow and be sustained by Church teachings for the next fifteen hundred years.

Legal restrictions soon followed. Anti-Jewish legislation adopted by the Church became the law of the land throughout most of what in the next centuries became "Christian Europe." Jewish-Christian marriages were forbidden, except in the case of conversion by the Jewish party. Christians were forbidden to celebrate Passover with Jews. Jewish property rights were restricted. Jews were barred from public functions and from practicing law. Jews were prevented from testifying against a Christian. The Mishnah, and later the entire Talmud, were banned (and in some places burned). Jews were forcibly baptized and their property forcibly expropriated. Eventually, some countries forcibly expelled their Jews. All this under the rule of the Church, and with its full backing.

There were some counter-tendencies. Sometimes a particular bishop or pope would come along with feelings of compassion or at least lower levels of hostility toward Jews. Some felt it important to keep Jews alive as living testimony to the degraded status of those who did not accept Jesus. Others were fundamentally humane people who did not wish to see Jews suffer. But overall, throughout the1500 plus years in which the Church had such a huge influence in shaping the fate of the Jews, the Christian world was permeated by teachings of hatred by just about every branch of the Christian church.

The first really massive slaying of Jews by Christians took place during the Crusades. As tens of thousands of West European Christians mobilized to take back Palestine from the hands of the Muslims who had conquered it, they swept through the Rhineland murdering Jewish communities wherever they could find them. The arrogant and racist attitude toward "the other" that would later manifest in Western colonialism and its reconquest of the Middle East from Arab Muslims in the nineteenth and twentieth centuries found first expression in the attempted destruction of Jews wherever they could be found. The Crusades proved traumatic for both Jews and Muslims, and shaped the historical memory of both peoples in ways that would place the question of "who owns Jerusalem" in the center of their consciousness, sometimes even mixed up with the notion that whoever controlled Jerusalem had proof that God was on their side. It is important to recall that the Crusades were a trauma for Muslims, and put them on alert to the dangers of Westerners trying to control the holy lands of Islam.

Not every outburst of anti-Semitism in Europe was the direct result of some intentional act by Christian leaders. Once anti-Semitism had been deeply ingrained in the culture of European life, it took on a life of its own, and was passed on from parents to children in every generation. Stories and prejudices about Jews became part of "shared wisdom," part of the socialization of people in European societies in much the same way that similar stories about African Americans became the shared legacy among whites in America.

Oppression forced Jews living in the West to band together tightly, to define rigid boundaries around their communities and lifestyles, and to develop compensatory fantasies about being "special" or "chosen" in contrast to non-Jews who were frequently perceived as being unintelligent and morally bankrupt (the latter founded in part on their racist behavior toward Jews). This clannishness and separateness, which was later used by non-Jews as an excuse for anti-Semitism, actually began as a response to Christian oppression— a defensive response to the legal arrangements that prescribed where Jews could live and travel and what Jews could do to make a living. The moment that legal restrictions on Jews were removed after the French Revolution, Jews poured out of the ghettoes and into the mainstream of European life, many attempting to leave behind all of the separateness and clannish behavior.

While medieval Jews erected powerful psychological defenses to protect themselves, the economic and political degradation of their daily lives, coupled with the constant feeling of being rejected and treated as pariahs, predictably generated a deep level of isolation, pain, and humiliation that scarred the Jewish psyche. The fierce barriers Jews erected to prevent social contact with non-Jews, the fantasies of revenge on those who had spilled Jewish blood, and the cultural denigration of the intelligence and moral sensibility of non-Jews were the flip side of this pain.

It was no wonder, then, that Jews rejoiced at the demise of feudal orders that had given official power to Christianity. Jews championed the new capitalist order with its promise of liberty, equality, and fraternity. Finally, Jews imagined, they would be able to participate as equals.

Imagine, then, the deep disappointment and despair that swept the Jewish people when the emancipation of Jews from legal restrictions did not, in fact, have the consequence of eliminating anti-Semitism. The impact of centuries of church-sponsored indoctrination against the Jews had led to a popular anti-Semitism that continued to flourish throughout most of the nineteenth and twentieth centuries. Ruling elites exploited anti-Semitic fantasies and used the Jews as a public target whenever resentment of the existing social order grew to threatening proportions.

Jews took the rap for the distortions in daily life that were rooted in the alienation of capitalist society. To ordinary citizens who had little contact with the real owners of wealth and power but had daily contact with Jews who were disproportionately prominent as the public representatives of "the system" in the courts, schools, welfare bureaucracies, media and the medical system, the Jews appeared to be the ones with real power. It didn't help that when Jews were finally able to compete for these kinds of professional positions (after being banned from them during the feudal period) they often assumed the ideologies and orientations of the ruling elites whom these professions served. Because of this, it wasn't hard for the elites to displace common people's anger onto the Jews.

No wonder, then, that as the hope that capitalism could provide equally for everyone began to disappear in the mid-nineteenth century, ruling elites began to finance anti-Semitic political parties to counter the appeal of socialist movements by deflecting anger away from the system and onto the Jews. The Jews were the group that most consistently opposed "the old order."

But while the new order worked for some, including many Jews, many ordinary citizens and non-Jews felt bereft of the traditional supports that the old order had provided for those most in need. The sense of being part of a community of people treating each other as connected through the dominant religious sensibility, the sharing of resources in the forms of "commons" (areas which were owned in common where farmers could feed their animals), the ethos of everyone having a place (however meager) in the social order—none of these had done much for the Jews during feudalism, but had given something real and valuable to everyone else. So while the Jews seemed unequivocal cheerleaders for undermining the old and replacing it with the new, for undermining communities and replacing them with the rule of the individual, for undermining the regulated feudal and mercantile-trade economy and replacing it with unlimited competition in the marketplace (at which the rest of the population was not equally skilled), there were many others who felt that the new order was hurting them. While some of these non-Jews joined (often Jewishly-led) socialist movements, many others responded to the appeal of "returning to the good old days" that was associated with anti-Semitic nationalist movements.

Imagine the Jews' surprise when they found themselves at the end of the nineteenth century facing the emergence of anti-Semitic parties and movements in European societies that had otherwise seemed to proclaim themselves committed to values of rationalism, science, humanism, and enlightenment. Imagine their surprise when scientific enterprises emerged to demonstrate the racial characteristics and defects of the Jews. All of this came to a head with the Dreyfus Affair in France in the 1890s, in which a Jewish army officer was falsely charged with treason, and what had seemed to be an enlightened French society was suddenly filled with anti-Semitic outbursts. The Jewish people were forced to confront a scary reality: they had been too optimistic in hoping that capitalism and legal equality would bring an end to anti-Semitism.

JEWISH RESPONSES TO MODERN EUROPEAN ANTI-SEMITISM

The reemergence of anti-Semitism in supposedly enlightened European societies in the late nineteenth and early twentieth centuries led many Jews to the conclusion that anti-Semitism was an irreversible aspect of non-Jewish societies, built into the structure of the non-Jewish mind. Jews responded to this conclusion in a variety of ways:

1. Zionists believed that the only solution for the Jews was to recognize that in an historical period when most people were finding their sense of mission and higher purpose through national identity, the Jews would need to have their own Jewish state for self-defense. Zionism became the name of the national liberation struggle of the Jewish people, a struggle based on the assumption that Jews must have the same national rights as every other people. But since those rights could not be exercised in Christian Europe, or Islamic North Africa, many Jews began to turn toward their ancient homeland as the place where this Jewish national destiny could be fulfilled.

2. Some religious Jews tended to see contemporary anti-Semitism as further proof of the degraded status of the non-Jew and of the need to avoid or protect oneself against non-Jewish culture and thought patterns. Thus, the ultra-orthodox built even deeper walls of restrictions around their communities, hoping that the repression of alternatives might protect the core of Judaism from pollution by the non-Jews.

3. The modernizing religious Jews, or "modern Orthodox," made accommodations to the modern world and sought to live and function within it. In sharp counter-distinction to the ultra-orthodox, they increasingly turned to Zionist solutions and articulated the notion that the (mostly secular and anti-religious) Zionist movement was actually a manifestation of God's will working through human beings who did not think of themselves as serving God (a version of Adam Smith's "invisible hand" in a different realm).

4. Assimilationists thought that if Jews converted or at least became as non-Jewish as possible (adopt Western forms of dress, cut our beards, get rid of our skullcaps, straighten our hair, get nose jobs, lower

our voices, be more polite, and adopt Western table manners), we would be safer from anti-Semitism. Assimilationist strategies seemed to have little impact on non-Jews, however. The German Jewish community appeared to be the most highly assimilated in the world, yet Nazis made a conscious effort to find "Jewish blood" that went back several generations. No matter how polite or goyish the individual Jew acted in his or her own life, they still ended up in concentration camps.

5. Internationalists thought the best way to overcome anti-Semitism was for the Jews to reject their national or particularistic identity. Jews should count on solidarity from the international working class, they reasoned, who would soon recognize that their real interests were to oppose every form of national chauvinism and racism.

The internationalists may seem to us today to have hit on the most progressive solution. The problem is that their comrades didn't join them in a true spirit of "equality and fraternity." Though socialists could "prove" that the "objective interest" of the working class was in international solidarity, the working classes of Europe too frequently responded to nationalism and anti-Semitism and passively or actively supported fascist regimes. The Jews inside the labor movement, the socialist movement, and the communist movement failed to make anti-Semitism a central issue of concern in those movements—fearing that doing so would only make them appear self-interested, proving the point of the anti-Semites that the Jews cared only for themselves and not for anyone else. So Jews played down the struggle against anti-Semitism to prove how internationalist they really were, and thus never really attempted a large-scale effort to challenge anti-Semitism within the Left itself.

Imagine the sense of betrayal these Jewish leftists experienced when communist or socialist groups who were involved in resisting the fascists were simultaneously filled with anti-Semitism; when groups of partisans fighting Nazi rule would sometimes reject or turn on Jewish escapees from concentration camps; when the Soviet Union began to discriminate against Jews; and when post-WWII Soviet regimes in Eastern Europe resorted to anti-Semitic purges of their own ranks in order to deflect anti-communist sentiments among the people they were ruling. The silence of the Left around the world in face of all this, and the insistence of Jews on the Left that they couldn't perceive any problem of anti-Semitism in its ranks, convinced many Jews who had once been drawn to liberal and progressive movements to be deeply suspicious of a Left solution to the problem of anti-Semitism. By the early 1950s many former Jewish leftists had turned to Zionism out of disgust at the way they were betrayed by the world communist movement, and many more turned away from the Left in the 1960s when they felt that Jewish concerns were either belittled or ignored by the New Left which championed the needs of other minority groups but were woefully inadequate in speaking to the situation of the Jewish people just a few decades after the genocide of Jews in the 1940s.

THE PALESTINIANS

Jews were not the only inhabitants of ancient Palestine. After the Romans had succeeded in crushing Jewish political independence and the locus of Jewish life moved to Babylonia, the land continued to be worked by peoples who remained there for the ensuing centuries. After repeated conquests by Islamic, Christian, and then Ottoman powers, the peoples of the land decreased in numbers so that by the end of the eighteenth century there were probably fewer than 300,000 people living on the land, including Muslims, Christians, and Jews (a figure that had increased to 500,000 by 1878 and to over 700,000 between 1880 and 1913).

These figures do not reflect the way in which Arabs from all over the Arab world have a very special and long-lasting relationship to the Land of Israel. From the very first days of Islam, and the subsequent Islamic conquest of Palestine, Muslims have treasured Jerusalem as a site of special religious significance. That attachment was not created in response to the Zionist movement or even to the Crusades, but has a long history in Islamic faith. The Al-Aqsa mosque, built atop the place that Jews believe to have been the site of the ancient Temple, is one of the three most sacred spots in Islam, and has been a popular pilgrimage site for centuries. Arab Christians as well had long valued much of ancient Palestine as the Holy Land where Jesus and his disciples had lived and taught. To imagine that these ties were suddenly created in the last hundred years as a way of stifling Jews is to deny a history of Arab attachment to this land that can be easily documented.

The exact lineage of the Palestinian people is murkier. Most of the inhabitants of Palestine in the eighteenth and nineteenth centuries were Arabs. Many of their families had worked the land for hundreds of years; many others had returned to the area in two immigrant waves—one after the invasion and subsequent rule of Palestine by Muhammad Ali's son Ibrahim Pasha, and the second as Western colonial forces started to show greater interest and created new economic opportunities. By the end of the nineteenth century, most people living in the area thought of themselves as Arabs, but not part of a particularly Palestinian nation. That is, they could be called Palestinian because they lived in the area once designated "Palestine" by the Romans, but they did not self-consciously identify themselves as part of something called the "Palestinian people."

It is hard for us to grasp that the idea of a nationality is a new idea. Before the eighteenth century, people thought of themselves as belonging to religious groups or tribes, or they identified themselves as citizens of cities and states, but few thought of themselves as belonging to a nation. This was true of the Jews as well. Before they became enamored of nineteenth century nationalism, most Jews did not identify themselves as part of a people living in Palestine, but as a worldwide religious people whose return to the Holy Land would take place after the Messiah arrived, and not sooner.

Contemporary Jewish national (as opposed to religious) identity was in large part formed by or in reaction to the modern Zionist movement. Before that, for example, Jews in Persia and Jews in Poland may have shared the same prayers and religious festivals, but they otherwise had little in common, had little contact, and showed little concern for each other's political situation. The religious references to "the people of Israel" had little to do with the notion of national identity or self-determination that emerged in the late nineteenth century.

Similarly, the Palestinians thought of themselves as part of a larger Arab nation. It was only through struggle with the Ottoman empire, and then with the subsequent divisions of the Middle East into distinct states by European colonialists, that the people living in Palestine started to define themselves as Palestinian.

Both Jewish and Palestinian nationalism originally emerged for reasons pertaining to the specific historical, cultural, and geographic situations these peoples faced. But once Zionism hit the ground in Palestine, at the earliest stages in the development of the nationalist

From *Before Their Diaspora,* Walid Khalidi, Institute for Palestinian Studies

consciousness of each people, both movements inevitably developed through their mutually formative, often mutually hostile, impact on each other.

Before the arrival of the Zionists, the people who would call themselves Palestinians had lived in peace with their religious divisions, which included the Islamic majority alongside minority Christian and ultra-orthodox Jewish Palestinians. Though subject to a special poll tax under Ottoman rule, Christians and Jews had autonomous authority to run their own family affairs and religious affairs, and their own courts. As the Ottoman empire dissolved, Greek Orthodox Palestinians played an important social role, as local Christians created hospitals, schools and orphanages while affirming their connection with the Arab world in general and the Palestinian people in particular. At the same time, a popular nationalist movement began to spring up which emphasized Palestinian consciousness as a common thread that transcended specific religious traditions. A revival of Arabic language and literacy

became a weapon of resistance to Ottoman Turkish ways, and intensified Palestinian identity.

Yet it was only after the arrival of a new breed of Jew, no longer waiting for the Messiah but intent on recreating a national homeland for
Jews around the world in Palestine, that Palestinians began to exhibit a
special awareness, and then a hostility, toward Jews (who had previously accepted their political powerlessness with docility and disinter-
est). At first Palestinian hostility was confined specifically to Zionist
Jews, and did not in the early decades of the Zionist enterprise poison
long-established relationships between the religious Jewish communities, which had existed in Palestine for many generations, and
Palestinian Arabs.

The hostility that did emerge toward Jewish newcomers was in part
a product of a larger resistance Palestinians felt toward European societies and their ways, which had been encroaching on Palestine for
much of the nineteenth century. In previous centuries, most
Palestinians were peasants "organized in patrilineal clans, surviving by
farming small plots of land, and living by norms, custom and values
anchored in their Islamic civilization" (Samih K. Farsoun with
Christina E. Zacharia, *Palestine and the Palestinians*, Westview Press,
1997). The clans, or *hamulas,* gave life stability and safety, protecting
the individual and kin, and providing access to land. The hamula
chiefs, or *shayks*, were responsible for collecting taxes for the Ottoman
authorities, who in turn appointed shayks and often helped foster competition between them.

It was a combination of local economic development (citrus and
soap, for example), tourism from Europe, and Ottoman centralization
and modernization policies that led to growing trade with Europe, a
trade that involved exchanging Arab agricultural commodities for
European manufactured goods. Europeans began to settle in Palestine,
and the Catholic population (both Eastern and Western) swelled. As
the Ottoman Empire declined in power, European states began to claim
special rights in the Middle East as "protectors" of the European populations that were living there.

The process of undermining local economies had already begun
before Zionist immigration became a factor. Nablus merchants played
an important role in the monetization of the economy, and moneylending led to massive indebtedness throughout the rural population.

Again Forsoun and Zahacharia paint the picture for us: "By the second half of the [nineteenth] century, a growing number of peasants lost their land and became sharecroppers and tenant farmers on land that their ancestors had tilled for centuries.... Usurious merchants transformed themselves into large landlords" and a growing stratification produced both landless and rich peasants. By the last half of the nineteenth century there was a marked decline in small and medium sized properties, a rise in huge estates, and an increase in land prices.

The decline of collective village work led many Palestinian peasants (*fellahin*) to seek work as wage laborers, either as free laborers in the fields or in unskilled construction jobs in the towns. In the towns a new class structure was emerging, comprised of a respected nobility tracing their roots to the days of Islamic conquest in the seventh century, a new commercial bourgeoisie (often Christian Palestinians who were favored by European powers), and Islamic merchants, artisans and a nascent working class.

From the standpoint of Palestinians, the Jews who began to arrive in Palestine at the end of the nineteenth and beginning of the twentieth centuries seemed to be part of the major changes in ordinary life brought on largely by European colonialism and trade. Whereas Palestinian Jews (Sephardim, mainly from North Africa and Mizrachim, mainly from Iraq and Iran, though these terms are sometimes used interchangeably to refer to all Jews coming from Africa or Asia) were well accepted by Palestinian society, and tended to be seen as part of their cultural landscape (in part because these Jews accepted their lesser status in the political hierarchy of the country), Ashkenazic Jews—primarily from Eastern and Central Europe, but also France, England and Germany (some with backgrounds in European imperial and colonial enterprises)—brought with them the culture of the West and the economic and political assumptions that went with it. So when the Ashkenazic Jewish population jumped dramatically between 1882 and 1914, so too did the concerns of Palestinians that these people were becoming the vanguard of European penetration of their land.

The decline of Palestine and the reduction of the fellahin to penury and sharecropping as well as the overall degeneration of the land began considerably before the resettlement of Palestine by the Zionists. It was accelerated by Jewish resettlement, a fact that Arab elites capitalized on to deflect resentment that might have otherwise been directed at them toward Jews. The Jews thus became the embodiment for many Palestinians of the worst impacts of the global capitalist market, and opposition to their presence in Palestine was a way of expressing (albeit irrationally) the anger that people were feeling at the changes that the new global order was imposing. No surprise, then, that many Palestinians were opposed to and deeply resented the increased presence of Jews in Palestine.

That opposition existed even before the Zionist movement's founding conferences, but it greatly increased after the Zionist movement declared its intention to form a home for the Jewish people in Palestine.

Chapter Two:

ZIONISM COMES TO THE LAND

Ever since the destruction of the Temple by the Romans (70 C.E.) and the subsequent defeat of the Bar Kokhba Rebellion in 135 C.E. Jews have perceived themselves in Exile from their homeland. Before the founding of the State of Israel, observant Jews would turn three times a day toward Jerusalem and pray for God's help in returning to Zion. After every meal they would call for the rebuilding of Jerusalem and pray for God to "lift the bonds of our oppression from our necks and lead us speedily back to our land." "Next year in Jerusalem" was so deeply inscribed in Jewish consciousness that it is amazing that Jews in larger numbers did not seek to return.

Religious interpretations of the Exile insisted that the time of return was God's will, and that it would be violating God's will to return to Zion until the Messiah arrived. Thus most religious Jews did not make any actual efforts to return to Zion.

As always, there were counter-tendencies. In Europe, both the followers of the Vilna Gaon and leaders of the early Hasidic movement sent some of their followers to live in Israel as part of a millennial messianic awakening that periodically reverberated through Jewish society in the centuries before the creation of Zionism. Some of these immigrants, particularly the less spiritually oriented Mitnagdim, developed an articulate ideology of redemption through natural, evolutionary means as opposed to miraculous means, of which the return to the Land of Israel was a key part.

We must also remember that a number of Jews continued to live in the Land even during the Exilic period. Crucial works of Jewish religious thought and law such as the *Schulchan Aruch*, the *Lurianic Kabbalah*, and the *Shnei Luchot Habrit* were composed in the Land of Israel. Yet the majority of Jews lived outside of the Land, and most of these held living in Israel more as an ideal than as a genuine realistic or religiously acceptable choice for the Jewish majority.

It took a powerful break from this traditional Jewish understanding of the Holy Land to take seriously the call of the secular nationalism that fueled the early Zionists. Because Israel had become a religious ideal more than a geographic location for a state, the religious traditionalists, and even more so the fundamentalists, wanted nothing to do with the Zionist movement, and saw it as "a rebellion against God" (the Messiah had not yet arrived, after all). Yet Zionism spoke to a yearning that had persisted in Jewish consciousness for two thousand years—a desire to return to the homeland and live a normal life as a people with a land.

Zionism took this yearning and gave it concrete political expression. The Zionists were overwhelmingly secular, and the dominant forces in the early Zionist movement were socialists who hoped to create a socialist reality in the context of a Jewish state. They were particularly hostile to what they saw as the passivity and powerlessness in Jewish life in the Diaspora, believing that Jews would only be able to achieve real dignity and empowerment when they transferred their messianic yearnings from the realm of religious mysticism to the realm of practical politics.

While it is probably true that Zionists exaggerated the degree of Jewish powerlessness throughout the centuries of Diaspora, as David Biale argues in his *Power and Powerlessness in Jewish History,* for many Jews the Zionist notion of creating a Jewish state in the land of their ancestors provided their first experience of healthy self-affirmation. Living in a larger society that increasingly demeaned Jews, Jews had tended to adopt a theology of self-blame. Religious Jews recited a prayer that proclaimed: "Because of our sins we were exiled from our land" while Jewish communists and socialists engaged in self-denigration and the forthright renunciation of Jewish interests. In this environment, Zionism was an affirmation that "Jewish is beautiful." It thus had the

Jewish refugees escaping death camps in Europe arrive in the Holy Land.
Courtesy of the Judah L. Magnes Museum.

same kind of appeal that Black nationalism had for African Americans or feminism had for women—it insisted that an oppressed group did not deserve its oppression.

WERE THE ZIONISTS AN EXTENSION OF WESTERN COLONIALISM?

Because the Zionists were overwhelmingly Europeans who settled a distant land based on nationalist claims and an aura of Western superiority, Zionism has sometimes been understood as an extension of Western colonialism. Palestinian Arabs, with the Crusades fresh in their historical memory (which may seem strange to Americans with their lack of historical memory, but not at all to Jews and Muslims whose lives are filled with rituals whose goal is to keep the past ever fresh), not surprisingly regarded the waves of Jewish immigration as a colonial phenomenon.

Yet, the claim that Jews were coming to Palestine to colonize it on behalf of Western colonial powers makes little sense once one understands the history of the Jews. The Jews were not an integrated and accepted element in colonial Europe. What brought most Jews to

Zionism was not a desire to extend European power and culture but the promise that Zionism could be a way to protect themselves against the oppression of Europe. In fact, the vast majority of Jews who actually came to Palestine in the early waves of immigration (aliyot) came from Eastern Europe, fleeing oppression and despairing of ever changing the deeply ingrained anti-Semitism of the Christian world. While the overwhelming majority of those who fled Eastern Europe sought refuge in the West (many in the United States), those who went to Palestine were the most idealistic, the most hopeful about the possibility of establishing a just and even socialist society, the most committed to a world of justice and peace. Their motivation was to escape centuries of oppression, not to overpower or exploit some other group.

The claim that Zionism is a movement of white people against people of color is similarly groundless. If we mean by "white" some description of skin color, then it is important to note that the vast majority of Jews who eventually came to Palestine were racially similar to the Palestinian people.

Nor does this characterization make sense if we mean by these terms that white people are the primary beneficiaries of the West, and peoples of color are those who have been victimized by Western powers. Given this definition, Jews are not white. For most of the past two thousand years, Jews have been the primary victims of Western colonialism, first as it took form in Hellenistic and then Roman imperialism, later as it manifested in the Church and in regimes influenced by the Church, and finally by the great nationalist forces of Europe, the overwhelming majority of which were explicitly anti-Semitic.

It was only in the second half of the twentieth century, after Europeans had managed to murder millions of Jews, that Western genocidal attitudes toward Jews were put on hold and Jews were allowed to succeed in the class struggle of Western society and reach positions of real power in the corporate and political world. But this is a very recent phenomenon that has little to do with the historical circumstances that led Jews to seek refuge in their ancient homeland. When Zionism conducted its struggle for a national homeland in Palestine, the Jewish people were an oppressed minority living in a largely hostile European environment.

Zionism was, however, a complex phenomenon, and both the European colonialist powers and the Zionist leaders had powerful political reasons to associate Zionism with Western colonialism. To understand Palestinian anger at the Jewish refugees fleeing Europe, we must recognize that many European Jews did, in fact, have contemptuous attitudes toward non-Jews (a contempt rooted in the morally abhorrent way that non-Jews had treated us), that was, unfortunately, easily transformed into racism when European Jews moved to a land where there was a group even lower on the social totem poll than they (namely, colonized Arabs).

Some European Zionist leaders sought to exploit anti-Arab racism of the European nations to gain support for the Zionist cause. The tragic reality of racism is that often victims of racism will join members of the dominant culture in bashing other victims of racism in order to advance their own status (this happens regularly in America, where minority groups will sometimes seek to get a leg up over other minority groups by identifying with the elites who run the corporate economy rather than with their potential allies in other oppressed groups). And in the course of the 20th century, both Jews and Arabs at times jockeyed for position by playing up to the English colonialists and other European colonial forces.

Some European Jews explicitly supported the Western imperial worldview, sharing with Western Christians an arrogant attitude toward Arabs and Muslims. This was best exemplified by the early Zionist claim that Eretz Yisrael, the Land of Israel, was "a land without a people for a people without a land." To Western minds, the native inhabitants were literally invisible, or, if their physical presence could not be ignored, their cohesion and identity as a people was.

Not all European Jews held these beliefs. The much beloved Jewish writer Ahad Ha'am, who was later known as a "cultural Zionist," may have shocked many Zionists when he wrote in 1891, after a visit to Palestine: "We abroad are used to believing that eretz ysrael is now almost totally desolate, a desert that is not sowed.... But in truth that is not the case. Throughout the country it is difficult to find fields that are not sowed. Only sand dunes and stony mountains ... are not cultivated."

Some Zionist leaders like Yitzhak Elezari Volkani, the founder of Zionist agronomy, were able to acknowledge that in many ways "traditional" Palestinian agricultural techniques were superior to "modern Zionist techniques." But most European and American Zionist enthusiasts were unable to see the strengths of this indigenous people, and instead continued to describe the land as empty of inhabitants, and to refuse to acknowledge the people who lived there.

According to Israeli historian Benny Morris, "the Arabs were generally seen by the *olim* (Jewish immigrants to Israel) as primitive, dishonest, fatalistic, lazy, savage—much as European colonists viewed the natives elsewhere in Asia or Africa." Many agreed with the Zionist activist Moshe Smilansky who by 1914 saw Palestinians "as a semi-savage people, which has extremely primitive concepts. And this is his nature: If he senses in you power—he will submit and will hide his hatred for you. And if he senses weakness—he will dominate you…. [They have the tendency] to lie, to cheat, to harbor grave suspicions and to tell tales … and a hidden hatred for the Jews" (quoted in Benjamin Morris' *Righteous Victims*).

These are perceptions of the Other that are near universal. You can read the same account, with only slight variations, by Europeans describing the lives of Jews of the shtetl, by American colonists of the lives of the Africans they enslaved or of Indians they exterminated, by Germans of Poles, by Spanish conquistadors of the civilizations they snuffed out, by Christians describing the people they forcibly converted to Christianity, or by Muslims of some of the populations they conquered.

The humanity of the Other remains invisible to those who imagine themselves on a higher or more civilized plane of existence, and it is that very perception which can legitimate acts of oppression.

On the other hand, we should distinguish between West European Zionists who had attempted to assimilate into the West and had assumed many of the Occidentalist attitudes toward native peoples, and the vast majority of Zionists who were from Eastern Europe and whose feelings toward Palestinians may have been based on a general discounting of non-Jews that had been developed throughout Jewish culture in the Diaspora and then brought to Palestine with the first major waves of immigration (particularly the one called Aliyah Bet).

The tendency toward "goyim bashing" was, in much of Jewish life, a defense against the dominant cultures in which Jews lived, cultures which not only demeaned Jews but also raped, robbed and murdered them. Jews used concepts like "chosenness" and jokes about the non-Jew to build up their own self-esteem and give themselves a cushion against feelings of bitterness and despair that might otherwise have colored their lives. Yet the meaning of these defenses against oppression shifted dramatically when brought into a new situation in which it was they who had many advantages that the Palestinian peasants lacked, not the least of which was literacy, ideological sophistication, and a sense of being connected to people all around the world who cared about their fate.

To be the victims of arrogance in one context does not insulate and sometimes may even encourage one to be the perpetrator of arrogance in another context. East European Jews who had been treated with little respect were often dismissive and arrogant toward Arabs and the Arab culture they encountered in the Holy Land. That attitude would soon extend to Jews who came from Arab lands (Sephardim and Mizrachim) who were perceived to be culturally backward by East European Jewish settlers. So it appeared to Ahad Ha'am, who wrote that the Zionist colonists "behave toward the Arabs with hostility and cruelty, trespass without justification, beat them shamefully without sufficient cause, and then boast about it."

In this circumstance it was not so surprising that Palestinian Arabs should develop an early antagonism toward these newcomers who did not speak Arabic, showed little interest in getting to know Arab culture, had little respect for the religion or the other institutions of Arab society (most of the early Jewish immigrants were socialists and atheists), and were ignorant of local customs (e.g. allowing local shepherds access to common pastureland). Nor was it hard to understand why Palestinians might perceive these attitudes as reflecting a kind of arrogance very similar to the arrogance of non-Jewish colonialists, despite the difference in origin.

DEALING WITH THE BRITISH

European colonialists encouraged European Jews' identification with European culture by giving Jews and Christians in African and Asian colonies some advantages over other native peoples, thereby creating antagonism between what otherwise would have been equally non-colonial minorities. The British, who would soon become the imperial masters of Israel/Palestine, were particularly skilled in using this "divide and conquer" technique.

Zionist leaders also had their reasons for associating themselves with colonialism. Theodore Herzl and Chaim Weizmann used the arguments of Western imperialism to convince the major colonial powers that a

Jewish state could be in their interests. For example, Herzl contended that a Jewish state would be "an outpost of civilization against the barbarism of the desert," and went so far at one point as to advocate the transfer of the indigenous inhabitants out of the country. We know that Herzl did not identify as closely with Western imperialism as quotes like this would indicate because he was simultaneously pleading his cause to the Ottoman Empire, using language drawn from Ottoman ideology.

Once the Zionists felt their goal was legitimate, they were not averse to trying to play power politics with whoever had power. In this sense they were "realists."

Nor was the attempt to make deals with colonial powers something unique to the Zionist movement. Every other national liberation movement has at one point or another formed alliances with one set of colonial powers to defeat another set. George Washington, Ho Chi Minh, Mahatma Gandhi, Nelson Mandela, Fidel Castro and many others were willing to play to the interests of forces whose long-term agenda was antithetical to their own goals, but who in the short run might help them advance their national interests

A national liberation movement does not automatically become an imperialist or colonialist venture just because it seeks support from imperial or colonial forces, not even if it does in fact advance the interests of that larger power. The African National Congress worked with and sought the aid of the communist party and of the Soviet Union, but the ANC was far more than a tool of the communists. It aided the Zionists to align with various colonial forces, including at times the British and more recently the United States, but the Zionist movement was far more than a tool of those from whom it sought aid.

The basic reality of the Zionist movement is that it grew out of Jewish despair at European Jews' inability to normalize their existence in Europe. Zionism began as a national liberation movement by a people who desperately wanted to move from a condition of homelessness and statelessness to a condition of being like other peoples with a state of their own in their national homeland.

Millions of Jews in the late nineteenth and early twentieth centuries were living in conditions of insecurity and threat, and these millions were all candidates to make aliyah to the land of Israel. The more those threats became overt—first in Western and Central Europe, then in Arab lands (from which hundreds of thousands of Jews fled in the period from 1948-1967) and finally in Ethiopia and the Soviet Union—the more the Zionists would need land to resettle Jewish refugees. No wonder, then, that the Zionists were always reluctant to define the borders of the state they desired—they knew that their borders would have to expand continually to meet the increased need for refuge. This is a very different kind of dynamic than a colonialism which expands in order to increase the wealth of some colonial mother country. Indeed, it was precisely because they acted out of a feeling of despair, fear, and weakness, rather than out of a belief in their overwhelming superiority and strength, that Zionists rarely understood how they could be perceived as colonialists by the native population of Palestine. Zionists could not see how their attempts to make deals with colonial powers could be taken as anything more than the requisites of survival imposed on an oppressed people.

Perhaps if the Zionists had been lousy dealmakers, Palestinians would not have been so worried. But the Zionists were great dealmakers, largely because their efforts played into the global strategies of the colonial powers. The Zionists' greatest success in this kind of deal-making came toward the end of World War I when they were able to gain the support of British Prime Minister David Lloyd George. Dedicated to overthrowing the Ottoman Empire and securing British control over the Suez Canal, the British planned on becoming the dominant player in the Middle East after the War. Lloyd George believed that a Jewish colony in Palestine would be helpful in advancing British imperial interests in the area.

A small part of this calculation included the belief among some in the British government that Jews in the United States (which had not yet entered the fray) were ambivalent about the War, but might become more supportive if they believed it would help the Zionist cause.

On November 2, 1917, the British Foreign Secretary Lord Balfour sent the following statement to Lord Lionel Walter Rothschild, the head of the Zionist movement in England: "His Majesty's Government views with favor the establishment in Palestine of a national home for the Jewish people and will use their best endeavors to facilitate the achievement of this object, it being clearly understood that nothing shall be done which may prejudice the civil and religious rights of existing non-Jewish communities in Palestine or the rights and political status enjoyed by Jews in any other country."

The Balfour Declaration gave important international legitimacy to the Zionist movement. Its use of the words "national home" was understood both by the British and by the Zionists to be a way of suggesting that the Jews would have a state of their own in their ancient homeland. Because of its clear and strong language in favor of a Jewish "national home," the Balfour Declaration is often cited as the legal basis for the Israel state.

From the standpoint of the Arabs, however, the Balfour Declaration was just one of many pronouncements by an invading colonial power, having no legitimacy beyond the practical fact that Britain had managed to conquer the land of Palestine by defeating the Ottoman Empire.

What concerned the Palestinians was that the Balfour declaration provided the first support outside of a small group of Zionists for a new political reality in the Arab world: a Jewish state carved out of what Arabs perceived to be their land. Here was a double land grab—a claim on Palestine by the British for the Jews with Palestinian Arabs left as little more than a footnote. Under the sponsorship of this major Western imperial power, the little group of Zionists moved from being a nuisance to being seen as a real threat. In that context, Arabs began to feel hostility not only toward the newly arriving Jews, but even toward the religious Jews with whom they had previously lived in peace but who were now welcoming other Jews into the land.

Palestinian concern about growing Jewish power was not pure paranoia. During a period which saw millions of Jews fleeing waves of anti-Semitism that were convulsing Europe and Russia between 1880-1920, it is clear that some of the Zionist leadership believed that the only real safety for their persecuted people would come through political control of the land of Palestine. Thus, for example, Meir Dizengoff, the first mayor of Tel Aviv, imagined creating a "state within a state" in Jaffa before the Jewish town was established, while Zionist leader Arthur Ruppin wrote in his diaries that the goal of Tel Aviv was to "conquer Jaffa economically." As it would turn out, this economic conquest of the land had at least as much significance as the political conquest to come.

CLASH OVER THE LAND

Though officially Zionists talked about a land without a people for a people without a land, in fact Palestine was densely populated and intensively cultivated except for some swampy areas, so the Zionists found that they would have to purchase land. The Jewish National Fund (JNF or Keren Kayemet LeYisrael) and the Keren Hayesod purchased land in the name of the entire Jewish people which was then restricted for exclusive Jewish use. This exclusivist policy was not one democratically endorsed by the Jewish people, but rather pursued by those who supported this particular project and donated monies on its behalf.

Much of this land was purchased from absentee landlords who lived in Beirut, Cairo, Damascus, and Baghdad, although some of it was purchased from landlords living in Palestine, and a smaller percentage from Palestinian peasants. Land purchased by the JNF often involved Palestinian villages or "commons" lands that had been used for generations by Palestinian families. The land was withdrawn from Palestinian use, and the people who lived on it were often forced to move and look for work in an urban economy in which Jewish-only economic institutions were making it hard for Palestinians to find employment.

The process of peasant displacement from the land was not initiated by Jewish immigration or Jewish purchase of the land, but was a universal phenomenon of the growing emergence of a world capitalist system. In fact, these dynamics, which had shaped the British industrial revolution back in the eighteenth century, had reached Palestine by the mid-nineteenth century and increased in the twentieth. But JNF land purchases greatly accelerated the process. Arab landlords and their political agents did not waste time redirecting peasant anger at the unfair class structure of the emerging capitalist economy towards property-buying Jews. Nor was this totally without foundation, because it was in fact Jews acting as Jews, in the name of the Jewish people, and not simply as individual capitalists, who were doing a significant part of the expropriation of the Palestinian peasantry in the twentieth century.

Imagine yourself living in a village whose agricultural lands have been worked for generations by your family and the families of your small community. Then one day someone arrives to tell you that he holds a piece of paper that indicates that he has bought all the land of your village and that you must move. To where? How will you and your family make a living? The land has been bought by "the Jewish people" and it has been bought from some absentee landlord whom you've never seen and maybe never even heard about. And you hear that this is happening to others around your country. The Jewish people are throwing you off your land and putting your family and the families of many many others into crisis. How would you feel?

And what would you think if not too long afterwards a group of Jews who speak no Arabic arrive on your land, telling you that they are "socialists" who are building a new world? They are building collective farms—kibbutzim—and in these kibbutzim they are going to experiment with shared ownership, raising children collectively, and developing a new consciousness for Jews who had previously never been allowed in European societies to own or work the land. But you can't join because you are an Arab. These socialists have no interest in your plight or your well-being. And when you express anger or rage at what is happening to you, they respond by calling your feelings "anti-Semitism," which they've known for hundreds of years from all non-Jews so they are not surprised that you are feeling it too. Your anger is discounted and dismissed as nothing more than an irrational holdover of prejudices that these "progressive" people don't have to deal with— except as pathology which they can defend themselves against by forming local defense militia (they called it "the Haganah" or Defense project of the kibbutzim). If some of your friends start getting involved in acts of terror against those who are taking your land, might you "understand" their outrage? Might you even wish that you could participate in some action to stop these people from coming and displacing your fellow Arab Palestinians? Might you even give credibility to anti-Semitic stories being told in Europe about Jews as being insensitive, selfish, and out for themselves?

Well, if you would do any of these things, you'd be morally wrong. I don't mean that Palestinians didn't have a right to feel wronged by the behavior of some of the Jews, but anti-Jewish violence and racism are not appropriate responses to economic exclusion and feelings of threat some Arabs were experiencing as the Jewish presence in Palestine grew (remember that we are talking about a time when the Jews were the minority and had no political power over Arab society). Nor are anti-Semitic or racist attempts to demean a whole people for the actions of a few (even if those actions are done "in the name of that people"). This way of blanketly blaming another entire people for some offensive behaviors of some of them leads people to blame all African Americans for the criminal activities of some, or blame all Muslims for the Bin

Laden/Al Queda acts of violence, or blame all Arabs or all Palestinians for the acts of violence by Hamas. They can be reasonably held accountable only to the extent that they could have known about the acts in question and had plausible (democratic) mechanisms to stop them. Palestinians would have been far more successful, and far closer to a moral course, had they sought a path of peace and mutual cooperation with the Zionists, something that would in fact have been possible for the first forty years of Jewish settlement up until 1920 and maybe even up until 1929.

Who Has a Right to the Land?

Jewish land acquisition was perceived by Palestinians as a threat. Shouldn't Jews have been more sensitive to this and known that they were taking over the land that "by right" belonged to Palestinians?

Not so fast!!

Jewish land purchase was based on the same market assumptions that were being used by nearly everyone: "If I buy the land, I have a right to it, and I do not have a responsibility to worry about the well-being of those who previously were tenants on the land and working it, but who did not personally own a piece of paper that gave them 'the right' to dispose of that land in the way that they wished."

Imagine that you had bought some land and the property on it, say a house and a barn, and then had been told that the people to whom the land had been rented in the past did not recognize the validity of your purchase. The government recognized your purchase, the person you bought it from recognized it, but the tenants didn't. Well, if you had no other place to live, after a while you might think about forcing those people off the land so that you could live there and work the land. Now suppose that the people forced off began to steal things from the land you purchased, or kill your livestock, or even kill some of the people in your community who are working the land. Might you not be inclined to call in the local police? And if the police were not functioning, perhaps because they didn't really care much about your needs because you were Jewish and they didn't like Jews, or because they were corrupt and taking bribes from whomever gave them the largest, or because they were incompetent and didn't really want to stick their necks out and get in between you and those feuding against you, might you not be inclined to create your own defense forces to protect your-self (which is what the Jewish settlers did when they created the Hagganah)? The focus on the legitimacy of buying land or not is becoming less relevant with time, as there is considerable evidence that the amount of land actually purchased by Zionists before 1948 has been vastly overestimated, giving the impression that the Zionists sim-ply bought their way into a Jewish state. This whole argument may be moot if we consider that by 1947, Jews only owned 1,734,000 dunums or 1,734 square km. of land—only 6.6% of pre-1948 Palestine. So the violence with which they were met cannot be explained away as a response to another people being dispossessed—because that had not happened—and yet by 1948 there had already been more than 20 years of violence against the Jewish settlers.

"Well," you might argue, "the Palestinians could foresee what would happen if the Jews were allowed to come without restraint—the Palestinian people would lose their land." But it could equally be argued that this was a self-fulfilling prophecy, and that a more open and gen-erous reception to Jewish immigrants, coupled with plans for how to include them in a new binational state and take seriously their need to help their families find a place of safety to live, might have produced a very different outcome.

My point, of course, is to show that both sides had a story to tell that seemed perfectly understandable and reasonable within the context of their own assumptions, and that neither had to be evil or racist or colo-nialist in order to think that what they were doing and how they were responding to the other made perfect sense.

We need to understand the whole context of capitalist society and its assumptions as it increasingly managed to turn every aspect of life into commodities that could be bought or sold. In the context of a global-ized capitalist society, market assumptions become dominant, and they enter into the consciousness of everyone. This was already happening in Arab society before the Jews arrived. Some Arabs were using their capital to buy land and were throwing villagers off the land before the Jews became a significant factor. But this was a minor phenomenon because the absentee owners needed people to farm the land in order to make any money. It was only when Jews offered inflated prices for the land that it became profitable for the landlords to sell the land to the Jews and thereby empower them to evict the Arab farmers.

So, if you want to argue within the context of an international capitalist society, the Jews who bought land were acting reasonably and those who used violence against them were not.

"But," you might object, "why should we allow the international capitalist system and its way of making land transferable into the arbiter. Are their not higher standards that give people rights to land? If they worked the land, why should it not be theirs? Isn't the conquest of Palestine by the Jews just like other attempts to throw indigenous people off their land by a new colonial group?"

Now, if you want to make an argument about rights to land being based on who worked the land, then lets look at the larger historical context. The original owners of the land of Palestine that you think of as "indigenous" owned it because someone had conquered the land from people living there previously and had devised a system of ownership and given some of it to some people and not to others. Ottoman, and before it Muslim, ownership of the land of Palestine was based on military conquest of the land from those who owned it previously, and their ownership derived from Roman and previously Greek conquest of the land from the Jews. And Jewish ownership derived from conquest from someone else, and so on, into the unknowable past. Jews were one of the indigenous groups whose previous working of the land gave them claims that were just as legitimate as every other group who had used force and violence to take it from some previous group. And that, by the way, is where all ownership is really rooted: in force and violence which is forgotten in subsequent generations.

Once we recognize that ownership of land is itself a questionable concept and that it is largely based on conquest and domination of one group over another, where do we go? Some people avoid discussing these issues at all on the grounds that we can't critique anyone's ownership of anything, because the moral foundations of ownership are so weak that all we can rely upon is the legitimacy of current arrangements. If we don't want to revert to a "war of all against all," they argue, then we have to accept the current distribution of land as legitimate and operate within the context of the actually existing power arrangements of the modern world. Within that kind of context, and using those standards, Jews who bought land in Palestine were operating by the same laws as everyone else and could not be faulted for acting immorally, and Palestinians who resisted the Jews coming and claiming the land that they had bought through the marketplace had no right to do so.

The Tikkun Community, whose roots are in spiritual and prophetic traditions, has a different take entirely on the very notion of ownership. In Torah, for example, God warns the people not to get excessively connected to what they have acquired through the marketplace. So every fifty years, Torah tells us, society should revert to its original (roughly equal) distribution of land, wiping out all subsequent market transactions. To underscore why the land must revert to this equal distribution, the Torah challenges any notion of private property, attributing to God the following statement, "The whole earth is Mine." Given that view, land can be held privately, but only with the constraint that it be used in ways that strengthen the larger system of love, justice, peace, and community. Human beings have a "right" to land only to the extent that they use it in ways consistent with their other moral and ecological obligations—to guard and protect it, to use it to produce food that will be available to all, and to use it as the foundation of creating a just social order in accord with the Torah mandate to "pursue justice" and to "love the stranger."

On these criteria, the original Zionist enterprise could be faulted. It was an attempt to acquire the land without regard to the well being of those already there, and it stands in sharp contrast with the Torah injunction to "love the stranger." But this criticism is only relevant for those who always and consistently use this criterion—and has no place in the discourse of those who regularly use market criteria rather than moral criteria to judge financial transactions and uses of the land on our planet. It's simply racist to use a higher standard for judging Jewish behavior than you use in judging your own or that of other national groupings. So, if you are willing to critique everyone, including yourself, and to judge your right to your own house and other property by the criterion established in Torah, then you have the right to fault the Jewish people as well for not having lived up to those spiritual standards. The reality is that neither Jewish nor Palestinian societies thought in spiritual terms—they both accepted market categories (as in "this is *mine* because I own a piece of paper that says so,") and they both accepted notions of ownership based on the flawed social system within which they lived.

So if we want to make a pragmatic argument, then we do so within the context of the current power relations and what they have established. But if we want to make an argument from the standpoint of a world that we really believe in, then we are not going to accept as a powerful argument the notion that somebody has property rights on a particular piece of land. Instead, we are going to ask about all land on the planet earth: how do we share it most effectively so that everyone can have enough and still be ecologically sustainable and responsible? And that is a very different kind of question than the question of "how do we reestablish previously existing rights to land that were unfairly taken away" (which is a difficult question in part because over the course of history many different people have mixed their labor with the same land, and hence have conflicting claims to it).

The Economic Clash

Though Jewish immigrants in the second wave of immigration after World War I brought with them a thick socialist ideology, it was their Jewish nationalism which eventually shaped their choices about how to relate to the Palestinian Arabs. Just as nationalism would ultimately undermine the internationalist aspirations of the European working class parties who lined up to support their own nations' involvement in World War I, so too nationalism overwhelmed the internationalist emphasis that had been part of the official ideology of early Zionist socialists.

The Zionists argued that Jewish life in the Diaspora was deformed, at least partly because Jewish existence had been separated from the means of production—from land and factory work. Jews had been economically marginalized, or allowed only into professions like moneylending and intellectual life, but had no intrinsic connection to the way that wealth was created in a society. So, the Zionists reasoned, the first priority for creating a healthy Jewish society would be to create Jewish farmers and Jewish laborers.

Yet that was not so easy, because Jewish capitalists, who put their class interests above their nationalist interests, were willing to hire Arab laborers who would work for low wages. If the Jews were going to build a working class, they would have to make it possible for Jews to work. The solution: make it a central demand of the Zionist movement that only Jews be employed in factories or agricultural enterprises that were to do business with the Jewish immigrants and their supporters abroad.

In this way, a new kind of socialist workers movement emerged—one which supported Jewish labor and excluded from membership Arabs who wished to work together with Jews. Political parties were formed, including Poaley Zion (led by David Ben Gurion) whose distinguishing ideology was their strong commitment to creating an exclusively Jewish economy.

As the labor movement became ever stronger, and took shape as the Histadrut, it established factories and other economic institutions which were meant to be exclusively for Jews. The Histadrut was a very unusual trade union organization because it not only represented workers, but it owned some of the institutions in which workers worked. Moreover, it created one of the most advanced and humanitarian networks of social services that the world had ever seen up to that point. It established a health insurance program or sick fund (Kupat Holim), pension programs, and training and educational programs. Through its outreach to workers, the Histadrut became the backbone of a powerful labor movement whose Labor Party became the major force in building the Israeli state. Yet all these benefits were restricted: Jews only.

Take, for example, the health program. Working with an international women's Zionist organization, Haddassah, Kupat Holim was able to create a health service that provided hospitals, nurses' training schools, school hygiene, school playgrounds, and public health programs which reduced trachoma and malaria among Jews. "As a consequence of these," argues Samih K. Farsoun, "the death rate among Jews was less than half that among the majority of Palestinians." It was only after the introduction of public health programs by the British that the entire population began to see the benefits of modern medicine and that population increase became possible among Palestinians.

Closely connected to economic strength was residents' level of education. Jewish culture had long given primacy to education, and was well positioned to take advantage of opportunities should they be available. Whenever European and American institutions allowed Jews to enter and advance on equal footing with their Christian neighbors, Jews excelled. But such opportunities were not abundant in the first half of the twentieth century. Many elite institutions had heavy formal or informal quotas on the number of Jewish students and faculty they would take. No wonder that some of the most talented thinkers and intellectuals were attracted to the Zionist movement with its promise that Jews could become "a people like all other people" and not face special disadvantages that came with their peculiar social location in Diaspora societies.

These intellectuals embarked on what many saw as an amazing feat—the revival of ancient Hebrew into a spoken contemporary language. In so doing, the Zionists were consciously breaking with the Yiddish language that had become the spoken tongue of the Jewish masses of Eastern Europe, and with religious Jewry's perspective that Hebrew was "lashon hakodesh," the holy language which should not be spoken in profane daily use.

With British consent, the Zionists were able to create a segregated Jewish school system which went from kindergarten through university (the Hebrew University in Jerusalem, the Technion in Haifa). But the British denied similar autonomy to the Palestinian Arabs who were forced to attend British government schools or private schools, and had to leave the country if they wished to attend university. As Samih Farsoun puts it, the educational systems were "separate and unequal in terms of quality, financing, levels, and delivery, especially in the rural areas." He quotes the director of education in the British mandate government to illustrate the extent to which the British contributed to a growing separation between the peoples: "The natural result of the disparity between the educational facilities offered to Arabs and Jews is to widen the cultural gap between the two races, to prevent social intermixture on equal terms, and to tend to reduce the Arabs to a position of permanent inferiority" (cited by Farsoun, p.87).

Now imagine you are an Arab Palestinian watching as this new group of people arrive in your society and begin to build economic institutions with the help of outside financial backing, institutions explicitly excluding you. Might you begin to feel that your own well being, and certainly the well being of your children and grandchildren, were being threatened by this group of immigrants? If you saw them as agents of European colonialism, if you listened to their publicly articulated desires to establish a Jewish homeland in your own neighborhood, if you heard the British declare in the "Balfour Declaration" of 1917 that they intended to support this Zionist movement, you might well see these institutions as pre-figuring a political state that would deny you your rights.

On the other hand, think of your own reactions when African Americans, women, gays and lesbians, and other previously oppressed groups to which you may not belong decide that they need to create Black-only, women-only, or gay-only institutions and gatherings. For many who are left out, the experience can be painful. Yet, as a whole, liberal and progressive people have tended to support this kind of development as a necessary step toward the empowerment of people who have previously been unable to develop their own identities and had been subject to demeaning and abuse. While we would oppose a government founded on such principles, most of us have been very supportive of voluntary organizations being formed on principles that allow previously oppressed groups to organize institutions that are exclusive, reasoning that for some (often unspecified) period of time it may be necessary for these people to have some institutions of their own so that they can overcome the internalization of demeaning self-conceptions that have limited their ability to function. Well, this is precisely the reasoning that was at the heart of the Zionist insistence for a Jewish-only economy in the midst of what was at the time a majority non-Jewish society. Creating Jewish-only institutions in an area that was majority Arab and in a country run by British colonialists could easily be understood as an act of national self-determination and resistance to oppression. That is certainly how the Jewish Bund had organized itself as a Jewish-only socialist organization in Europe.

One might object that whether or not Jews intended to be agents of British colonialism, they came to Palestine with the active support of the British after 1920, and were often helped by the British in settling in to their new homeland. This is quite different from the experience of other minority groups in advanced industrial societies.

As is often the case in this history, the relationships here are complex and call for a sophisticated understanding of the situation. The British were far more ambivalent about Zionism than their official pronouncements often suggest, and wavered between moments of support for aliyah and moments of hostility. The hostility was real and led to an actual armed struggle between the Yishuv (the Jewish settlement in Israel) and the British army. In particular, the Zionist embrace of socialism scared British capitalists—if the Holocaust had not led to the prevalence of a nationalist-protective discourse in the Jewish people, Israel might have become a socialist country aligned with anti-capitalist forces. Just because the British at times showed hostility toward the Yishuv, some Zionists have gone in the other direction, and argued that Britain was actually against the Zionists. That was not the case either because, as Tom Segev has demonstrated in his recent book *One Palestine, Complete* the Zionists cooperated with the British far more than traditional Zionist histories acknowledge.

The government in England veered sometimes toward the interests of the Yishuv but more frequently toward the interests of the Arabs (since doing so was necessary to preserve British access to Arab oil and support for their continued rule over India). However, the Brits who actually lived in Palestine were often more supportive of the Yishuv. The British shared with the leadership of the Zionist movement a discourse of development which led them to see the Zionist movement as an agent of modernization and progress even at moments when political circumstances set them in opposition to each other, while their inherent racism led them to see the Arabs as backwards and incapable of transformation

On the other hand, there were many Brits in Palestine who had a deep anti-Semitic revulsion against Jews which played out in attempts to curtail immigration and in sending illegal immigrants to detention camps in Cyprus.

The very idea that the victims of oppression can be wholly "co-opted" if they ever align with ideologies of their oppressors is or should be a suspect notion. Take the example of former African Americans slaves and their descendents, who were supported in moving north by "big capital" interests that used them as a source of cheap labor and as strikebreakers to counter the power of white working class unions. White workers resisted the introduction of African Americans into their communities, sometimes through restrictive covenants on where they could live, enforcing defacto segregation in schools, and using police and the court system in a discriminatory way to make things more difficult for African Americans. These restrictions were in turn challenged by the Federal government in alliance with big capital.

Would we conclude that because big capital used its power to support the introduction of African Americans into northern and western communities that these African Americans were merely tools of big capital, and that therefore the resistance of white workers was legitimate? Or would we nevertheless condemn the racism of white workers and say that they were morally wrong to have opposed African Americans coming and settling in their communities?

The point here, as throughout this discussion, is not to justify the choices of the Zionist settlers or the Palestinian farmers and the Arab elites, but to see how both sides could have had reasonable foundations for doing what they did, and both sides could have had some reasonable grounds for feeling that the other side was acting in ways that were insensitive, provocative, and hurtful.

Chapter Three:

THE EMERGENCE OF A JEWISH STATE

When the League of Nations incorporated the Balfour Declaration into its "Mandate for Palestine" it essentially was giving international approval to British rule and to the British elevation of Jewish interests over the interests of the Palestinians. As a result, Jewish immigration dramatically increased, and many Arab Palestinians were outraged that these outside forces were now imposing their vision on an Arab society. By 1920, Arabs had begun to riot against the Jewish immigration, causing many deaths on both sides. Attacks against Jewish settlements increased. Though the official leadership of the Palestinian movement—usually the scions of the wealthy and powerful land owners and feudal families who traced their lineage back to the early conquest or to the struggle against Crusaders—was organizing in the large cities, it was the peasantry who was most radicalized by the growing economic power of the Jewish community and its land purchases. It was largely the peasantry, rather than the Palestinian movement's official leaders, who demanded of the British Mandate authorities that taxes be reduced, schools and roads be built, and agricultural cooperation be fostered.

Violence broke out again in 1929, and 133 Jews and 116 Palestinians were murdered by angry mobs before the British authorities could restore order. Though precipitated by specific struggles over conflicting claims to Jewish and Islamic holy sites, a British investigatory commission concluded that the basic cause of the riots was the feeling of many Palestinians "of disappointment of their political and national aspirations and fear for their economic future." Yet listening to the actual language being used by those engaged in violence, it would be hard to deny that anti-Semitic themes on the Arab side and anti-Arab prejudices on the Jewish side played into the willingness of both to believe a set of rumors about the other side's having already massacred people which provided "justification" for more violence.

In particular, I want to note the outrageous slaughter of innocent Jews in Hebron. For centuries a small group of religious Jews had attended the Machpelah, the traditional burial site for Abraham and Sarah (and, in some accounts, of Adam and Eve). It was on this site sacred to Jews that Muslims had chosen to erect a mosque, and so it became for many years a shared site of holiness. The Arab mobs who murdered religious Jews in Hebron in 1929 left a scar in the memory of Jews that would resurface in the eventual establishment of a Jewish settlement in the late twentieth century by fundamentalists who recall this earlier massacre to justify their hatred of Palestinians.

The underlying conditions continued to fester and radicalize both sides. Gradually, an increasing number of Jews agreed with Chaim Arlosoroff, the director of the Jewish Agency's Political Department from 1931 until 1933, that force would be necessary to achieve Zionist aims, while politically sophisticated Palestinians became increasingly convinced that an armed conflict with the British would be necessary to preserve Palestinian society. When economic conditions worsened in 1936, many Palestinians were ready to join a general strike in protest of continued Israeli immigration (which had escalated dramatically in the few years since Hitler had come to power in Germany—only 4,075 Jews immigrated in 1931 but by 1933 the number was 30,327, and by 1935 it was 61,854).

The Palestinians called not only for an end to immigration and opposition to Zionism, but also an end to the British Mandate and the creation of a parliamentary Palestinian Arab government. Guerilla bands (Ikhwan al-Qassam or Brothers of Al-Qassam, named after a guerrilla leader who was killed by British troops) attacked Jewish immigrants and British officials. The goal of these primarily young nationalists, known as "the shabab," was not only to stop the Zionists but also national liberation for the Palestinian people from British colonial rule. Older and more established Arab voices tried to calm or restrain the shabab for fear of an open conflict with the British Mandatory authorities.

The "Arab Revolt" of 1936-39 began with a general strike which lasted six months and an armed insurrection which lasted longer. The British declared the strike illegal, censored or closed down newspapers, imposed tough curfews, imposed collective punishments and jailed or deported key leaders. It set up a new investigation, the Peel Commission, which came to the same conclusion that earlier studies had: the central cause of the revolt was the desire of the Arabs for national independence and their hatred and fear of a Jewish national homeland in Palestine.

Many Jews were shocked. While Ben Gurion, a leader of the Jewish community in Palestine, understood that Arabs feared losing their homeland and hence had resorted to a violent struggle, other Zionist leaders saw the revolt as little more than an extension of centuries of hatred of Jews. It was easier to see the Palestinians as an extension of Jew-hating Cossacks and street gangsters than as representatives of an Arab nationalist movement with equal claims to legitimacy as the Zionist movement. To the extent that they were willing to acknowledge the Arab Revolt as a nationalist movement, they would only character-ize it as an immoral and terroristic movement. As Yitzhak Tabankin, one of the ideologues of the kibbutz movement, put it: "The swastika, waved aloft in Hitler's Germany, and the green flag, the Arab 'national' flag, now upraised by reactionary leadership of the Arabs of Palestine—they are the same flag, the flag of national hatred." This response of delegiti-mating the other was prevalent on both sides and with equal intensity.

The Peel Commission concluded that the struggle was "irrepress-ible," the Mandate unworkable, and the solution was to partition the territory. The Jews would receive 1/5 of it, including most of Galilee, Emek Yizre'el, and the coastal plain, while the Arabs would receive the Negev, the southern coastal plain, the Gaza strip, the Judean hills and central plains, and would be united with Transjordan into one large Arab state. Peel also recommended exchange of populations—the transfer of some 225,000 Arabs from the Jewish state to the Arab state and the transfer of 1,250 Jews from the Arab state to the Jewish state. Picking up themes that had been part of Zionist thinking since Herzl,

Jews welcomed the idea of transfer because they believed that a Jewish state would be impossible without a solid Jewish majority. Though few talked about this publicly, many believed that the Palestinian Arabs should be resettled in the lands of their brothers and sisters across the Jordan if their transfer were well compensated, done in a humane manner, and was not forced.

While Jews publicly welcomed the partition plan and privately celebrated the legitimation of "transfer," few of the Zionist leadership believed that the Jewish state would be able to live within the narrow boundaries proposed by the Peel Commission. Yet by 1937 there was a perceived urgency to have some place to settle the Jews of Europe unrestricted by quotas, and the possibility of transferring Arab populations to neighboring states made the Peel Commission proposal seem reasonable to the Zionists.

But the Peel Commission proposals did not seem at all reasonable to the Arabs, who were outraged at the idea that their homeland should be divided. The Arabs of Galilee led the opposition, unwilling to consider either transfer or living under Jewish rule. Thirty years before there had been few Jews; now the Jews were going to transfer them from their homes or make them live as a minority in a Jewish state? The revolt continued and intensified.

Until 1937 the Jews had followed a policy of restraint, but an increase in acts of Palestinian Arab terror in October 1937 provided the "grounds" for a Jewish terrorist group, the Irgun, to plant bombs in Arab civilian crowds and Arab buses (in the same sense that Israeli Army acts of violence against Palestinian civilians today provides "grounds" for Palestinian acts of violence against Israeli civilians). As Benny Morris reports, "Massive bombs were placed in crowded Arab centers, and dozens of people were indiscriminately murdered and maimed—for the first time more or less matching the numbers of Jews murdered in the Arab pogroms and rioting of 1929 and 1936. This 'innovation' soon found Arab imitators, and became something of a 'tradition'; during the coming decades Palestine's (and, later, Israel's) marketplaces, bus stations, movie theaters and other public buildings became routine targets, lending a particularly brutal flavor to the conflict." (p. 147).

The Arab Revolt was put down forcibly by the British, as the approach of World War II reinforced British fears about their ability to keep control of the routes to Arab oil and to India. Yet for the same reason the British backed away from the Peel Commission notion of partition and focused instead on winning Arab support for the coming conflict with Germany, Italy, and Japan.

Given Nazi anti-Semitism, the Jews had no choice but to side with the British in a struggle against Germany, but the Arabs' anti-colonial feelings gave them reason to find a Hitler victory potentially appealing. So the British issued a new statement of policy designed to appease the Arabs, The White Paper of May 17, 1939, which proposed a ceiling of 75,000 on Jewish immigration during the next five years, severe limitations on Jewish land purchasing, and promised an independent Palestinian state within ten years. The British hoped that the White Paper would appease the Palestinians and buy Arab support for the war in Europe. But because the proposal did not provide immediate Palestinian independence, it was rejected by the Arab militants; because it restricted immigration, it was rejected by the Zionists. So the British were forced to implement their policy unilaterally.

Jews had already sought to break the British immigration quotas through illegal entry by sea. Between 1934 and 1938 about 40,000 Jews arrived illegally. But after 1939, with the British more determined to keep Arab support, the number of illegal entries decreased, with less than 16,000 making it into Palestine between 1940 and 1945. Seeking to appease Arab anti-Zionist sentiment, the British captured boats filled with Jewish refugees seeking escape from Nazi Germany, and sent them to special island camps in Mauritius and later in Cyprus.

These policies did little to convince Palestinians that the British were really on their side. The British had consistently prevented Palestinians from developing their own democratic institutions, still refused to give Palestinians their independence, and were not challenging Zionist aspirations for the future. Many Arabs cheered when the Nazis began to defeat the Allies militarily in the early war years, hopeful that England's and France's weakened military would eventually lead to a loosening of their colonial power throughout the Arab world (France played a major colonial role in Syria and Iraq). Given the absence of a strong democratic tradition inside the Arab world, the dictatorial approach of the Axis countries did not cause huge tensions, though the racist ideologies of the Axis (Hitler once had called the Arabs "half-apes") would certainly have come into conflict with Arab aspirations had the Nazis succeeded in dominating the world. But for many Arabs the immediate need to free themselves from British or French colonialism made an Axis victory seem preferable.

In 1941 the Iraqi military revolted in favor of the Axis. There were mass riots in Baghdad and in other Arab cities against the Jewish populations there, and hundreds of Jews were killed (setting the stage for the subsequent mass exodus of Sephardi and Mizrahi Jews to Israel as soon as that became possible after the creation of a Jewish state). The exiled ex-mufti of Jerusalem, Amin al-Husseini, a leader of the Arab revolt, tried to organize support for the Axis among Arabs and eventually fled to Berlin where he was greeted as "a great champion of Arab liberation and the most distinguished antagonist of England and Jewry." He later helped organize Arab volunteers to fight on the side of Germany, and tried to interfere with the emigration of Jewish children to Palestine.

This history of Arabs tilting toward the Axis, though motivated largely by anti-colonial feeling rather than by any allegiance to Nazism (just as the Zionist tilt toward the British had been motivated by Zionist national interests and not by a fundamental affinity for colonialism), made it easier for the Zionist cause to be more fully supported by the Allies, whom Jews were in any event unequivocally supporting. And the legacy of Arab willingness to close the doors of Palestine when Jews were seeking refuge would set the stage for similar moral insensitivity when Jews shut their ears to the cries of Palestinian refugees.

THE HOLOCAUST

The destruction of European Jewry by the Nazis was a decisive factor in convincing Jews that they needed a state of their own to provide protection from what was seen as the inevitable and periodic resurfacing of the world's basic anti-Semitic tendencies. On this account, the German Jewish population had fooled itself into believing that they would be safe simply by assimilating into German life. There was no Jewish community in the world that had been better integrated into the life of its host country in all of Jewish history than the German Jews. Jews had reached positions of commanding power and respect in academic and cultural life, in the media, in the professions, and in some corners of the business world. Yet none of this was enough to provide Jews with ultimate protection from the recurring curse of anti-Semitism. Even those

A Nazi officer walks over victims of the World War II Bergen-Belsen concentration camp on April 29, 1945.   AP Wide World Photos

whose families had converted to Christianity were not safe. The Nazi doctrine of racial origins led them to trace birth records back several generations, unearth hidden "Jewish blood" in families that had no previous knowledge of their Jewishness, and send them to the death camps along with other Jews.

There is little question that the Nazis were the indispensable element in organizing the mass murder of the Jews. But, on an experiential level, Jews were equally shocked at how quickly their non-Jewish neighbors abandoned them, refusing to take risks to stand up on their behalf, or even actively betraying them to the Nazis. In some places in Eastern Europe, large numbers of Poles, Latvians, Estonians, Lithuanians, Ukrainians, Croats, and Russians joined enthusiastically in hunting down Jews who were seeking to escape, and then murdered the Jews in large numbers and with disturbing brutality. Even in the "more cultured" Austrian, Czech, French, and Dutch populations there were all too many people eager to cooperate with the Nazis and turn in the Jews. Neighbors, coworkers, employers, employees—no matter where Jews turned, they were amazed to find so little support. There were, of course, righteous gentiles who did risk, and in some cases actually lose their lives defending, hiding, or protecting Jews. A room in the Yad Vashem Holocaust memorial in Jerusalem commemorates these courageous people. But by and large the picture was one that tended to reenforce the worst fantasies of who non-Jews "really are."

There was nothing secret about Hitler's plans. The Left had plenty of warning, yet it did little to counter the growing anti-Semitism in the left-wing parties in Europe. Jews in the Left were often reluctant to raise this issue, perhaps subconsciously aware that their non-Jewish comrades were unwilling to campaign seriously against anti-Semitism, or perhaps unwilling to seem parochial in a movement whose central theme was to overcome nationalism and become internationalists. When the war came, many socialists were unwilling to protect their Jewish comrades, and instead allowed racism to triumph. After the war, communists again used anti-Semitism to provide them with a common link to the people, show their nationalist credentials, and reestablish their credibility with a people whom Soviet troops had conquered in repelling the Nazis.

Meanwhile, the Allies did little to save Jews. There was no concerted effort to destroy the death camps, interdict trains bringing Jews to their deaths, or give support for refugees who had managed to get on ships taking them from Europe. The gates of the United States were closed, and Arab influence managed to ensure that the gates of the much closer Palestine would be closed as well.

And so Jews were rounded up, herded into ghettoes where they died by the tens of thousands by being slowly starved to death, then shipped to concentration camps where they were worked to death or simply sent to the gas chambers and crematoria. As tens of thousands turned to hundreds of thousands, and then millions of Jews being murdered, the world paid little attention as the death machine worked with remarkable efficiency toward the stated aim of exterminating every last Jew on the planet.

It should be stressed that the goal of the destruction of the Jews was quite unique in that it did not flow from some other economic or political goal. Even when destroying Jews required a diversion of resources and energy away from the front lines and the military struggle, the Nazis gave the gas chambers first priority: they were willing to sacrifice other goals, even the goal of winning the political war, to accomplish this evil end.

The impact of these events remains a major factor in Jewish consciousness in the twenty-first century. The humiliation of being treated like vermin who ought to be exterminated, the murder of one out of every three Jews alive at the time, the fear facing every Jew on the planet as they contemplated their fate should Hitler win, coupled with the subsequent lies by people who had collaborated, the denial of what had happened, the failure of the world to allow Jews to find refuge from Nazism (most countries simply refused Jews entry and none provided any resources to assist Jews in escaping), the failure of the world to come to grips with what had produced this tragedy and what could be done to prevent future recurrences—all these combined to create an ongoing trauma for the Jewish people which has never been healed.

The political impact of the Holocaust on Jewish consciousness went into opposite directions. For some, the horror of racism and genocide led to a deep commitment to never again allow any people to face this kind of horrible reality. Though Jews had already played a leading role in the labor, socialist, and communist movements, and various other liberatory enterprises, the overwhelming nature of the Holocaust gave a deeper immediacy to the need to fight racism and other forms of oppression. No wonder, then, that young Jews growing up in advanced industrial societies in the 1960s, born immediately after the Holocaust yet having their childhoods dominated by its stories, became leaders of movements against racism and imperialism and advocates for the civil rights of African Americans, women, homosexuals, the disabled, and other victims of neglect and abuse.

Many—perhaps most—other Jews, however, drew a quite opposite set of conclusions. "We Jews cared about everyone else, but no one cared about us, no one protected us, and no one ever will. We are alone in the world and we can't count on anyone but ourselves, so we need to focus all our energies on protecting ourselves to ensure that it will never happen to us again." These Jews tended to focus more of their attention on building the Jewish state, and became impassioned advocates for Zionism. Indeed, they became increasingly intolerant toward anyone who criticized it. From their perspective, history had "proven" that the Jews could only count on themselves, and that therefore the need for a Jewish state was paramount in importance.

Moreover, in the aftermath of the war there were hundreds of thousands of Jews in D.P. (displaced persons) camps around Europe—homeless, hopeless, and in need of urgent care. To the Zionists it was obvious that the place for them was the ancient homeland of the Jewish people, though many of those refugees had never been connected to Zionist aspirations before the war.

So, as soon as it appeared clear that the Allies were going to defeat the Axis powers, the fight for Palestine resumed. But this time the Zionists managed to bring in another important ally: the United States. The strong Jewish population of the United States played an important role in the Democratic Party, and their influence in electoral politics helped to balance the still very large clout of American global interests, which tended to lean toward accommodating Arab oil. The historical gains of democratic movements in the American past made it possible for ordinary citizens to have an impact on global politics, even when their perspectives conflicted with those of ruling elites. So the Jewish people were able to effectively use the influence that those democratic processes had made available in order to move popular revulsion at what had happened to the Jews into political support for the Zionist enterprise.

Of course, this was not the only way Jews might have chosen to use the democratic arena. Jews might have argued for the elimination of all immigration quotas toward Jews and for the mass importation of hundreds of thousands of Jewish refugees into the United States. But this choice was unthinkable to Jews under the influence of Zionism, for whom this was the moment to claim national sovereignty and not just national safety. And it was a choice unthinkable to many leaders of

American Jewry who still felt wary about testing American tolerance by daring to bring in to the U.S. large numbers of Jewish refugees. All the better, all agreed, to send them to Palestine (and some leading anti-Semitic figures in the U. S. Senate concurred, hoping that perhaps American Jews would also depart for the Holy Land).

As the United States started to lean on Britain to provide a more satisfactory arrangement for Jewish immigrants, the Yishuv also stepped up its struggle for statehood. The Yishuv now included tens of thousands of men who had participated in the Allied armies of WWII, and many had stolen or illegally purchased arms that could be used in the coming struggle. With the post-war British seeming more tentative about the Zionist enterprise, two Jewish terrorist organizations—the Lehi and IZL (the Irgun led by Menachem Begin)—initiated an armed struggle for Zionist independence in February 1944. The press dismissed them as "misguided terrorists" and "young fanatics crazed by the sufferings of their people into believing that destruction will bring healing." But even before the war fully ended the more mainstream Hagganah joined in attacks on the British. For the next three years, from 1945 to 1948, a guerrilla war was fought between the British and the forces of Jewish national liberation (the Zionist movement). The most notorious act of this guerrilla war took place on July 22, 1946, when the IZL placed bombs in the King David Hotel, killing ninety-one people (Britons, Arabs, and Jews). The Hagganah condemned the attack.

Yet the British were far less repressive toward the Jewish revolt than they had been toward the Arab revolt of 1936-39. For example, during the Arab revolt thousands of Palestinians were killed by the British forces and the entire leadership of the Palestinian movement was either arrested, detained or deported; during the Jewish revolt from 1945 to 1947, the British killed just 37 Jews. The standard Zionist claim that the British systematically tilted in favor of the Arabs throughout the Mandate period ignores the relatively benign way that the British fought against the Yishuv.

Without U.S. support for the Mandate, the British were in an untenable position and began to make plans to leave. They proposed a British-run international "trusteeship," with local autonomy for Jews and Arabs over municipal affairs, agriculture, education, etc. leading eventually to a binational state. Neither side agreed. The Palestinians wanted majority rule (they were still the majority in Palestine in 1946) in an independent Palestinian state; the Zionists insisted upon partition and a separate Jewish state.

Instead of solving the problem themselves, the British, limping from the War, resolved to leave, turning the issue over to the United Nations where both the United States and the Soviet Union announced support for partition. Using its considerable political power, the United States pressured some of its client states into voting with it, and partition received the two-thirds vote necessary for passage in November 1947.

The partition agreement gave the Jews, who were 37 percent of the population in 1947, some 55 percent of the land. The Arabs believed that they were being asked to pay the price for the pain Jews suffered during the Holocaust. Why, they wondered, shouldn't the Jews be given a portion of Germany or some other country that had actually persecuted them, rather than part of the Arabs' homeland? And if Jews didn't want to be a minority in a Palestinian state, why should Palestinians have to be a minority within a Jewish state? Outraged, Arab states walked out of the United Nations and declared that partition, if implemented, would lead to war.

There were a few Jewish voices in Palestine who called for compromise with the Palestinians and a bi-national state right up to the outbreak of the war of 1948. The Jewish philosopher Martin Buber, author of *I and Thou* and a popularizer of the wisdom of East European Hasidism, Judah Magnes, president of the Hebrew University, and others argued that a Jewish state created under these circumstances would be in perpetual conflict with Palestinians and with its Arab neighbors. Jews, they believed, should do more to seek accommodation with the Palestinian people before declaring independence. Most Jews felt that these idealists were out of touch with reality. With hundreds of thousands of Jews incarcerated in displaced person's camps, with Palestinians involved in guerrilla actions against the Yishuv, there was no time to waste. After 1800 years of statelessness, and three years after the conclusion of the Holocaust, the Jewish people were no longer willing to wait for the fulfillment of messianic dreams—they wished to take control of their own history by creating their own state.

In grabbing the opportunity that history had presented them, the Zionists embodied the ethos of activism and self-affirmation which had been so long absent in Jewish history. A people who had faced 1800 years of cultural demeaning, oppression, and genocide, a people who had developed a culture of passivity and otherworldliness, had been transformed in the course of fifty years of Zionist education, anti-Semitic attacks, and economic and political security in the West into a people who could act decisively in their own self-interest and shape their own future. From the standpoint of social psychological development, this was a powerful indication that an oppressed people could revive and rejuvenate; or, from a spiritual standpoint, an indication that "dead bones" (in the words of the Prophet Ezekiel) could still live.

There is little recorded of Palestinian voices calling for acceptance of the 1947 partition plan. Many Palestinians were convinced from the public statements of Zionist leaders in the 1920s and 1930s that once the Jews had established an independent state in Palestine, they would push for more and more land, continuing the expansionism which had been a central dynamic of the Zionist movement till that point. It's not hard to see why Palestinians, who had been the vast majority of people in their own land a mere thirty years before, should imagine that millions more Jews might soon arrive and continue the dynamics which had already resulted in the loss of Palestinian land and livelihood.

And yet there is little doubt in retrospect that the failure of the Palestinian leadership to accept partition and to attempt to negotiate a peaceful transition to statehood for both Jews and Palestinians had disastrous consequences for the Palestinian people. For all their bluster, the Arab states were in no position to win a war with the Yishuv. The Yishuv had used the years of the Mandate to build the infrastructure of a state, complete with mechanisms for taxation, a school system, settlement agencies, a well-functioning labor movement, and a governmental apparatus (the Jewish Agency). Meanwhile, the Palestinian infrastructure and leadership had been severely crippled by the British occupation, particularly during the Arab revolt. Further, while Jews were developing the institutions of a parallel government underground in preparation for potential statehood, the Palestinians continued to work through the British Mandate authority and to rely on its institutions. They had built no independent infrastructure to create a state or run it. Nor could the Palestinians really rely on their fellow Arabs. Surrounding Arab states had huge populations but tiny armies that had less military supplies available to them than the new Jewish state. Militarily, the Zionist movement had vast superiority over the Palestinian Arabs in command and control, weapons production, trained manpower, and political unity.

Nevertheless, the Yishuv faced serious challenges from Palestinian guerrilla forces who began a civil war in November 1947 and continued to be a major factor in the conflict until Arab armies invaded in May of 1948, the day after Israel declared its independence. These guerrilla forces were not strong enough to conduct a frontal war. Instead, they focused on cutting off the roads between settlements, isolating and in some cases seriously threatening their survival. The Jewish population of Jerusalem (100,000 Jews) was cut off from the rest of the Yishuv and under intense siege in the spring of 1948. Convoys of Jews bringing supplies to Gush Etziyon and to Jerusalem were massacred. Jews in Jerusalem faced a desperate food situation in March of 1948, and the attack on convoys bringing relief made them feel cut off and scared.

Meanwhile, as the civil war raged, the IZL killed or wounded hundreds of Arab civilians. There were moments when the Hagannah joined with IZL in reprisal attacks on Palestinians, but mostly the terror against Palestinian civilians was perpetrated by IZL and Lehi. As in all such situations, the cycle of violence and counter-violence made it difficult to say, "who started first." Jewish terror attacks in response to Palestinian guerrilla actions were met by vicious attacks on Jewish civilians by Palestinians which led to more Jewish terror attacks. Throughout most of Palestine, both Jews and Palestinians felt that they were deeply threatened by the other side. And both used violence against civilians as part of their strategy to demoralize and terrorize the other side.

The campaign to secure the road to Jerusalem was particularly intense. Jerusalem had not been part of the area given to Israel in the UN partition plan—it was to be an international city. Yet the attack on its Jewish residents by Arab guerillas and the cutting off of its food supplies convinced the Yishuv that it must become part of the new Israeli state. So several convoys were sent to Jerusalem and a set of battles took place involving Palestinian villages along the road, in the course of which the most prominent Palestinian military leader was killed.

One of those villages was Deir Yassin, a village which had gone out of its way to establish good relations with the nearby Jewish neighborhoods of Western Jerusalem and had refused to host Palestinian units or to let them use the village as a base for attack against Jerusalem. In coordination with the Hagannah, the IZL and Lehi planned to expel the inhabitants of this village to further secure the road to Jerusalem. Hagannah machine gunners provided cover for the attack. The Deir Yassin residents resisted the attack, and five of the IZL and Lehi were killed in the battle, and thirty were wounded. But Deir Yassin stands out in the memory of the Palestinians because of the atrocities committed there against Palestinian civilians, as men, women and children were massacred by the IZL and Lehi troops. Benny Morris quotes an Israeli commander who reported on April 12: "The conquest of the village was carried out with great cruelty. Whole families—women, old people, children—were killed, and there were piles of dead. " In a report the next day, this same Hagannah commander reported, "Lehi members tell of the barbaric behavior of the IZL toward the prisoners and the dead. They also relate that the IZL men raped a number of Arab girls and murdered them afterward." The number of dead has been estimated at about 250, with some pro-Zionists insisting that the count was much lower (around 120 dead) and some Palestinian partisans claiming numbers closer to 350.

The Jewish Agency immediately condemned the massacre (though many Palestinians took that condemnation with the same kind of doubtful skepticism that decades later Israelis would use to greet Yassir Arafat's condemnation of acts of terror against Israelis).

Some historians believe that this and other acts of terror in the pre-1948 period played an important role in pushing surrounding Arab states to move beyond empty rhetoric and actually enter the war against the Yishuv. But its greatest impact was on demoralizing and terrifying many Palestinians, becoming a major factor in their flight from their homes. Deir Yassin, after all, was a village that had sought to have good relations with the Israelis, which had resisted attempts to recruit it into the civil war, and which had expected that it could live in peace with the emerging Jewish state. If even these people were brutalized and massacred, many Palestinians reasoned, what could they personally expect from Israeli forces?

It made little impact on the Palestinians that many unarmed Jews had also been killed in the course of the previous years, or that a few days later Arab militiamen from Jerusalem attacked a convoy of mostly unarmed doctors, nurses and others on their way to the Hadassah Hospital and Hebrew University camps on Mt. Scopus, murdering over seventy Jews. Just as today acts of Palestinian terror are not put into the context of the larger cycle of violence generated by both sides, so too in the Palestinian world of 1948 the terrible massacre at Deir Yassin was not contextualized to the larger struggle, nor did Palestinians see their own acts of violence as anything more than defensive acts against Jewish terrorists. So when the news of Deir Yassin became known, it spread panic among Palestinian civilians who drew the conclusion that unless they left their homes quickly, they too would be targets for massacre. Nor was this panic without foundation. Future Israeli Prime Ministers Menachem Begin and Yitzhak Shamir were leaders of the terrorist groups that were proud of their accomplishments at Deir Yassin, and openly advocated that Palestinians should be terrorized into flight.

In the next weeks in April and the beginning of May the struggle accelerated. From the standpoint of the Jews, the struggle was to save Jewish populations in cities and kibbutzim whose supply of food was being cut by Palestinian forces controlling access. From the standpoint of Palestinians, the struggle was to save Arab villages that would soon be wiped out just as villagers at Deir Yassin had been. The Jewish forces prevailed in many of these battles. After rebuffing an attack on Kibbutz Mishmar Ha'emek, Jewish forces counterattacked and wiped out ten surrounding Arab villages. Teverya, Haifa, and the Arab Katamon section of Jerusalem were conquered. In the case of Haifa, the Jewish mayor urged Arabs not to flee, though Arab leaders were asked to make an unconditional surrender to the Jewish forces; instead, fearful of what might happen, most Arabs fled.

The pattern spread: Jewish forces conquering Arab neighborhoods or villages, Arab civilians fleeing for their lives. So in Jaffe, in Eastern Galilee, and in Western Galilee. In fact, by May 15, many of the population centers of Arab Palestine had been conquered by the Jews and much of the Arab flight had already taken place. It was only in the Etziyon bloc of settlements that the pattern was reversed and the Jewish settlements were crushed by an Arab offensive; in this battle, angry Arab villagers yelling "Deir Yassin" proceeded to massacre over 160 Jewish civilians.

From the standpoint of Palestinian Arabs, the rapid conquest of many Palestinian population centers and the resulting flight of Arab civilians reconfirmed their worst fantasies about what would happen under Jewish rule. Surrounding Arab states showed little real interest in the fate of Palestinians, but after having postured about caring for the fate of Palestinians, the developments of April and early May forced the hands of Arab feudal regimes and required that they show at least token support.

Once it became clear that the Zionists were intent on declaring their own independence and the creation of a Jewish state would begin with the departure of the British on May 15, 1948, the Arab states began to talk about exterminating the Jews and eliminating the Jewish state. They were awash with talk about sweeping the Jews into the sea. A few hours after the Yishuv leadership declared independence and created the State of Israel, Arab countries invaded with the intent of wiping out that state. Yet the Arab elites had done little to educate or mobilize their own masses into this struggle, and they were not invested enough in their struggle to give more than token support to the Palestinians. The Arab forces were much smaller than the Zionists had calculated, and only parts of their strength were ever used in Palestine. Things might have been different for the Palestinians had the huge Arab world responded to their plight with hundreds of thousands of volunteers to fight against Zionism. In fact, not more than 5,000 volunteers from the Arab world joined the Palestinian cause—far less than the number of Jews and non-Jews who came to volunteer for the Yishuv. Most Arabs were not invested enough in this struggle to want to get directly involved, and though they may have felt some sense of solidarity with their fellow Arabs in Palestine, it was not sufficient to overturn the rhythms and customs of what were in fact largely peaceful village societies in order to respond to the hateful diatribes of their unelected feudal leadership and reactionary anti-Semitic Islamic clergy. There is little reason to doubt that the Arab armies sent to invade would have wiped out the Jewish state if they had prevailed, but historical revelations from that period now make it possible for us to know in retrospect that the Arab leaders mostly doubted that they could achieve such a result. Certainly, their military experts cautioned them that they would not be able to win an out-and-out war with the Zionist state. Most entered the conflict with the goal of grabbing as much land as possible while avoiding blame for the loss of Palestine which they knew was inevitable.

Yet the fact is that their clearly stated intentions were to destroy the Jewish settlement, and with that commit a potential genocide of the Jews of Palestine. It was this recognition that made the Yishuv leaders ever more determined to mobilize every possible resource to resist this invasion. And that proved easier than anyone had expected. The Arab states had fewer men able to take up arms than the Israeli Yishuv.

The constant intrigues among the Arab states about how to divide Palestine made it impossible for them to develop a serious coordinated effort. Instead, there were several separate Arab armies with little in the way of shared plan or cooperation. The one plan developed by the Arab League Political Committee was ignored by Jordan, whose Legion (the only force which had any previous battle experience) was directed instead to capture the West Bank for Jordan.

There was no attempt to incorporate the Palestinians into planning or participation in the struggle, partly because no one in the Arab countries was willing to take seriously the needs of the Palestinian people. The Arab countries' own disregard of the Palestinians made it easier for the Zionists to discount the Palestinians after 1948.

The war was bloody and horrific on both sides. Over 1 percent of the Jewish population of Palestine at that time were killed in (that would be equivalent to a war in the U.S. that killed approximately 2.7 million Americans). Arab forces massacred Jewish settlements. Jewish forces massacred Palestinian civilians and prisoners of war (at Eilaboun, Saliha, Safsaf, Jish, Hule, Major, Al-Kurum and more). Israel won a powerful military victory and secured its existence; the Arab states were shown to be militarily powerless.

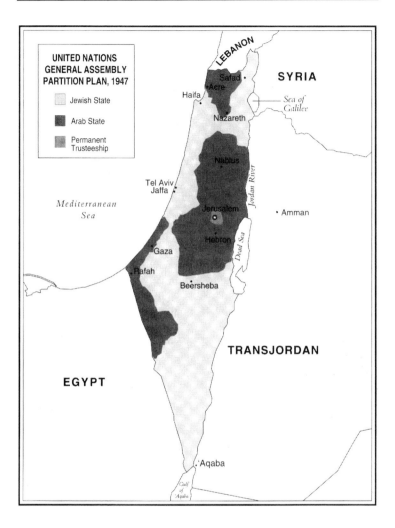

UNITED NATIONS
GENERAL ASSEMBLY
PARTITION PLAN, 1947

Jewish State

Arab State

Permanent
Trusteeship

LEBANON

SYRIA

Safad

Acre

Haifa

Sea of
Galilee

Nazareth

Nablus

Mediterranean
Sea

Tel Aviv
Jaffa

Jordan River

Jerusalem

Amman

Hebron

Dead Sea

Gaza

Rafah

Beersheba

TRANSJORDAN

EGYPT

Aqaba

Gulf
of
Aqaba

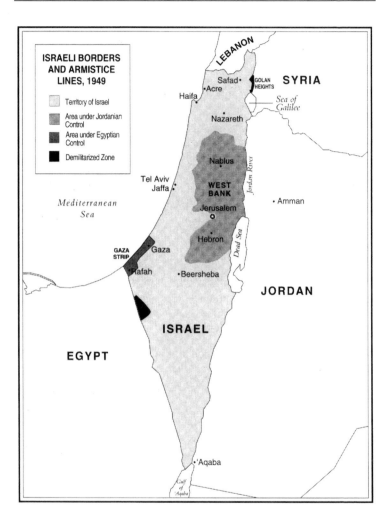

ISRAELI BORDERS
AND ARMISTICE
LINES, 1949

Territory of Israel

Area under Jordanian
Control

Area under Egyptian
Control

Demilitarized Zone

LEBANON

SYRIA

Safad
Acre
GOLAN
HEIGHTS

Haifa

Sea of
Galilee

Nazareth

Nablus

Tel Aviv
Jaffa

WEST
BANK

Jordan River

Mediterranean
Sea

Jerusalem

• Amman

Hebron

Dead Sea

GAZA
STRIP
Gaza

Rafah

• Beersheba

JORDAN

ISRAEL

EGYPT

• 'Aqaba

Gulf
of
'Aqaba

Chapter Four:

AFTER THE 1948 WAR

PALESTINIAN REFUGEES

One of the terrible and lasting consequences of the war was the creation of a large population of Arab refugees.

Israel claimed that there were 520,000 Palestinian refugees, while the Palestinians claim somewhere between 900,000 and one million. Benny Morris' classic *The Birth of the Palestinian Refugee Problem 1947-1949* (Cambridge U. Press, 1988) shows that neither the official Israeli account—that Palestinians left voluntarily or in response to an appeal by Arab leaders—nor the Palestinian account—that all refugees had been systematically and with premeditation expelled—turn out to be true. Morris cites private statements by Ben Gurion and other Zionist leaders in the 1930s and 1940s that show they had a penchant to use "transfer" of Arabs as a solution while simultaneously acknowledging that they could not talk about this publicly without endangering their own cause. It was this proclivity to see transfer as an appropriate way to deal with "the Palestinian problem" which set the background for many specific military actions during the 1947-49 struggle in which there were outright acts of expulsion either by Lehi/IZL or by the Hagannah. Morris argues that almost every instance of Palestinian mass flight from April through June of 1948 "was the direct and immediate result of an attack on and conquest of these neighborhoods and towns. In no case

A Palestinian refugee camp in Hahr al-Barid in northern Lebanon, winter
1948.   Courtesy of the Institute for Palestine Studies.

did a population abandon its homes before an attack; in almost all cases
it did so on the very day of the attack and in the days immediately following." (*Righteous Victims*, pa. 255) But Morris is equally insistent that
during the first stage of the war "there was no Zionist policy to expel the
Arabs or intimidate them into flight, though many Jews, including Ben
Gurion, were happy to see the backs of as many Arabs as possible. And
without doubt, Jewish—both Hagannah and IZL—retaliatory policies
and the IZL/LHI terror bombings were precipitants." (p.256).

On June 16, 1948, the Israeli cabinet resolved to prevent the return
of Palestinian refugees, and to greet them with live fire should they
attempt to return. Morris writes that "Abandoned villages were razed or
mined or, later, filled with new Jewish immigrants, as were abandoned
urban neighborhoods; fields were set alight, and landowners still in
place were urged to sell out and leave; and new settlements were established and began to cultivate the abandoned fields."

In the next phase of the war, in July 1948 and then again in October
and November of 1948 another three hundred thousand Arabs were
made refugees.

Morris' gripping account of one battle illustrates how Palestinian civilians became refugees ("The New Historiography: Israel Confronts its Past" originally published in TIKKUN in Nov. 1998, and then reprinted in *Best Contemporary Jewish Writing* edited by Michael Lerner , JosseyBass, 2001): "On July 12 and 13, the Yiftah and Kiryati brigades carried out their orders, expelling the fifty to sixty thousand inhabitants of the two towns, which lie about ten miles southeast of Tel Aviv. Throughout the war, the two towns had interdicted Jewish traffic on the main Tel Aviv-Jerusalem road, and the Yishuv's leaders regarded Lydda and Ramle as a perpetual threat to Tel Aviv itself. About noon on July 13, Operation Dani HQ informed IF General Statt/Operations: 'Lydda police fort has been captured. The troops, led by Lt. Col. Yitzhak Rabin [later to become Israeli Prime Minister] are busy expelling the inhabitants." Lydda's inhabitants were forced to walk eastward to the Arab legion lines, and many of Ramle's inhabitants were ferried in trucks or buses. Clogging the roads (and the Legion's possible route of advance westward), the tens of thousands of refugees marched, gradually shedding possessions along the way. Arab chroniclers, such as Sheikh Muhammed Nimr al-Khatib, claimed that hundreds of children died in the march, from dehydration and disease...Many of the refugees came to rest near Ramallah and set up tent encampments which later became the refugee camps supported by the United Nations Relief and Works Agency [UNRWA] and the hotbeds of today's Palestinian rebellion."

Yet Morris, who carefully investigated the Israeli archives, insists that there is no evidence of a systematic expulsion policy at the level of the Cabinet or IDF staff. Individual commanders in the field made their own decisions, some expelling villagers, others leaving them in place. Morris concludes that the attacks by the IDF were the major precipitants to flight, but "the exodus was, overall, the result of a cumulative process," rather than a premeditated plan. In the countryside, many factors were involved: "isolation among a cluster of Jewish settlements, a feeling of being cut off from Arab centers, a lack of direction by national leaders and feeling of abandonment by the Arab world, fear of Jewish assault, reports and rumors about massacres by the Jews, and actual attacks and massacres." (*Righteous Victims* p. 257-258).

Morris' conclusions have been subsequently challenged by Arab and Israeli post-Zionist Jewish historians who believe that the evidence is far more ambiguous, and who point to the ways that many Zionist leaders were privately (and a few, publicly) endorsing the notion of "transfer" of Arabs from their homes as early as the 1930s in order to achieve a Jewish majority in some part of the land of Israel. The problem had long predated the actual war: If Zionists were to have a state that went beyond the narrow areas around Tel Aviv, they would have to find some way to move the Arab majority, and that is exactly what happened. On this account, though the transfer may have never been consciously planned, it was the inevitable consequence of the logic of creating a Jewish state in a society with a majority of non-Jews.

Yet it matters to many Israeli historians that at the time there was far more chaos than plan, and that many more Palestinians left their homes than Israelis had imagined or planned for. The Palestinian flight went far beyond anyone's expectations.

Historian Avi Shlaim says that although there were many reasons for the Palestinian exodus, including the early departure of the upper classes and Palestinian leadership when the going got tough, the most important reason was Jewish military pressure. The infamous Plan D called for the Hagannah to capture Arab cities and destroy Arab villages. The objective of the plan was to clear the interior of the country of hostile and potentially hostile Arab elements. Though that plan was defined in narrow military and territorial objectives, Shlaim argues that "by ordering the capturing of Arab cities and the destruction of cities it both permitted and justified the forcible expulsion of Arab civilians" by the Israeli army (the Hagannah) and that is exactly what happened even before the official outbreak of hostilities on 15 May, 1948. (*The Iron Wall*, p. 31).

Once the flight began, there were explicit orders to not allow refugees to return. One such, from General Moshe Carmel on October 31, told troops to "Do all in your power to clear quickly and immediately from the areas conquered all hostile elements in accordance with the orders issued. The inhabitants should be assisted to leave the conquered areas." This was understood by the IDF commanders as orders to expel. In the course of subsequent expulsions, the IDF perpetrated massacres at Mujd al-Kurum, al-Bi'na, Dayr al-Assad, Nahf, Safsaf, Jish, Sasa, Sliha, Ilabun and Hula. Historian Benny Morris argues that the "uniform or at least similar nature of the massacres points to a belief among the perpetrators of central direction and authorization....

Almost all the massacres followed a similar course: a unit (of the IDF) entered a village, rounded up the menfolk in the village square, selected four or ten or fifty of the army-age males...lined them up against a wall and shot them. Some of the massacres were carried out immediately after the conquest of the village by the assaulting troops, though most occurred in the following days."

In July 1949, Israel offered the Arab states an overall peace settlement in which 100,000 refugees would be let back if the rest were resettled in Arab lands as part of a peace settlement; or, if Egypt would give up the Gaza strip, Israel would take its 200,000 refugees and let them stay there. But the Arab states insisted that Israel allow all the refugees return to their homes. In subsequent years, Israel insisted that the Arab states resettle the refugees, but the refugees insisted on remaining in camps, hoping someday to return home.

Who could blame the refugees from being outraged at not being allowed to return to their homes once the hostilities had stopped? Many of them had been forcibly evicted. Others had fled from a war zone, imagining that they would be able to return home once the war was over. No wonder the creation of the State of Israel was for them "Al Naqba," (the disaster), because it had meant the loss of their homes and the transformation from a life of some stability and regularity to a situation of economic desperation living in refugee camps.

The decision to not allow refugees to return was the single most significant decision on the part of the Israeli government. It guaranteed incalculable human suffering for the Palestinian people—and a time bomb for Israel which would explode in the coming decades.

Yet from the standpoint of many Zionists, the expulsion of Palestinians was a necessity. Even though most Palestinians had not joined the armed struggle against the Yishuv, many had. And how could one be sure that those who had not yet joined would not soon join? There were few Palestinian voices calling for co-existence and peace in 1948. The Yishuv perceived itself as faced with a huge threat both externally from Arab states and internally from a hostile Palestinian population. Moreover, these Palestinians had seemed united in their opposition to allowing Jewish refugees to enter the country just a few years earlier. Perhaps, reasoned some Jews, the Palestinians would get a taste of what they had done to the Jews whom they had prevented from entering the Land of Israel during the Holocaust.

But the central claim made on behalf of preventing refugees from returning was that they were people who had proven that they were not trustworthy, and if allowed to return would become a group that would destabilize and perhaps destroy the Jewish state from within. Ben Gurion frequently would tell Westerners, "Israel did not expel a single Arab." The official story became that they had all left voluntarily, in response to the appeal of their Arab leaders who wanted a clear path to massacre all of the Jewish inhabitants of the land, and in so doing they had proved that they were an element who sought the destruction of the Jewish state, a goal that they would be empowered to advance should Israel allow them to return.

This fear was not without foundation. The new Israeli state was surrounded by hostile Arab states. Even after the mass flight of Palestinians, there were at least 150,000 Palestinians who remained within Israel's total population of 850,000. To bring back the refugees could easily have guaranteed turmoil and possible internal dissolution of the Jewish state. Instead, Israel turned its attention to resettling Jews who had been living in camps in Europe and elsewhere after the War, and to opening its gates to the hundreds of thousands of Jews who had previously lived in the Muslim world and who now sought refuge from the anti-Semitic backlash that the Zionist movement had produced in Islamic countries.

The Zionist movement argued that what had in effect happened was a population transfer similar to what had happened in India/Pakistan after India had achieved independence and millions of Muslims fled to Pakistan while millions of Hindus fled to India. Yes, a large number of Palestinians had lost their homes. But hadn't that happened to millions of people after World War II as well as during the breakup of the post-WWII colonial world? What was important to note, these voices said, was that other refugees had been resettled. From the standpoint of the world's refugee problem, Israel had been a net gain—resettling more refugees than it had dislodged.

The Palestinian people, of course, did not see things quite that way. They were not looking at the situation from the standpoint of the world refugee problem, but from the standpoint of their own lives. In that context, what had happened was an outrageous wrong that Israel refused to acknowledge. Instead, Israel had resettled Jewish refugees in Arab homes and villages, and given some of the Arab agricultural land to kibbutzim.

Over 350 Palestinian villages had been destroyed. The long Israeli path of "creating facts" on the ground which would make the return of Palestinians to their homes virtually impossible had begun.

It is hard to fully grasp the impact of what Palestinians later were to call "the Disaster" (Al Naqba). At the beginning of 1948, historian Rashid Khalidi points out, Arabs "constituted over two thirds of the population of the country and were a majority in fifteen of the country's sixteen sub-districts. Beyond this, Arabs owned nearly 90 percent of Palestine's privately owned land. In a few months of heavy fighting in the early spring of 1948, the military forces of a well-organized Jewish population of just over 600,000 people routed those of an Arab majority more than twice its size ... more than half of the nearly 1.4 million Palestinian Arabs were driven from or fled their homes. Those Palestinians who did not flee the conquered areas were reduced to a small minority within the new state of Israel (which now controlled about 77 percent of Mandatory Palestine). At the end of the fighting Jordan took over the areas of Palestine controlled by its army west of the Jordan River, while the Egyptian army administered the strip it retained around Gaza, adjacent to its borders.... The Palestinians found themselves living under a variety of alien regimes, were dispossessed of the vast bulk of their property, and had lost control over most aspects of their lives." (Khalidi, "The Palestinians and 1948: the underlying causes of failure" in *The War for Palestine*, edited by Eugene L. Rogan and Avi Shlaim).

I have been telling this story in a way that attempts to show that this outcome was a product not of evil intentions, but of the ways that both sides perceived and defined their realities, and both sides ignored the needs and legitimate concerns of the other. There is no question that had the Palestinian people responded to the needs of Jewish refugees for a place to come they would have been in a much stronger position to have argued for one democratic country and against partition. On the other hand, had they embraced partition and accepted the needs for a Jewish state, they would have ended up with far more land and security than a war yielded for them. Conversely, had the Zionists been able to understand the legitimate concerns of the Palestinian people to not lose their identity and rights to national self-determination, and had they extended a hand of cooperation and friendship rather than perceiving the Palestinians to be an extension of all the hurtful forces that had ever confronted the Jewish people throughout our history, they would have been able to work out agreements and arrangements that could have prevented Israelis from continuing to fight the same battle for legitimacy for the next fifty-five years of Israel's existence.

It makes little sense to demonize either side. Both were incapable of seeing the pain of the other. Both were so caught up in their own suffering that they could not grasp what the other side was talking about. And that denial has made it impossible for either side to talk in an honest way with the other or to find a path to heal the wounds without destroying the current State of Israel.

It certainly would have been better for the long term well-being of the Jewish people if they could have found a way in the early years of 1948–52 to start a process of bringing back refugees. If, for example, they had allowed back 50,000 a year, on condition that they live in peace with their neighbors, and with the clear understanding that the process of bringing them back would stop if violence from these returnees became a significant reality, that would have been the kind of humane gesture which could have influenced Palestinian consciousness. If, in addition, Israel had sought to reach out to the refugees in a spirit of conciliation, trying to separate their fate from the politics of the Arab world, recognizing them as victims and not as a monolithic group of enemies, there might have been a very different relationship established.

But now imagine the Jewish people in 1948, three years after the Holocaust, just barely even beginning to acknowledge the level of pain and trauma it had suffered, and then fighting for what it perceived to be its survival in Palestine. Imagine the experience as fear turned to jubilation and it appeared as if a modern miracle had taken place—the dead bones of Europe had been revived, the people who had been destroyed were resurrected, the people who had been treated as dispensable had now shown that they would not allow themselves to be pushed around any more. At such a moment, talk of compassion for the enemy that refused to allow your refugees to escape the Holocaust, and that fought you rather than allow those living in displaced persons' camps to find refuge in their homeland, was perceived to be utopian foolishness.

Now imagine if, on the other side, the Palestinians had produced a new leadership, one willing to repudiate the horrible choices of the past. Imagine if the Palestinians had denounced the Husseini clan which had allied itself with Hitler, had spurned the leadership of those who had foolishly turned down the Partition proposal of 1947 which would have given the Palestinians a far better deal than they were forced to settle for in 1949, had repented of the moral scandal of refusing to allow Jewish refugees to come to Palestine, and had turned to the Jewish people with a simple plea: "Give us an opportunity to prove that we can live as loyal citizens and a minority within a Jewish state and we will show you that we can do so and acknowledge the validity of your having created such a Jewish state." If the Palestinians had been capable of that, it would almost certainly have changed the politics of Israel.

Now think your way into the consciousness of the Palestinian people by the end of 1948, a few months after having been thrown out of their homes or having fled for the complex of reasons described above. Imagine the rage you would feel at having your worst fantasies confirmed: that the Zionist enterprise was in fact causing you to lose your homeland. You would hardly be able to believe your ears and eyes that the Zionists were now going to keep your house or apartment, forbid you to return to your village (if, indeed, it even existed anymore), and were rejecting resolutions calling for the return of refugees (Resolution 194) from the very United Nations whose vote had been used to legitimate the State of Israel in the first place. At such a moment, talk of acknowledging past errors, repudiating their leadership, or pleading for another chance with the State of Israel would have been perceived as utopian foolishness.

And yet, it was precisely this kind of prophetic thinking that was necessary. Without what some would dismiss as "utopian foolishness," both sides dug themselves into a deeper and deeper hole.

In the early years of the State, Palestinians would seek to return to their land, sneaking over the borders, attempting to work their own farm land, and occasionally to grab back property that had been theirs; eventually these incursions led to acts of stealing food or property from the kibbutzim or others who occupied the land that had previously been theirs. At first, they came to steal crops, to graze their flocks, to engage in smuggling, or to reach the other side of Israel into the Jordanian-occupied West Bank. They were mostly unarmed at first, but after the IDF began to use violent repression (the IDF gave orders to shoot at any Arab "infiltrator," armed or unarmed, who attempted to cross the lines, killing several thousand Palestinians in this way) more and more of them carried arms, and some came to commit acts of revenge for what they had lost. They perceived Israel as an immoral robber that had stolen Arab lands, and they felt justified in striking back. After 1954 they were joined by Egyptian fedayeen ("self-sacrificers") who struck against Israelis. In the period 1948-1956 approximately 200 Israeli civilians and scores of soldiers were killed by this combination of Palestinian infiltrators and fedayeen.

Some Israeli leaders understood the motivation of the Palestinians seeking to cross the borders back into Israel. Benny Morris cites the following quote from General Moshe Dayan, responding to criticism after a particularly horrendous anti-infiltration move by the army (at the end of May 1950, when a whole group of "suspected infiltrators" were pushed across the Jordanian frontier in the desert land of Arava, thirty of whom died of dehydration and exhaustion):

> Are [we justified] in opening fire on the Arabs who cross [the border] to reap the crops they planted in our territory; they, their women and their children? Will this stand up to moral scrutiny…? We shoot at those from among the 200,000 hungry Arabs who cross the line [to graze their flocks]—will this stand up to moral review? Arabs cross to collect the grain that they left in the abandoned villages and we set mines for them and they go back without an arm or a leg…. [It may be that this] cannot pass review, but I know no other method of guarding the borders. If the Arab shepherds and harvesters are allowed to cross the borders, then tomorrow the State of Israel will have no borders.
> —*Righteous Victims*, p. 275

Had the Israelis retained this consciousness, they might have found a better way to deal with the infiltrators. But increasingly these infiltrators were defined not as hungry Arabs looking for some means of physical survival, but as terrorists seeking to destroy Israel. The IDF turned in 1951-53 to strikes against villages on both sides of the border that were suspected of harboring these infiltrator/terrorists. A special IDF commando group, Unit 101, was created in August, 1953 to execute these retaliatory actions—commanded by Ariel Sharon. In response to a grenade thrown into a house in the settlement of Yehud, killing an Israeli woman and two children, Unit 101 and a paratroop company struck at the Palestinian border village of Qibya, killing sixty inhabitants. In this case, the IDF acted according to orders from above, because they had been told to execute "destruction and maximum killing."

Chief among the hardliners was Ben Gurion himself, who at the time publicly denied the IDF involvement in the Qibya massacre. But privately he and others made clear to his Foreign Minister Moshe Sharrett (the voice in the ruling party Mapai most critical of these policies) their belief that Arabs understand only the language of force and that Israel would be destroyed unless the Arabs could see clear examples of Israel's willingness to use force in a devastating and highly effective manner.

In construing their situation in this way, the Israelis refused to take seriously the desperate plight of the Palestinian people. Instead, they focused only on the activities of the surrounding Arab regimes, believing that all reference to the Palestinian refugees was nothing more than ideological window dressing. After all, if the Arabs "really" cared about the Palestinians, Israelis reasoned, they would resettle them in decent economic conditions, rather than use them as a political football for the sake of mobilizing the masses behind the anti-Israel policies of these dictatorial governments. The anger of the Palestinian people was dismissed as little more than a replay of the anti-Semitism that Israelis had experienced through the ages. Unable to recognize or acknowledge their own role in the creation of that anger, Israelis brought to this most pressing problem the ghetto mentality, which Zionism had originally thought to transcend.

STRUGGLE WITH THE ARAB STATES 1949–2002

The belief that the Arabs understand nothing except force, the inability of Israelis to imagine that any Arabs really cared about the Palestinian people, and the dismissal of the needs of the Palestinian people as having any reality independent of the way that "the Palestinian issue" was being misused by Arab states set the basic frame for Israeli/Arab relations over the next fifty years of Israel's existence. There are the refugees, increasingly bitter and ready to take up arms in acts of violence to express their ongoing outrage at the awful conditions of their lives and the failure of Israel to allow them to return. There are the Arab states, using the issue of the Palestinians, sometimes with genuine caring, often with cynical intent, to manipulate their own populations into acquiescence to oppressive circumstances which can be blamed on the Jews. And there is Israel, seeing itself as surrounded by hostile forces whose sole motivation is to destroy the Jews, and who interpret the rage of the Palestinian people as pathological anti-Semitism rather than legitimate anger at Israel's treatment of them, and as an expression of the crude mentality of ethically underdeveloped people who have an instinctive affinity to violence and terror.

What I've found is that the struggle between Israel and the Arab states, like every other part of the story, can be told persuasively from each side's perspective. I have listened to Arabs tell the story of growing anti-Semitism in Arab states as a logical outgrowth of the anger that their own peoples felt at the terrible treatment they were seeing being inflicted on their fellow Arabs by a group of people they perceived as Westerners, and, to the extent that they had historical memory, as part of yet another wave of "crusaders" seeking to establish and maintain a Western presence in a Muslim society.

Though these sentiments were, to be sure, manipulated by the ruling elites in various destructive ways, the core of these sentiments was a genuine and legitimate outrage at what had happened to their fellow human beings. Some Arabs have used the anaology of American politics after September 11 to explain these dynamics. It is certainly the case that George Bush, Dick Cheney, and other opportunistic politicians manipulated the legitimate outrage Americans felt at the attack on the World Trade Center and channeled it into militaristic justifications for imperial ambitions that long predated that attack. Yet the core feeling of outrage at the unjustifiable suffering of our fellow citizens was not a product of media manipulation alone, but in part a genuine feeling of deep empathy as well as (somewhat exaggerated) feelings of vulnerability that it might happen to us as well. It was this same kind of dynamic, some Arabs have told me, that helps explain why Arab states could manipulate legitimate anger at Israel in ways that were fundamentally illegitimate and more intent on propping up support for Arab elites than relieving the suffering of the Palestinian people.

Yet the case for understanding Arab nation's behavior as irrational anti-Semitism could also be made. Arab countries allowed the widespread dissemination of classic anti-Semitic literature including *The Protocols of the Elders of Zion* (as recently as 2002 the Egyptian television was relying on this classic forgery to demean the Jewish people). Arab countries integrated into their defense and intelligence system former Nazi scientists and operatives. They refused to allow Jews from anywhere in the world to visit their countries (including American Jews who were in the diplomatic or military service). They did little to distance themselves when Arab terrorists in countries around the world struck at Jewish targets that had nothing to do with the State of Israel (Jewish community centers, for example). It was not hard to make the case that a deeper dynamic than identification with the suffering of the Palestinians was being played out in these dynamics.

Indeed, there is a story that can be told of how the Arab countries, after overthrowing the old feudal regimes and starting to create new modernizing elites in the 1950s who sought to mobilize support for a new Arab nationalism, used the struggle against Israel as a rallying point to take attention away from the fact that for all their courageous anti-imperialist rhetoric, these nationalist regimes had little interest in seriously empowering ordinary people or redistributing the wealth that could be amassed through Arab oil. The supposed danger of Israeli expansionism was used as the excuse for why democratic processes could not be introduced, why a free press was impossible, and why the wealth of the country, instead of being redistributed, had to be spent on arms procurements (which in fact were used to strengthen the power of ruling elites that congealed around figures like Nasser, Mubarak, Asad, and Saddam Hussein).

Nor were the Arab countries unique in their behavior. In the post-colonial period following World War II many countries around the world sought to separate themselves from Western domination and to find another way to begin a process of modernization and economic development. At first, many were attracted to the ideals of socialism or communism and to their supposed embodiment in the Soviet Union. But as the Soviet Union never adopted a real communist path, but instead merely used the language of communism to cover the reality of an oppressive authoritarian elite engaged in a struggle for world dominance with the West, third world countries began to sour on those ideals and to accommodate to the reality of Western power. The result was the spread of a new version of nationalism and/or religious fundamentalism which preached national independence, supported small national economic elites who sought to separate themselves from Western domination and to work out arrangements that would allow the elites to benefit while cooperating with Western corporate penetration of their country, and found some "demeaned other" to blame for the inability of the elite to share its wealth with the rest of the population. In the Arab world, that Other was Israel and the Jews, though in other parts of the Islamic world it was alternately Hindus, Westerners, and Americans.

It's not hard to understand the reason why Jews would appear to be Other to many Arab nationalists. For hundreds of years Jews had lived as second class citizens in Arab lands in northern Africa and the Middle East, enjoying a higher level of safety and well being than they experienced in Europe, but nevertheless being scorned and demeaned in Arab culture. When European colonialists in the nineteenth century managed to impose domination on these Arab societies, their standard colonial "divide-and-conquer" strategy led them to align themselves with the Jews, who were given the same equal rights that Jews had been given in the post-emancipation Europe of the nineteenth century. Under these circumstances, Jews tended to align themselves with the colonialists, and against Arabs who were seeking independence. When those Arab nationalists identified with the anti-Yishuv forces in Palestine, the Jews of Arab lands felt all the more antagonistic to this burgeoning nationalist movement, and all the more committed particularly to the French and English colonialists, and this was only intensified when those two colonial powers became the primary antagonists to Hitler's Germany while many Arabs flirted with fascism precisely because it would weaken the colonial powers.

The tensions between Jews and Arab nationalists spilled over into outrageous campaigns of anti-Semitism (and occasionally anti-Semitic violence) in some Arab countries in the 1940s (particularly Iraq, but also in Egypt, Syria, Algeria and Morocco). By the time of the creation of the State of Israel, large sections of Jews in Arab countries felt themselves imperiled and many responded to the vigorous recruiting being done by Zionist agents who fanned the flames of discontent and urged Jews to leave. What followed was a mass exodus of Jews from Arab countries, many of them leaving what had been relatively secure lives, and a mass flight to the newly established State of Israel. The hundreds of thousands of Jews who left these Arab countries were not facing Arab armies going from neighborhood to neighborhood and forcing Jews from their homes, nor were they facing systematic campaigns of anti-Jewish terror. But they nevertheless were leaving what had been their homelands, and leaving under conditions in which they perceived themselves to be in grave danger.

The newly arrived immigrants in Israel had different customs and styles of life from that of the (European-origin) Ashkenazim who were at the time the majority of Israelis, and they were greeted with more than a little ambivalence. On the one hand, they were proof of the continuing need for a Jewish state even after the Holocaust refugees had been integrated in to Israel. On the other hand, the socialist parties that ran the State of Israel were predominantly Ashkenazim who saw these new immigrants as primitive, culturally undeveloped, religiously medieval, ethically stunted (particularly in their treatment of women), and generally Other (almost Arab, some would have said). Though it taxed the resources of the new state, Israel made huge efforts to absorb these new immigrants at a moment when it had little resources to do so. Arab sections of cities that had been emptied by Arab flight were now filled with these new refugees. Massive housing projects created flimsy new housing in immigrant towns, some in the Negev, others in areas of the Land of Israel that the Ashkenazim had found to be undesirable for themselves. Resentment that these new immigrants felt at the way they were being treated translated into a general alienation from the Ashkenazic establishment who ran the dominant Labor Party of the Israeli Left, so that these communities became the core element in the voting blocks of right-wing parties. But since the anger that Sephardim/Mizrachim felt at the Ashkenazim was seen as disloyalty at a time while Israel was being threatened externally, it was displaced onto Arabs (with whom, according to the Israeli Right, the Left was being too gentle and accommodating). Given the experience of having fled from Arab lands, it was not a difficult step for these new immigrants to feel lots of resentment at Arab societies, and to focus that resentment in ways that would prove their patriotism to their new homeland—by hating Palestinians.

All this contributed to the ease with which Israel came to portray itself as a lone island in a sea of hostility from surrounding Arab states and to develop a "Left" that was progressive on social and economic issues but highly hawkish on issues relating to Arabs in general and Palestinians in particular. It was this socialist Left, embedded in the Labor Party, that became the shaping force in creating an ethos of hostility to Arabs that persisted long after the creation of the State of Israel. And in this they were in part responding to the actual hostility being evinced by Arab nationalists and fundamentalists who were portraying

Israel to their own masses as little more than an incursion from the West and the symbol of continuing Western colonialism and expansionism.

ARAB STATES

It would be impossible in the course of this short book to tell the whole story of the ins and outs of the history between Israel and the Arab states in the fifty years from 1948-2002. The central argument of this book does not rely much on the brief summary presented in the next few paragraphs, which are here only to point out that even this story can be told from both people's standpoints.

From the standpoint of many of the Arab elites, the perception that Israel was the tool of Western expansionism was based in part on the fact that the United States gave so much economic aid and political support to Israel. But it was also based on the reality of Israeli behavior. When the Egyptian nationalists overthrew the feudal elites who had chosen to make war on Israel, their new leader Gamal Abdul Nasser in 1955 challenged the right of the British and French to continue to control the Suez Canal which ran through Egypt and allowed the West unimpeded access to the oil of those Arab countries whose elites were dominated by Western interests. In 1956 the French and English responded by invading Egypt and attempting to grab control over the canal, and the new State of Israel joined them in this enterprise, seizing the Sinai peninsula and supporting the colonial invasion. Though Israel claimed it was only interested in stopping any further incursions into its own borders from Palestinian refugees, its association with British and French colonial interests was now confirmed for the world to see. Even the United States reacted with hostility, insisting that all three countries withdraw their forces and allow the Egyptians self-determination. Israel agreed only when a UN force was set in place in the Sinai to separate Israel and Egypt and guarantee an end to incursions from Palestinian refugees.

For most Israelis, the notion that the new Jewish state was an extension of Western colonialism seemed absurd—they perceived themselves as the victims of Western anti-Semitism, and they had made common cause with the British and French only to provide greater security for their own fledgling state. With the United States abandoning them by demanding withdrawal from the Sinai, Israelis perceived themselves as isolated. That isolation reached a crescendo when in 1967 Gamal Abdul Nasser generated a new crisis by calling for the UN to withdraw from Sinai and enflaming the dormant anti-Israel feelings in Egyptian and Syrian societies. Egyptian radio repeatedly broadcast messages talking about "pushing the Jews into the sea," and calling upon Arabs to join in this struggle. Recent diplomatic and military papers in the Israeli archives give some evidence to believe that the top military leadership of Israeli society had reason to believe that Nasser had no serious intention of invading Israel, and that like the Arab states of 1948 was posturing with no mechanism to follow through. It's hard to know whether they believed that evidence or whether their own perceptions of powerlessness might have led them to feel more endangered than their information would have warranted. But for the vast majority of the Israeli people, and for Jews around the world, the rhetoric of "pushing Jews into the sea" that poured forth from Arab states restimulated the anger and fears lingering from the Holocaust, feelings that had largely been suppressed during the intervening years when the Jewish state had to focus its attentions on survival and resettling of immigrants. For many of us who lived through the spring 1967, the possibility of the destruction of the State of Israel and a new Holocaust seemed very real. Once again the nations of the world sat silent.

No wonder then that so many Jews around the world experienced almost religious ecstasy when Israel's leaders used this moment to launch a preemptive military strike against Egypt and Syria. The Six Days War was so short, many Arabs pointed out, because there was no serious plan on the part of Egypt and Syria to attack and hence no serious mobilization of those societies in preparation for war. I believe that the evidence so far uncovered makes claims about who was planning what far more ambiguous than either side claims, and in any event the perception of imminent destruction that Egypt and Syria created in the population of the Israeli people cannot be attributed solely to displaced Holocaust fantasies and must be placed squarely on the irresponsibility of Nasser and his demagoguery.

In the days leading up to its sneak attack on Egypt and Syria that launched the 1967 war, Israel made overtures to King Hussein of Jordan, seeking to keep him out of the war. Instead, he joined, and attacked Israel a few days after Israel's attack on Syria and Egypt. Israel's counterattack conquered the Arab sections of Jerusalem, and from there proceeded to conquer the West Bank. There was little resistance to Israeli forces moving into the West Bank for two main reasons: 1. The Palestinian people had been living under Jordanian rule since 1948, and did not feel particularly attached to that occupying power any more than to the Israeli power who now took over. 2. The Palestinian people had nothing to do with starting or engaging in the war in 1967. They would be amazed to later be told "you lost the war in 1967, so now you have to bear the consequences," because most Palestinians had not been involved except as passive witnesses to a swift battle fought by foreign armies.

Israeli forces occupied the West Bank, and very soon thereafter many sane voices in Israel, including that of Moshe Dayan and David Ben Gurion, both of whom had quit the Labor Party they had previously led, called upon the Israeli government to withdraw and create an independent Palestinian state in this territory. Unfortunately, the Labor government did not respond to these pleas. Drunk with the blindness of instant and glorious military victory, the "Leftists" who were now leading Israel could see no point in making an accommodation with the Palestinian people. In fact, many of them denied there was such a thing as a Palestinian people, insisting instead that there was only an Arab people and that the only problem regarding Palestinian refugees was that they were not being resettled in Arab lands.

A new religious group, the "block of the faithful" (Gush Emunim), would soon argue that it was forbidden for Jews to return the land to the Arabs, because the land had been given to the Jewish people by God in Torah, and that now it was being given back to us again by God's will. Just as former Chief Rabbi Kook of the Yishuv had once argued that Zionism was God's way of using secular people to do His will, so Kook's disciples now argued that the outcome of the wars by the Israeli army were actually a product of divine intervention, and God's will had thereby been made known. So, while the Israeli government argued that it needed to hold on to the West Bank and Gaza for strategic and military reasons, a growing number of "modern Orthodox" (to distinguish from the more Haredi-fundamentalist orthodox who largely refused to acknowledge the legitimacy of the State of Israel, seeing it as an unfortunate secular reality that had to be dealt with but which had no religious significance whatsoever) began to see a different reason: God's manifest destiny for the Jewish people. It was these "modern

Egyptian president Anwar Sadat, second from left, stands next to Israeli prime minister Menachem Begin, third from left, during a visit to Yad Vashem, Israel's National Holocaust Museum in Jerusalem, 1977.

GPO HO/AP Wide World Photos

Orthodox" who created settlements in the West Bank, and have been at the center of pushing the agenda of Israeli expansionism. Over the course of the next twenty-five years they encouraged some 120,000 Israelis to settle in the West Bank and Gaza, in the process sometimes buying land, but often occupying and expropriating land from Palestinian farmers and landholders.

The return engagement of the 1967 war occurred in 1973 when the Egyptians launched a retaliatory strike to win back what they had lost in 1967, only to face an Israel newly armed by the United States, which had become convinced that Israel could be a useful ally in the global struggle against communism. The 1973 war produced a stalemate, and much suffering among Israelis, so it was with great joy that Israelis welcomed Egyptian president Anwar Sadat to Jerusalem in 1977 and then proceeded to sign an agreement with him which returned the Sinai desert to Egypt in return for a peace treaty that has kept the border mostly quiet, and has allowed Israelis and Egyptians to visit each other's country over the course of the past decades.

Yet even with a peace treaty with Egypt, and after the Oslo Accord a peace treaty with Jordan, the Arab states continued to put forward deep hostility to the State of Israel. In the 1970s they used their considerable power to get the United Nations Assembly to pass a resolution condemning Zionism as racism. Yet this move itself was a racist singling out of the Jewish people and its particular sins, as though somehow their transgressions were qualitatively worse than the oppression of Tibet by China, the suppression of millions of people in the then Soviet Union and the East European states that its army was occupying, the pervasive denial of human rights in Arab countries, the systematic denial of rights to minorities in many countries at the time, etc. Yet other countries went along with this double standard, in part out of genuine and legitimate sympathy for the ongoing plight of the Palestinian people, and in part out of cynical disregard for "fairness" so that they could build good relations with the oil-producing Arab states.

In singling out Israel, a world that had previously abandoned the Jewish people during the Holocaust was once again showing a particular willingness to ignore the suffering of the Jews and focus only on our sins. This kind of behavior, in turn, strengthened the hands of those in the Jewish world who would say, "The world is filled with so much anti-Semitism that there is no point in paying attention to what they think. Our only hope is to develop our military strength in Israel to protect ourselves against the inevitable resurgences of anti-Semitism of which this UN resolution is an example." Right wing forces in American politics were similarly able to use this unfair and racist resolution as an important weapon in their campaign to discredit the United Nations more generally. Thus, the distorted attack on the Jews, an attack motivated at least in part by genuine and legitimate outrage at the fate of the Palestinian people, took a form that was so unfair and unprincipled that it gave strength to the forces most willing to ignore the well being of the Palestinian people. And this is an important lesson: Sometimes the tactics of support for a cause can generate more distraction from the cause than aid to it.

Back to Israel. The growing resentment by Sephardic Jews at the Ashkenazi elite, combined with disillusionment about the military smarts of the Labor government in the aftermath of the 1973 war, had produced a radical change of government in 1977 when the Likud came to power and former Jewish terrorists Menachem Begin and Yitzhak Shamir became the leaders of a new Israeli government. It was they who concluded peace with Egypt, and they who, having pacified the Arab country with the largest population, turned their attention to consolidating their power over the larger Land of Israel that had been acquired in the conquest of 1967.

The Palestinian people, themselves largely apolitical and still traumatized into quiescence by the shock of al Naqba and the daily problems of surviving in horrendous refugee camps receiving minimal rations from the United Nations, had begun to awaken to the challenge of Occupation, and had begun to develop a national liberation struggle which called for the elimination of Israel and the return to a single democratic Arab dominated state, and to support the Palestinian Liberation Organization under the leadership of Yassir Arafat. But as Arafat became more successful in mobilizing and radicalizing exiled Palestinians, it became increasingly obvious to PLO activists that the first goal would have to be the replacement of repressive Arab regimes which had used the Palestinian cause for their own purposes but not provided serious support for a struggle against Israel. Needless to say, that kind of analysis was not welcomed by the conservative Arab elites, and so it was no surprise that the PLO and its supporters were physically driven out of Jordan by King Hussein's forces, and later were the subject of attack by Syrian and Lebanese forces in Lebanon. But as the Lebanese were not able to fully defend themselves against an increasingly militant PLO which had, by the late 70s, moved its main presence to Lebanon, the PLO became a major factor in shaping the lives of people in Southern Lebanon. It was on the flimsiest of pretexts that Menachem Begin sent the Israeli Army under Gen. Ariel Sharon to wipe out the PLO in 1982, thus beginning a struggle that would leave tens of thousands of Lebanese and hundreds of Israelis dead over the course of the next eighteen years.

Israel's behavior in Lebanon contributed to the continuing hostility of Arab states to Israel. Even Egypt, having contracted a peace agreement with Israel, made this into a "cold peace," one in which there was little real friendliness. Though Israel was anxious to develop deeper ties, it paid little attention to Egyptian sensitivities about the role Israel was playing in the Occupation of the West Bank or in the invasion of Lebanon. In turn, the Egyptians, while scrupulously living up to the terms of their treaty, continued to teach hatred of Jews, hostility to Israel itself, and participated in the ever shrill anti-Israel rhetoric that pervaded the Arab world.

Rock-throwing Palestinians challenge the Israeli Occupation in Ramallah,
1988.   AP Wide World Photos

Though Israel did succeed in routing Arafat's forces (who withdrew
to Tunisia), the war produced a powerful anti-war movement in Israel,
Peace Now, started by army officers who opposed the war in Lebanon,
and broke what had until the early 1980s been the virtual uniformity in
Israeli society supporting aggressive action against Arabs. Meanwhile,
Palestinians in the West Bank and Gaza began to demand self-determination, and claimed that their real representative was the exiled PLO.
When Israel ignored the repeated appeals for democratic self-determination, the Palestinian people began a spontaneous uprising called the
Intifada (I) in 1988, a war of stones against the bullets of the occupying
armies and the Jewish settlers.

The response of the Israeli government ranged from that of IDF
general and then defense chief Yitzhak Rabin who ordered his forces to
"break the bones" of the teenagers throwing rocks, to that of Ariel
Sharon who used his new position as housing minister in the coalition
government (he had previously been forced to resign for his role in the
massacre of hundreds of civilians in Lebanon) to provide massive assistance to Israelis who would agree to buy an apartment in West Bank
settlements (which, as a result, mushroomed in size and in suburban
accoutrements).

But Israel was unable to end the Intifada, and it only sputtered out after Bush Sr.'s war against Iraq in 1991 was followed by the US convening a new set of peace negotiations in Madrid whose goal was to develop a comprehensive Middle East settlement.

To Israelis, the idea that the Arab states could demand a resolution to the conflict seemed ludicrous, both because the Arab states had been proven militarily powerless (and hence from the standpoint of "realists" they were inconsequential) and because the Arab states had so transparently never really cared about the fate of the Palestinian people.

The proof text is the way Arab states used the Palestinians as a political football, without really caring about them. Edward Said, writing in 2001, wrote about this behavior of Arab countries as "a scandalously poor treatment of the refugees themselves. It is still the case, for example, that the 40,000–50,000 Palestinian refugees resident in Egypt must report to a local police station every month; vocational, educational, and social opportunities for them are curtailed and the general sense of not belonging adheres to them despite their Arab nationality and language. In Lebanon the situation is direr still. Almost 400,000 Palestinian refugees have had to endure not only the massacres of Sabra, Shatila, Tell el Zaater, Dbaye and elsewhere, but they have remained confined in hideous quarantine for almost two generations. They have no legal right to work in at least sixty occupations, they are not adequately covered by medical insurance, they cannot travel and return, they are objects of suspicion and dislike." Though this was not true in Jordan, it was true in most other Arab countries that the fate of refugees became the pretext for anti-Israel mobilization, but not for actual concrete measures to protect and care for the refugees themselves. And it was this continuing cynicism by Arab states which gave credence to the supposition of some Israelis that they were surrounded by people who were implacably opposed to them and that the particulars of Arab grievances should not be given too much credence, but were only a cover for underlying irrational anger at the Jewish people.

From the standpoint of the Palestinian people, the interventions of the Arab states in attempts to keep the Palestinian refugee issue alive, no matter how laced with cynicism, were a blessing in a world that would just as easily have forgotten the fate of these refugees. No matter how cynical the intent of the interventions of the Arab states, their own perceived need to keep the refugee issue alive may have served the interests of the refugees. Or maybe not—maybe the refugees could have been resettled in Arab lands, and taken the same stance toward return to their homes that Jews took after the Roman defeat—maintaining the dream but building new lives for themselves in the lands of their diaspora. The refugees themselves had a very clear message: "We want to return to our homes and villages" (homes and villages which, unfortunately, mostly no longer existed, having long been replaced by Israeli villages and towns and apartment complexes in which new generations of Israelis had been born and which they also claimed as their homes).

Nor would it be reasonable to say that it was only the Arab states that were playing a cynical role. Facing the growing upsurge of support for the PLO and its secular nationalist vision of Palestinian independence, Israel decided to help support the newly emerging Islamic fundamentalist movement in Gaza called Hamas. While Hamas is best known in the West for its acts of horrific terror against Israeli civilians, its large base was built by providing the social services to the Palestinian population that international law requires of the occupying force but which Israel was unwilling to provide (e.g. health care and education). Imagining that Hamas would be a counterweight to the PLO, Israeli agents worked with and provided material support for the development of the Hamas infrastructure, though Hamas was 100% clear in its total opposition to the existence of a Jewish state in any part of Palestine at any time. In this they were following a path that had also been followed by the United States which at the time was funding Osama Bin Ladin to organize Afghan "freedom fighters" to struggle against the Soviet occupation of Afghanistan.

It was to please the Arab states, which had allowed George Bush, Sr. to station troops in Saudi Arabia to fight against Saddam Hussein during the Gulf War of 1991, that the United States pressured Israel to participate in international negotiation in Madrid to develop a multilateral peace agreement. But while Israel agreed to participate, its Likud government felt no incentive to concede anything. As then Israeli Prime Minister Shamir later revealed, his strategy was to sit in negotiations for the next ten years, because as long as Israel continued to occupy the West Bank and to expand settlements, there was no problem in having representatives sit through an essentially meaningless process that was preordained to produce nothing.

George Bush, Sr., however, was determined to reward Arab states in some way for their support, so when Prime Minister Shamir requested that the United States back "loan guarantees" (which would help provide housing and support for Russian immigrants who had suddenly been able to move to Israel now that the old communist regime had collapsed) to the tune of ten billion dollars, he refused unless Israel agreed to a complete freeze on new settlements in the West Bank. Shamir refused, Bush stuck to his guns, and though some of his supporters later argued that this move cost him his reelection because it so alienated American Jewish conservatives that they were unable to mobilize Republican votes in the 1992 election, it also was seen by many as a central cause of why Shamir lost the election of 1992 to Yitzhak Rabin of Labor (because many Russian immigrants whose conservative politics inclined them to the Right felt that Shamir had shown he could not "deliver" the help that they needed).

Although the public negotiations continued to go nowhere, a private channel was opened in which Yossi Beilin and others representing the new generation of Israeli leaders met with the new generation of Palestinian leaders, and by the Spring of 1993 they could publicly announce a breakthrough that became known as the Oslo Accords. It was clear to both sides who were party to those negotiations that for a moment the two sides had taken the time to get to know each other and each other's needs, and it was in that context that they could recognize each other's humanity and begin to work out a plan that would not be about one side winning, but about both sides winning. This new attitude, the spirit of Oslo, did not survive the 1990s.

Chapter Five:

Difficulties
Sustaining Peace

The signing of the Oslo Accords in September 1993 at the White House ushered in a new period of hopefulness. Finally, it appeared that an end to the conflict had been negotiated! The center of the agreement was mutual recognition between the Palestinian Liberation Organization (PLO) and the State of Israel. The agreement itself was far smaller than the hoopla around it. It called for a three-staged negotiation, beginning with a short negotiation period, followed by an interim period of self-government for the Palestinian people in the West Bank and Gaza that would last no more than five years, accompanied by three stages of Israeli disengagement from the territory, after which would come a per-manent solution to be negotiated during the five year period. The best part was the preamble, which states that "it is time to put an end to decades of confrontation and conflict, recognize mutual legitimate and political rights, and strive to live in peaceful coexistence and mutual dignity and security and achieve a just, lasting and comprehensive peace settlement and historic reconciliation."

Privately, Israeli officials involved in the negotiations told the Palestinians flat out that the interim "self-government authority" (SGA) was a fancy, yet indirect way to say that the Palestinians would have a state of their own in five years and that Israel would be out of

Doug Mills/AP Wide World Photos

the territories. The first few years would involve gradual transfer of authority to the Palestinians, during which time the Palestinians would build a strong police force to guarantee public order and internal security, while Israel would have the right to defend the security of Israelis in the territories.

From the standpoint of Israeli negotiators, the gradual process of transfer of power would be critical, because it would allow for the building of confidence among Israelis who had, over the course of decades, developed deep anger and antipathy toward the Palestinian people. If the Palestinians could demonstrate to Israelis during this period that they were using their new power in responsible ways, that would make it easier for the government to build the political support it would need to implement the final settlement.

For this same reason, the Israelis left many issues undefined, hoping that as support built for the peace process in Israel they could make greater concessions in the future without endangering the political support that the Yitzhak Rabin government would need to survive inevitable critiques from the Zionist Right. The great fear shaping the

Ultra-nationalist Jews try to march on the Haram al Sharif mosque. May, 1995.   Photo by Ruben Bittermann/Impact Visuals.

strategy of Israeli negotiators was that somehow they would provoke the Israeli Right into resistance, and that resistance could lead to civil war. The Rabin strategy was to gradually show the Right that there was nothing to fear from Palestinian control of the West Bank (something which the military experts agreed upon, and which had become obvious to a large section of the Israeli public during the Gulf War when missiles from Iraq sailed over Jordan and the West Bank, proving that holding these extra few miles of territory did not necessarily enhance Israeli security in an age of advanced technology weaponry). Rabin would have to ease out of the territories the now close to 120,000 Israelis who had moved there (some for ideological reasons, others because it was cheap housing and convenient commuting to Jerusalem or Tel Aviv). So Rabin and others imagined that this interim period would allow him the wiggle room to establish trust and to win a larger and more solid majority in the Knesset which would allow him to negotiate a more generous final settlement agreement.

Many Palestinians, on the other hand, saw the agreement as a massive sell-out of Palestinian interests. The settlements were not uprooted. The IDF would continue to exercise control over most of the West Bank and Gaza. The borders with Egypt and Jordan would still be controlled by the Israelis. The future stage of final settlement had not been defined. And, in return for all this, what Israel was seeking was the use of the Palestinian Liberation Organization as an internal police force to ensure that there would be an end to the terror attacks on Israel from a people which considered itself "occupied."

Many Palestinians felt that the real winner at Oslo was not the Palestinian people, but the PLO, which claimed to represent their interests. The PLO was granted the right to bring in large contingents of police (12,000 in the West Bank and 18,000 in Gaza Strip), as well as machine guns, rifles, and light armored vehicles. Yet the Palestinians had not freely chosen the PLO for this role.

It was Israel that had chosen the PLO, not the Palestinian people. Israel's focus was on its own security, which it believed the PLO could enforce, rather than on creating a democratic process for the Palestinian people. It is thus ironic that Israel later would denounce the lack of democracy in Palestinian-held areas, when in fact it was Israel that had chosen to impose the PLO before conducting elections of the Palestinian people. Though it is certainly true that local representatives of the PLO like Faisal Husseini rejected the notion of local elections and insisted that only the PLO could speak for the entire Palestinian people (including the majority who were in exile), there were others in the Palestinian world who would have participated in these elections and a representative voice could have been established for the Palestinians living in the West Bank and Gaza.

Yet Israeli fears of such elections were also understandable. In the absence of a peace-oriented PLO policing the West Bank and Gaza, the elections might have been unduly influenced by the power of Intifada militants and Hamas, the Islamic fundamentalist group which Israel had helped build in the 1980s but which was now committed to using terror attacks on Israel. Even if the Israeli army could have ensured quiet and orderly elections, Israeli leaders feared that these militants would win the election and thus determine the shape of Palestinian politics. While professing a commitment to democracy, Israel did not have a similar commitment to allowing Palestinians their own national self-determination.

Despite this essential problem at the core of the agreements—the introduction of guns to the PLO to run the West Bank—most Palestinians welcomed the Oslo Accord as an important first step toward the ultimate goal of a Palestinian State living at peace with Israel. Many had insisted on the PLO as "the sole legitimate voice of the Palestinian people" because the PLO represented not only the people who would be in a position to vote inside Gaza and the West Bank, but also those Palestinians scattered around the world (many in refugee camps) who had no other way to have their views expressed except through the PLO. Yet the PLO and the Palestinian Authority they set up was from the start riddled with opportunists who were far more interested in self-enrichment and power-aggrandizement than in the best interests of their own people. Over the course of the ensuing decade, the irresponsibility of some of these people in the PLO and in the P.A.helped discredit the larger Palestinian Authority leadership in the eyes of many Palestinians.

There originally was widespread approval in Israel for the Oslo Accords—polls indicated about the same percentage of Israelis and Palestinians supported the agreements (roughly 2/3 of the population). In the few weeks following the signing, jubilation spread through much of the Israeli population. That jubilation was equally intense when, a year later, Prime Minister Rabin and Jordanian Premier Abd al-Salam al-Majali signed a Treaty of Peace.

Israel's political system, however, gives a great deal of power to minor parties, including the religious parties and the Sephardic parties, who held the balance of power in the Knesset. They did not share the popular enthusiasm for the Oslo Accords, nor did the right-wing secular party, Likud, nor did even some of the more settler-oriented leaders of the Labor Party (Ehud Barak, for example, had been critical of the proposals when they were voted on by the Cabinet a few week before the signing in Washington).

Because of this internal opposition, Yitzhak Rabin made a fatal choice in the aftermath of Oslo. He had the opportunity to use that moment to try to challenge the anti-Palestinian discourse and rhetoric which had been taught in schools and which dominated the media for decades. He had the opportunity to proclaim that this was a moment to move from enmity to friendship.

In a private conversation I had with Yitzhak Rabin at the signing of the Oslo Accords at the White House, and in numerous conversations with his top advisors, I proposed to him that he could use this moment to define the highest patriotic duty of Israelis as reconciliation with their former enemies. I asked him to ask Israelis to make it their patriotic duty to make friends with at least one Palestinian family, to learn of their situation, and to find ways to help them as the process of ending the settlements proceeded. I asked him to propose a massive fund to resettle settlers inside the Green Line (the pre-1967 borders of Israel). I asked him to start talking in explicit terms to the Israeli public about what the terms of a final settlement would be—to use this moment of enthusiasm to prepare people for the ending of the Occupation and the turning over of the settlements to the Palestinian people, and the sharing of Jerusalem as the joint capital of two states. Now was the moment to act decisively to change the dominant discourse in Israeli society, and Rabin had the opportunity to do so.

Instead, Rabin chose another path. Instead of building on the two-thirds of the population who supported him, something he could have done by dissolving the Knesset and calling for an election to give the Israeli people an opportunity to ratify Oslo, Rabin decided to play to the people who did not support the agreement or whom he felt might be influenced by right-wing critiques. In many ways the Right and its ways of thinking were closer to Rabin's army mentality than talk of reconciliation and emotional bridge building with Palestinians. So his focus went not to building the self-confidence of the peace forces and the spreading of a peace mentality, but rather to speaking to the Right. Here, as in the negotiations for Oslo, the great fear was to prevent a civil war—and with that at the top of his agenda, placating the Right rather than mobilizing the Center was where he put his energy. He did this in a series of speeches whose main point was not how to build peace, but rather to focus on how little he had given away, on how clever a negotiator he had been, on how he still didn't really trust the Palestinians, on how he would not move too quickly to implement various parts of the agreement, on how he and Israel would remain "tough." Thus he reinforced the tendency in Israeli media and public discourse to distrust the Palestinians at the very moment when what was needed was the building of a climate of trust.

Perhaps if more of his advisors had shown him a different path, Rabin would have taken it. Instead, many of his advisors, and even many of the leaders of the Israeli peace movement, opposed any attempt to push Rabin in a direction which would have led to an explicit confrontation with the Right. The fear of civil war with the settlers dominated public discussion, and peace movement leaders like Avi Ravitsky, Moshe Halbertal, MK Avrum Burg, and Peace Now leader Janet Aviad told me that the path Yitzhak Rabin was following was the one that made sense: show through confidence building measures that land could safely be handed over to the Palestinians, and then, once Rabin had been re-elected in 1996, he would have the mandate he needed to more forcefully and unequivocally bring peace. In the meantime, this logic went, Rabin had to show the Israeli "middle" that he was tough and restrained, that he would fight terror as though Israel still had the right to do whatever it wanted in the West Bank.

What happened instead was that Rabin's confidence-building measures gave new credence to the right-wing critics of Oslo. The latent content of Rabin's message was this: we may have reached an agreement, but we still can't trust those Palestinians and we have to be careful that we don't give them too much. And that's how Rabin acted. When a series of terror attacks came, instead of seeking to target responses to the specific terrorists who had attacked Israel, Rabin responded by closing the borders with Palestine and imposing restrictions on access to the mosque on The Temple Mount. Check points were established between various Palestinian towns, making transit more difficult for the Palestinian people (and, as later military authorities were to concede, only created more hassles for Palestinians without increasing Israeli security). The underlying assumption was that Israel was still at war with the entire Palestinian people, who would be punished collectively for whatever action was taken by the minority who wished to thwart the will of the majority.

Moreover, Rabin did little to confront the settlers with a new reality. On the one hand, he talked in ways that were experienced as demeaning to the settlers. On the other hand, he did not actually dismantle the settlements. As a result, settlers felt both under attack and free to mobilize counter-attacks with impunity. And some showed that by taking aggressive actions against their Palestinian neighbors. Expansion of existing settlements continued.

In the first phase of implementing Oslo, Israeli troops were withdrawn from major Palestinian cities. From Israel's standpoint, this, together with the creation of a Palestinian Authority democratically elected to run the new reality, was a major accomplishment for which the Palestinian people ought to be grateful and recognize Israeli generosity. Palestinians, after all, could now run their own municipal services (education, taxation, municipal policing, garbage collection, etc.). Israeli police were no longer shooting Palestinian youth for the offense of waving a Palestinian flag (something that had happened frequently in the previous years). Yet this was a long way from what the Palestinian people wanted: independence as a separate country with their own borders (which under the Oslo Accords were still under Israeli control), their own representative in the United Nations, their own ability to participate in international affairs. But quite apart from the dignity and self-respect that would only come with national independence, something which Israelis had fought for themselves in 1948, there was a much more concrete reality: daily life was becoming more, rather than less, oppressive.

Implementing Oslo involved the creation of different zones in the West Bank, and to go from one zone to another Palestinians found themselves standing in long lines, sometimes for hours, to get from one town to another (try to imagine yourself in this situation every day). The decision to respond to acts of terror by the then still marginal Hamas by punishing the entire Palestinian people was implemented under Yitzhak Rabin, and it proved to many Palestinians that they were still being treated as "the enemy" and not as a friend which had just signed a peace treaty. The collective punishments involved closing the borders between Israel and Palestine, and since Israel had for much of the time of the Occupation prevented the Palestinians from developing their own economic infrastructure, Palestinians were economically

A Palestinian man is denied entry through a checkpoint north of the West
Bank city of Hebron, 1997.   Nasser Shiyoukhi/AP Wide World Photos

dependent on jobs that many held in Israel and on tourists who came
through Israel. And when the Israeli government found that border
closings were hurting the Israeli economy, they moved to a whole new
tactic: importing foreign workers to take the jobs that Palestinians were
no longer able to fulfill (because of the border closings).

No wonder, then, that the Palestinian people became disillusioned
with Oslo and found it increasingly difficult to argue against the Hamas
militants who were claiming that Arafat had sold out the entire
Palestinian people. What the Israelis really want, Hamas contended, was
for Arafat to be the jailkeeper for the Palestinian people, enforcing the
Occupation in exchange for pathetic gains of municipal self-governance.

Arafat could have countered Hamas by laying out to the Palestinian
people a vision of national independence that would be achieved if only
violence could be stopped. After elections were held and the PLO
received a mandate, he could have used that moment to announce a
relentless campaign against violence and in favor of absolute non-violence in response to the ongoing struggle for full liberation of Palestine.
And then he could have followed through by actually arresting and then
trying and jailing Hamas leaders who were organizing acts of violence.
Moreover, he could have built a popular understanding of why it was so

important for the Palestinian people to involve themselves in "confidence building measures" to reassure Israelis that what they were "giving up" was not going to make them less secure, nor was it going to provide a base for future violent struggle against Israel.

But Arafat was as incapable of this as Rabin was incapable of validating the aspirations of the Palestinian people to Israelis. So instead of stopping terrorism in the period 1994–1996, Arafat mostly made empty pronouncements. But without an end to the terror, the Israeli Right could easily argue that the Oslo Accord had not brought security, but had only given away land to the Palestinians in exchange for zero peace.

Within this context of distrust, both sides had a point. Even after Israel began to withdraw its troops from Gaza and small slivers of the West Bank, most Palestinians found their own lives just as oppressive as ever. Palestinians still found their land occupied by Israeli settlers who continued to expand their settlements and continued to consume vastly disproportionate amounts of scarce water supplies. So even when Israeli troops withdrew from some of the major cities, the Palestinians felt that their lives were not vastly improved and felt that the prosperity promised by some as the certain accompaniment to Oslo never materialized.

The failure of Oslo to deliver the goods was also connected to the dominance the Israelis essentially had given the PLO. Many Palestinians came to believe that the PLO was rife with corruption, and that buddies of Arafat and other top leaders were embezzling funds meant for the needs of the Palestinian people, or were directing those funds to projects that were of use to the PLO elite and not to the masses of impoverished Palestinians. This same perception played a role in explaining why the aid promised to the newly created semi-governmental Palestinian Authority by donor countries failed to materialize. While Israeli peace activists tended to see the emergence of the PLO in Palestine as proof that Israelis had been willing to give Palestinians what they wanted, some Palestinians felt that the PLO was itself part of the problem and was a gift of questionable value.

In retrospect, we can see another way. Just as Rabin could have appealed to the Jewish people to be patient, and to see the basic needs of the Palestinian people, the Palestinians could have seen that Israeli society had within it a significant group of people who were wanting to move toward an end of the Occupation, and who were celebrating Oslo as a step in that direction. Had the Palestinian people used this moment to renounce all forms of terror and create instead a massive movement for nonviolent civil disobedience against the remnants of the Occupation, they could have continued to publicly express their disapproval at the way Oslo was not being fairly implemented, but done so in a way that conveyed a sense of respect for the Israelis and made the Israelis feel secure about continuing down the path to peace. Had they been able to stop acts of terror, they would almost certainly have created the conditions under which Rabin would have been able to proceed toward dismantling of the settlements. Though he still might have faced a civil war from armed settlers, most people would have backed a heavy repression of the settlers had the settlers not been able to point to acts of Palestinian violence as "proof" that it was not just they, but all Israelis, who were in danger from the Palestinian people.

I can't make this criticism without simultaneously acknowledging that the Palestinians faced many violent provocations from the settlers in this period, including attacks on Palestinian towns and the shooting of random Palestinian civilians by settlers who were rarely restrained by the IDF. The most well known was the slaying, on February 25, 1994, of twenty-nine Muslim worshippers, and the wounding of dozens more, inside the Tomb of the Patriarchs in Hebron by a Jewish settler doctor named Baruch Goldstein. In the riots that followed in Hebron, many more Palestinians were killed by the IDF, which was stationed there to protect the 500 Jewish settlers who had provocatively set up a Jewish encampment in the heart of this Arab town. Goldstein became a hero for the Jewish Right, and to this day his grave has become a place for pilgrimages by Jewish opponents of the peace process to honor his murderous deed. How could Palestinians be expected to build a nonviolent movement in this kind of a climate, some of them asked?

Yet, in the end, settler attacks on Palestinians were the actions of a fringe minority in Israel—and when the Palestinians attributed these acts to "Israelis" that was as misleading and racist as Israelis attributing Hamas or Islamic Jihad violence to "Palestinians."

Sometimes partisans on each side of this struggle point to the actions of the other side and seek to show that a large percentage of people on "the other side" are covertly supporting the actions of the extremists. Very often the media contribute to this by putting before the viewing audience the most extreme (and therefore most visually interesting) scenes of support for some extremist act. "You see," say the partisans, "just look at those people—they prove that there is no real possibility of dealing with them." This dynamic happens repeatedly on both sides. When SCUDS landed on Israel in 1991 during the Gulf War, a small number of Palestinians publicly celebrated, but the world was made to believe that this was the universal response of the Palestinian people; or again, when two Israelis were brutally lynched in the fall of 2000, the footage of the crowd of Palestinian extremists celebrating and pulling their bodies through the streets was presented without ever giving public voice to the many Palestinians who opposed these acts. Similarly, when Israel developed policies that literally caused widespread malnutrition among Palestinian children (the 24-hour curfews that became a tactic of the IDF in 2002), the media gave no attention to the many Israelis who protested and organized attempts to deliver food to the besieged population. One aim of this book is to help readers step back from this kind of "see, the other side is really bad" posturing. Anyone who has spent substantial time speaking in depth to people on both sides, as I have, will have discovered that most people—on both sides— actually deeply want peace and reconciliation, even though most people are doubtful about whether the other side really wants that.

Rabin himself finally broke through this sort of "blame the other side for everything wrong" dynamic. Two years after the first Oslo accords were signed, Rabin was deep into negotiations on the next step, called Oslo II, which was to involve the withdrawal of Israeli troops from the West Bank and Gaza. At this point, however, the Right began a political insurrection, led in part by Benjamin Netanyahu, who said that Rabin had "established the Palestinian terrorist state." The Right explicitly claimed that Rabin was turning over Israel to the terrorists, and that his government was acting as the Nazis had acted to destroy the Jews. Right-wing forces sponsored daily acts of (sometimes violent) civil disobedience, blocking entrances to Jerusalem and attempting to wreak havoc in Israeli society. Thus began the Israeli civil war which Rabin and others feared so much.

It was under this circumstance that Rabin made a sharp turn in his public rhetoric in the last three months of his life. The path of compromise with the Right was not producing results, and Rabin was furious that his strategy to position himself as a center-right moderate was not succeeding. So Rabin unexpectedly took a turn toward a more compassionate and accommodating attitude toward Arafat and the

Palestinians, for the first time actually beginning to sound as though he not only had negotiated a peace accord but actually believed in peace.

The response of the Israeli Right was dramatic: posters appeared throughout Israel talking about Rabin as an enemy of the Jewish state, some comparing him to Hitler. In the religious world, a discourse of hate was aided by quotes from the Torah which authorized people to kill someone who is coming to kill you (literally "a chaser," or *rodeph*). The argument that the entire Palestinian people were such *rodephim* who were seeking the destruction of the Jewish people gave support to the notion, articulated in public discussions in some corners of the Orthodox world, that Rabin had either aided the rodephim or was himself a rodeph, and hence a legitimate target of murder. It was this kind of discourse which contributed to the climate in which a young Orthodox Jew named Yigal Amir, brought up in the Orthodox schools and yeshivas of Israel, assassinated Rabin after Rabin gave his first talk at an Israeli peace rally on November 4, 1995.

The unthinkable had happened—a Prime Minister of Israel had been assassinated, and not by a Palestinian but by a right-wing fanatical supporter of the settlers. The civil war had in fact already started, and had claimed the democratically elected leader of the Israeli people.

This was a moment when it would have been possible to change the dynamics of Israeli society and accelerate the peace process. A decisive peace-oriented leader could have called for an immediate referendum of the Israeli people to authorize the government to evacuate the key settlements that had sponsored opposition to the peace process—Kiryat Arba, Ariel, Hebron and dozens more—and to begin immediate resettlement of these ultranationalist religious zealots into the Negev where new houses would be constructed for them. Simultaneously, such a leader would have immediately negotiated an End to the Occupation, returning to the pre-1967 borders, with slight border adjustments to allow the continuation of Gush Etziyon and the sharing of Jerusalem (while retaining the neighborhoods which in 1995 had a majority of Jewish inhabitants).

A powerful leader could have won the support of the Israeli majority at this moment when it was clear that the democratic process had been thwarted by violence from the Right. A forceful campaign to explain why the Occupation and settlements constituted a clear and present danger to the continuation of Israeli democracy could have produced democratic authorization for the IDF to move decisively. (Though I strongly disagree with the content of his politics, George Bush showed precisely this kind of leadership when he used the tragedy of the September 11, 2001 terror attack against the World Trade Center to become the springboard for a bold right-wing political initiative which dramatically changed American politics. The murder of an elected peace-oriented Prime Minister by a right-wing fanatic might have provided a similar opportunity for peace forces, had they been more courageous).

AFTER RABIN

Shimon Peres, who succeeded Rabin as Prime Minister, was the wrong man for the moment. Peres had a career as an appeaser of the Right, and though he was known to be a dove in comparison with the even more right wing circles of the Labor party, he shared the contempt for Palestinians that had been fostered through decades of struggle. So instead of defining the settlers and their ideology as the source of Israel's woes, Peres defined the possibility of civil war as the main enemy.

The Jewish world was told that the central post-assassination task for friends of Israel was to emphasize Jewish unity—including unity with the very forces that had created the circumstances of the assassination. Instead of confronting the settlers, Jews around the world were asked to embrace them and the ultra-orthodox fanatics whose ideology had defined Rabin as an enemy of the Jewish people. Thus, the actual civil war which had begun and which had manifested in this dramatic act of killing the democratically elected leader who was moving toward peace was now repressed from awareness and denial became the order of the day.

This was a moment of truth for the Israeli peace movement. Had they rejected Peres' appeal and demanded serious moves to end the Occupation, they might have created a political crisis inside the Labor Party which might have allowed for the ascendancy of more dovish voices, like Knesset members Yossi Beilin and Avrum Berg, to key leadership positions. But the Israeli peace movement had demobilized itself in the years since the Oslo Accord, accepting the strategy that everything would work out by allowing Yitzhak Rabin to be a moderate. Now suddenly faced with his assassination, the peace forces fell into line behind Shimon Peres, imagining that his accommodationist strategy, while unprincipled, would be smart politics and allow for his reelection.

That still might have happened had Peres made some genuine moves of accommodation to the Palestinian people. Instead, Peres decided to use all the political credibility the assassination had given him (the repository of hopes after the death of the father figure) to attempt to negotiate a deal with Syria, a deal which failed because Peres was not prepared to return to the pre-1967 borders of Israel (as Rabin had indicated he was willing to do in secret messages sent to the Syrians through the United States).

Rather than make a new set of overtures to the Palestinians, Peres chose this moment to allow the Israeli security apparatus to take vengeance on Palestinian terrorist leaders. Here was a way to show that he was not the "wimp" that one might have thought by standing up to the Palestinian terrorists. Rabin had allowed the assassination of Islamic Jihad leader Fathis Shkaki in Matla in October, so in January Peres authorized GSS operatives to kill Hamas' Yahya Ayash, known as "the Engineer," for his bomb-making skills and allegedly responsible for major terror attacks inside Israel during 1994 and 1995. In short, a moment that could have been used to close down the settlements was instead being used to take vengeance on a suspected mastermind of Palestinian terror.

Hamas is an organization committed to the creation of an Islamic state in all of Palestine. Its strength has grown directly in proportion to the degree to which Palestinians have despaired that there could be a peaceful path to Palestinian rights under the leadership of the secular government of the Palestinian Authority. Hamas had no desire to see the peace process succeed, a process that would have credited the Palestinian secularists and provided this-worldly satisfactions to the Palestinian people. Instead, the Islamic fundamentalist movement has been committed to the full destruction of Israel, and so has a stake in proving to the Palestinian people that any path to peace is just a sham and a false start. For the same reason, Hamas seeks to discredit the Palestinian Authority, seeing it as the enforcement arm of the Israeli Occupation.

Peres' attempts to be perceived as "strong" after Rabin's death by murdering a Palestinian suspected of terror activity (charges that had never been brought to any judicial body for consideration, a precedent which would soon lead to many more such Israeli assassinations of "suspected" Palestinian terrorists) gave Hamas just the excuse it might have wanted to break through the relative quiet that had followed in the months after the Rabin assassination. In early February, Hamas began retaliating against Peres' strike against them (the assassination of Yahya Ayash) by killing Israeli civilians and soldiers in acts of terror. It was a predictable response that Peres could have known would undermine his popularity in the forthcoming elections (and for that reason, some people argued at the time that it was an action taken by members of the Mossad who sought to undermine Peres; but if so, Peres could have publicly disassociated himself and critiqued the assassination, which he did not do).

So, instead of Israeli society dealing with the terror from the Right, Peres' strategy now allowed for the public discourse to once again be focused on how to stop Palestinian terror (and which party could do so most effectively). There was only one thing that could have changed this. At this moment, it would have made sense for Yassir Arafat to do what he could to combat Hamas and to preclude it from being able to take steps of violence against Israel. Yet Arafat did nothing to undermine Hamas' ability to deliver retaliatory blows against Israel. Perhaps he believed that Israel's failure to move forward on the peace front should not be rewarded. If the Israeli right wing was to be allowed to kill the Prime Minister, and if the new people in power in Israel made their priority not the dismantling of settlements but rather retribution for the past, then there was little incentive for Arafat to clamp down on Hamas. Yet failing to do so gave the Israeli Right the opportunity to say that Hamas and the PLO were in effect identical, and that support for Peres was in effect a ticket for further Hamas violence.

Free to proceed without interference from Arafat, Hamas got what it wanted: a provocative attack on Israel followed by an Israeli retaliation against the entire Palestinian people. Thus rewarded, Hamas continued in March and April with more attacks, guaranteeing a right-wing shift which undermined the momentary swing toward the peace forces that occurred in late 1995. Though Arafat finally seemed to understand the disaster that was happening and arrested Hamas leaders, the switch in Israeli sentiments was hard to overcome.

Even the convening of the Palestinian National Council in April 1996, and its annulling of the clauses of the Palestinian Covenant that called for the destruction of Israel, a move that would have been seen as a significant step toward peace in a different environment, was not sufficient to switch the mood of despair that had been caused by the killing and wounding of large numbers of Israelis by what the media constantly described as "Palestinian terrorists." (For contrast, the American news-papers never described the people who blew up the Oklahoma City Federal Building as "white terrorists," "Christian terrorists," or "right wing terrorists"—because they had no interest in generating anger at any of these groups of which the terrorists were members).

It should be said that it is not clear Arafat had the power to stop these acts of terror. Hamas and other Arab fundamentalist groups often were as inspired by a desire to undermine Arafat and the peace process he subscribed to as by a desire to advance the interests of the Palestinian people. Hamas was armed and able to defend itself against Palestinian Authority forces, and the demand for Arafat to jail (and keep jailed, because sometimes he would jail and then quickly release) those aiding in the cycle of Hamas violence may have been unrealistic. But what can be said with certainty not only about this moment, but about the entire period from 1993 to the present, is that Arafat could have done a lot more to show his abhorrence of the violence, if that is what he indeed felt. Arafat could have done more to mobilize ordinary Palestinians to act in opposition to Hamas and other terrorist groups, and more to apologize in a sincere and serious way to the victims of terror and to the Israeli people.

For example, had Arafat, as a symbolic gesture, attempted to give some of the monies his people were receiving from international sources directly to the Israeli victims of terror, had he created a media campaign to have members of his cabinet speak out against terror and why it was hurting the Palestinian cause, had he made a serious attempt to explain to the Israeli people why he was unable to stop the terrorists and yet why he was reluctant to have Israeli security officers dominat-ing the Palestinian state and suspending normal civil liberties for every-one (a position that could have been explained in the same way that we in the United States explain why we oppose Bush administration con-straints on civil liberties in his war on terror), he would have made a serious dent in Israeli consciousness and made it much harder for the Israeli Right to benefit from Hamas violence.

Without that effort, Israeli politics moved quickly from the hope of the Rabin years to a new despair about peace, and it was that which helped create a very narrow electoral margin for Likud, making Benjamin Netanyahu the new Prime Minister in the election of June 1996. Again, Hamas had its strategy rewarded: drive out the moderates and show the world that "the true face" of Israel is that of reactionary chauvinism.

Benjamin Netanyahu was under strong pressure from the Clinton Administration to show that the change in government in Israel would not destroy the peace process. However, apart from removing IDF troops from most of Hebron in 1997, the most populated Palestinian city, Netanyahu refused to implement the three scheduled redeployments of IDF troops called for by previous agreements. He also refused to allow the Palestinians to open seaports in Gaza or to allow the promised West Bank-Gaza safe passage that had been promised in the Oslo Accords. Under these circumstances, the Palestinian Authority was not willing to take further action against Hamas. Both sides argued that the other should be taking the next confidence-building step.

New pressure on Netanyahu from President Clinton resulted in a new set of negotiations with the Palestinians at Wye River. Those talks led Israel to agree to implement more of the Oslo accord by actually withdrawing troops from more of the West Bank. Both sides agreed to prevent acts of terrorism against each other and to punish incitements to violence, and the Palestinians agreed to round up terrorist suspects and to confiscate illegal weapons.

When Netanyahu returned to Israel, he found that his right-wing base was outraged at his having signed the Wye River accord, and after a first withdrawal of IDF from some areas around the Palestinian city of Jenin, he quickly backpedaled. But not enough for his right-wing allies whose criticism of Wye led to the dissolution of his government and the calling of new elections for 1999. The Palestinians, meanwhile, invited President Clinton to the West Bank, where, in his presence, the Palestinian National Council once again nullified the clauses in the Palestinian Covenant that called for Israel's destruction. And, though Israel was clearly not implementing its side of the Wye agreement, Arafat did not allow a repeat of the Hamas terror of 1996—he suppressed Hamas activities so that the forthcoming Israeli election would not be thrown by Hamas to the Israeli Right.

Former IDF Chief of Staff Ehud Barak, the Labor Party candidate whose military credentials helped undermine fears of "selling out" the interests of Israeli security, was elected Prime Minister in May of 1999, with 56 percent of the vote to Netanyahu's 44 percent. Barak raised many hopes for a return to the legacy of peace of Yitzhak Rabin. Yet

Two Palestinian women try to avoid crossfire in Hebron, 1997.
Heidi Levine/AP Wide World Photos

Barak had never been part of the peace wing of the Labor party, and had opposed the Oslo Accord in the weeks before it was signed. He was an authoritarian leader, and it is a testimony to the desperation of the Israeli Left that they invested so many hopes in him rather than seek to create a genuine peace party with a genuinely committed peace leadership. But the leftists inside Labor argued against that—it would be, they thought, "more realistic" to get a rightwing Labor general elected than to insist on a principled peace person who might lose. Their calculations proved a tragic historical error.

Barak's electoral majority was only achieved through overwhelming support from Israeli citizens of Arab ethnicity (approximately 15 percent of Israeli citizens claim Arab ethnicity). Without that support, Barak would not have won. In the days immediately before the election the Arab candidate for Prime Minister, Azmi B'Shara, withdrew from the race so that Arabs with strong political consciousness would switch their votes from him to Ehud Barak. The tactic worked, and over 95 percent of the Arab votes went to the Labor Party.

The political Right immediately jumped on Barak's Israeli-Arab constituency to challenge the legitimacy of Barak's election. Deeply committed to the view that Israel must be a Jewish state, the Right argued that a Prime Minister could not claim legitimacy as the leader of the Jewish state if he did not receive the vote of a Jewish majority.

For Barak to have continued the peace process, he would have had to use the moment of his electoral victory to vigorously challenge the racism inherent in this right-wing position. An immediate counter-offensive at the moment when the Right had lost the election could have effectively isolated the Right and put them on the defensive. In any democratic country, the electorate is defined as those who are eligible to vote, not just those who are part of the majority ethnicity. Had Barak used this moment to affirm the legitimacy of Arab voters (who had, after all, given him the margin of victory) he would not only have solid-ified that constituency electorally, he would also have sent an important message to the Palestinian people: Arabs are no longer "second class" in the estimation of the Zionist leadership.

Unfortunately, Barak's own Labor Party had many within it who agreed with the Right's vision of legitimacy. Though there are many Zionists who do not believe that an Israeli government is illegitimate when it bases itself in part on Arab votes, there are enough who do to have made the position seem plausible to the leadership of the Labor Party. So rather than challenge the Right, Barak sent the opposite mes-sage. He implicitly accepted their definition of political legitimacy (namely, Jewish ethnicity) by declining to appoint even a single Arab to his cabinet. And this proved fundamentally self-destructive.

Barak's Labor Party and the pro-peace Meretz party under the lead-ership of Yossi Sarid, without counting the Arab parties and a few other minor ones, failed to win enough votes in the Knesset to form a gov-ernment. Once he had rejected the Arab parties, Barak had to make coalition with others in order to govern. The parties he invited into his governing coalition, the Sephardic Shas party and a few Ashkenazic religious parties, were fundamentally hostile to the peace process. The decision to make his government dependent on the right-wing forces with whom he disagreed politically, rather than to ally himself with the Arab parties, was a further extension of the fundamental position that has distorted Israeli politics at least since the time of signing Oslo: that it is more important to have peace with the Israeli Right than peace with the Palestinians. The Israeli Right had, in effect, won even when it lost: it had intimidated the so-called Left into making peace with the Right the most important priority.

These dynamics played out in a bizarre way throughout Barak's Prime Ministership. Barak would make pronouncements that seemed to indicate he was willing to move in a progressive direction, then he would immediately capitulate under pressure from the Right and take a path that was largely indistinguishable from what they would have done were they in office. To justify these moves, Barak's top advisors would point to the fact that the Barak government had no choice but to capitulate to his coalition partners, lest they quit and his government fall. Because his partners were fundamentally hostile to the peace process, whenever he seemed ready to make a move to actually implement the peace agreements Israel had signed, Shas or the religious parties would make a move to quit the coalition, and Barak would then back away. Because of these dynamics, Barak, supposedly the peace prime minister, failed to implement even the terms of the Wye River agreement that Benjamin Netanyahu had negotiated. Understandably, Arafat felt even further betrayed by Israel. The assassination of Yitzhak Rabin, the bus bombings by Hamas, the subsequent election of Benjamin Netanyahu had all made it understandable why Israel was dragging its feet in implementing the Oslo Accord. But with a prime minister now elected who had explicitly committed himself to fulfilling the terms of Oslo, it was difficult to understand why no progress had been made in implementing the intermediate steps that even Likud Prime Minister Netanyahu had agreed to. It appeared to many Palestinians as if the only part of the agreement that had any interest for Barak was the part requiring the Palestinian Authority to act as Israel's West Bank and Gaza police force to rein-in potential terrorists. Not surprisingly, the Palestinian Authority had little enthusiasm for that task when it was separated from the rest of the peace agreement, and so it did little to prevent terror attacks from continuing on a small scale.

Israeli society has a very strong sector of the electorate which is hostile to the ways that minority religious parties have often dictated their will to the Israeli majority, coercing Israelis into public policies that prohibit secular marriage and divorce, impose limitations on Sabbath activities, and use state power to require Jews to follow some religious laws. Yet each party has capitulated to the religious parties in order to stay in power, causing a great deal of contempt for politicians by ordinary Israelis. So when religious parties began to quit Barak's coalition in the first half of 2000, Barak suggested that he was on the verge of a secular revolution in which he would free Israelis of religious coercion. Had he followed through, he would have become a hero to many Israelis who might not have been so excited about his policies toward Palestinians, but who would have admired his courage in facing up to the ultra-orthodox whose power they resented. Unfortunately, in this, as in every other significant arena, Barak showed little courage, and after a week of dramatic announcements about his willingness to promote a secular revolution, Barak backed away and abandoned this promise.

By this point, in mid 2000, few Israelis felt any confidence that their prime minister stood for anything but his own political survival. And that was in danger of immediate collapse, because the minority parties had made it clear that they would soon abandon Barak's government, and that new elections would be needed. It was at this moment that Barak, desperately needing to pull off something dramatic to win reelection, decided that he would use the peace issue.

BARAK'S "GENEROUS OFFER"

After having ignored the agreement to implement Oslo through the steps decided upon at Wye, Barak turned to President Bill Clinton and asked him to convene a meeting at Camp David at which a permanent solution to the struggle with Palestinians would be negotiated. In the summer of 2000, Clinton had his own political problems. His presidency had been so severely tainted by his affair with Monica Lewinsky that he had reason to believe he would be remembered for little else. One of the most hopeful moments in his presidency had seemed to be the Oslo Accords, and now, with Oslo faltering, a last minute success in securing Middle East peace might obscure his other presidential failures and might even strengthen the chances for electoral success of his chosen successor Al Gore (whose election, among other things, might have alleviated any possibility of further criminal charges against Clinton, something by no means assured in the summer of 2000).

Clinton accepted Barak's plan to convene a summit at Camp David, but Arafat was uninterested at first. The Palestinian Authority argued that before a summit could be useful there needed to be more agreement on critical points, so that the summit could be productive. At the very least, something should have to change on the ground (meaning,

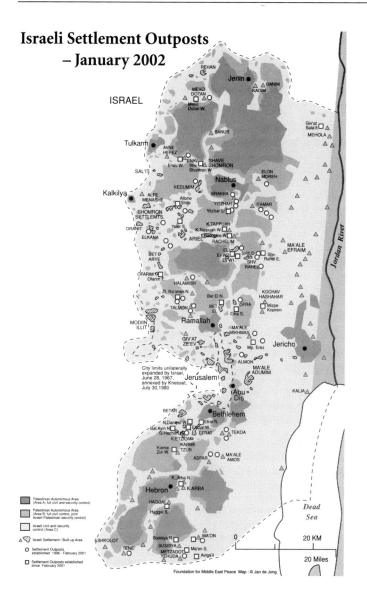

Israeli Settlement Outposts – January 2002

Foundation for Middle East Peace Map : © Jan de Jong

some change in the extent of Israeli Occupation) so that the Palestinians would feel more confident that they were not being pushed into the same kind of meaningless agreements that Wye had proved to be.

Clinton and Barak, however, faced immediate domestic political challenges that made them anxious to have a victory in the Middle East, and managed to pressure Arafat into coming. Once there, Arafat was confronted with an offer he was told he could not refuse. There is no agreement about what that offer was, because it was never put into writing. In fact, there were two offers being made at the same time.

First, there was the offer put on the table by President Clinton. That offer included a promise of 95% of the land of the West Bank and a fund of $30 billion to finance a Palestinian state. Had this been the sole offer being discussed, things would have been much clearer. But Ehud Barak, while accepting the Clinton offer as "the basis" of the Israeli position, had many reservations and differences in direction. So one of the things that Arafat was trying to do at Camp David was to clear up what part of Clinton's offer was really being accepted by Barak. When the Palestinians tried to piece together a coherent picture, here is what the came up with in what Barak later described as "the best deal the Palestinian people would ever receive":

Offered	What Palestinians Needed
1. A state	1. A state
2. Somewhere between 85–92% of the 22% of pre-1948 Palestine that constituted the West Bank and Gaza.	2. 100% of the West Bank and Gaza, constituting 22% of pre-1948 Palestine.
3. Israeli control over Palestinian borders.	3. Palestinian control over Palestinian borders.
4. Capital in Jerusalem.	4. Capital in Jerusalem.
5. Incorporation of some sections of Arab Jerusalem into a Palestinian state.	5. All sections of Jerusalem with majority Arab population into a Palestinian state.
6. Free access to holy sites supervised by Israeli army and as long as there are no security problems.	6. Free access to holy sites without Israeli army given power to determine access on security grounds.
7. Israel retains sovereignty over Temple Mount.	7. Palestinians have sovereignty over Temple Mount.

8. Israel retains military presence in Palestine including check points as it determines them to be necessary.	8. No Israeli military presence and no checkpoints.
9. Palestinians say that this agreement ends all claims on Israel.	9. Since the 3 million refugees remain in refugee camp, there is no way to abrogate future claims on Israel.

When Arafat refused this supposedly wonderful deal, both Clinton and Barak portrayed Arafat's refusal as the ultimate betrayal of the peace process and a sure sign that Arafat had no interest in building peace. This was, both claimed, the best offer that the Palestinians would ever get, and yet they had turned it down. What better proof to the world that these two men had gone as far as they could on behalf of peace, and had suddenly found that there was no real partner for peace!

It's not surprising that both men and their communities could come to this conclusion. Barak's supporters pointed out that Israel had never before explicitly and in public offered to share Jerusalem (the public formula was that Jerusalem was "the eternal capital of the Jewish people"). Yet from the Palestinian perspective, the offer did not include sections of Jerusalem with physical contiguity to each other and to the Temple Mount, and Israel would continue to rule the Temple Mount where Muslims had built two mosques at which they had been worshipping for the past several hundred years. This was not an issue of principle alone—Israel has regularly declared the Temple Mount shut to people coming from outside the Old City of Jerusalem in order to preserve security, thus effectively making it impossible for Muslims to reach one of their most important holy spots. As long as this power remained in Israel's hands, the Muslim majority is kept from the free exercise of their religion (just as Palestinians had prevented Jews from exercising their religious freedom in the period 1948-1967 when Jews were prevented from gaining access to the Western Wall).

From the perspective of Barak and Clinton, Israel had offered a great deal of the West Bank to the Palestinians. From the Palestinian perspective, the central deal of Oslo was that the Palestinians would agree to live in peace with Israel, and to accept that 78 percent of pre-1948 Palestine would become part of Israel, if in return the Palestinians could have a state on the remaining 22 percent (the West Bank and Gaza).

That those were in fact the terms promised to the Palestinians was confirmed publicly by Yossi Beilin, one of Israel's chief negotiators at Oslo who was Minister of Justice in the Ehud Barak cabinet. Given that promise, the point of future negotiations was solely about the timetable of implementation of the withdrawal of Israel from the Occupied territories, and from the settlements in them. Yet Barak was instead planning to retain 8 to 10 percent of the land that had been promised to the Palestinians. This small percentage of land was not empty, but contained the vast majority of settlers and Jewish settlements in the West Bank. Nor was the land Barak wished to keep contiguous—instead, it was scattered throughout what would have become the Palestinian state, creating pockets of Israeli control in the middle of the Palestinian lands.

There was some ambiguity about exactly what Israel was proposing. It never put a written offer on the table—which is one reason why many people coming out of Camp David had different versions of what was actually offered versus "floated" for discussion. But what is not disputed is that Israel planned to retain military roads that criss-crossed the new Palestinian state and checkpoints that would have made passage from one part of the Palestinian state to another a matter of choice by Israel. From the standpoint of Palestinians, this was like someone who has occupied your home and then offers to return 90 percent of it to you, but insists on retaining control of the hallways, so that whenever you want to go from one part of your house to another you still need his permission. That, they perceived, lessened the supposed generosity of the offer.

Yet the absolute deal-breaker of this last set of Camp David talks was and has always been the fate of the Palestinian refugees.

Sometimes Israelis point to the fact that conditions for the refugees could have been made better by the Arabic host countries, had they been interested in resettling the Palestinians there, and that their failure to do so was proof of their determination to use these refugees as a political football to justify endless struggle with Israel. As I've suggested above, I think that this claim has some validity. But it cannot explain why Israel, occupying Gaza and the West Bank for some thirty-five years, did not itself build decent housing, provide schooling and medical care, or help build an economic infrastructure so as to alleviate the poverty and oppression of Palestinians living under the Occupation.

In any event, the reality is that the refugees have been the nub of the problem for much of the past fifty years, and that Barak's offer gave them nothing. Though Arafat could sign an agreement in 1993 that would leave the fate of the refugees for later negotiations, no Palestinian leader could have signed what Barak demanded at Camp David: that the refugee issue be ignored and that Palestinians give up all their claims against the State of Israel. To thereby abandon the refugees to perpetual refugee status would have been perceived as an unforgivable betrayal by the three million Palestinian refugees, many of them living in some of the worst conditions human beings face anywhere on the planet.

Given that their reasons for rejecting the Clinton-Barak proposal were clear and convincing, the Palestinians in general and Arafat in particular were at a unique moment to explain to the United States and to the Israelis what they needed to sign an agreement. They could have put forward a clear counter proposal incorporating their own terms for a final settlement, using this moment to let the world understand that their vision did not require the destruction of Israel. If, as they maintained later, they actually could envision how the Right of Return of refugees could be implemented without the destruction of the Jewish character of the State of Israel, this was the moment to share that vision with the world. They did not.

From the Israeli perspective, the Palestinian people had once again shown their tendency to "never miss an opportunity to miss an opportunity" as Abba Eban, former Foreign Minister of the State of Israel, put it.

In retrospect, many Palestinians share this criticism of the Arafat circle of leadership. But at the time, Arafat was also aware that he was sitting on a powder keg ready to explode. According to Oslo, which was a signed agreement, an interim Palestinian government was supposed to have been established two years earlier. Promises of a return of the land to the Palestinian people had been made and remade, and still remained unfulfilled. And the facts on the ground were irrefutable: the peace process was supposed to end the settlements and return the land to the people. Instead, in 1993 there were 120,000 settlers; in 2000, when Barak met with Arafat, that number had increased to 200,000 settlers. Though

Barak had been elected as a peace candidate, he had allowed settlements to expand their numbers, and the IDF had increased the roadblocks through which Palestinians had to pass when they went from town to town in the West Bank. The peace process seemed like a sham. Now, Arafat had been pressured to come to negotiations, and what he had been offered was not a plan to implement Oslo, but much less, and on top of it he was being told by Clinton and Barak to symbolically abandon the Temple Mount and the refugees. It is not hard to understand the resentment that Palestinians felt at this offer, the sense of being treated disrespectfully, a sense underscored by the fact that the talks had been scheduled to respond to internal US and Israeli politics more than to actually solve a problem the Palestinians had lived with intimately for at least fifty-two years.

Yet in retrospect we can see how tragic it was that there was no Palestinian leadership capable of transcending all this and enthusiastically embracing what was good in the Barak proposal, allowing Barak and Clinton to claim a victory, and then moving from there to insist on the changes that Palestinians would need to sign a final agreement. Had Arafat been able to imagine these people as potential allies instead of as enemies, he might have been able to strategize toward a path of reconciliation. Instead, he simply rejected what had been offered and made no proposal of his own. It is not true that he walked out of the negotiations or called them off in favor of starting a new Intifada. It was Barak and Clinton, not Arafat, who had set a time limit of one week. But it is true that he gave the impression of not really having a view of how to resolve the conflict, and seemed to be giving off confusing messages. Whatever may have been the real limits of the Camp David offer, however ridiculous to describe it as "giving the Palestinians everything they had been asking for," it is nevertheless true that a relatively sympathetic observer of the Palestinians like American envoy Dennis Ross could come away from this procedure with a sense that it was Arafat and his way of handling the situation that had been the fatal problem.

Barak and Clinton were now faced with a public relations disaster. They had gambled on pressuring a powerless people into accepting a deal at Camp David that they felt they could easily sell to their own electorates as a triumph. Instead, they had come home with nothing. Having created expectations of a miracle, they were shown to be failed magicians. And both were furious, and lashed out at Arafat, blaming him for the failure of the negotiations rather than asking themselves if there was some way to provide a more palatable deal for the Palestinian people. In return, Arafat positioned himself as the person who would not trade away any more Palestinian claims to their homeland.

If Israel expected the Palestinian Authority to continue its role as surrogate policeman for a Jewish state, while Israel continued the Occupation, people around Arafat would show that that could not happen unless Israel produced some dramatic change on the ground. The Palestinian leadership knew that their own people were likely to explode, and there is some evidence that at least some of that leadership had developed plans to fan an explosion even before it happened.

It was in this circumstance that Ariel Sharon, the right-wing militarist who had assumed leadership of the Likud Party after Netanyahu's electoral defeat, decided to make a symbolic visit to the Temple Mount as a way of demonstrating that Israel had no intention of giving up power over this place where two Muslim mosques had been built centuries before. The Temple Mount has symbolic importance for both Jews and Muslims. Muslims had taken a provocative stand in relationship to the Jewish historical claim to the Mount, both by excavating and removing historical relics that may have religious significance for the Jews, and by denying that Jews have ever had a legitimate claim to the Mount. On the other hand, a religious Zionist yeshiva in the Old City, supported directly by Ariel Sharon, has been making preparations to tear down the mosques and restore Temple worship in light of the assumption that Jews will soon reoccupy and rebuild their ancient Temple.

Most religious Jews do not follow that path, and in fact will not go to the Temple Mount, because it once contained the Holy of Holies, and it would be a desecration to walk on that holy ground. Religious Jews will only go to the Temple Mount once the Temple is rebuilt, and for most religious Jews, the Temple can only be rebuilt when the Messiah comes. Until that day, Jews pray at the Western Wall located below the Mount. For this reason, Israel's continuing insistence on sovereignty over the Temple Mount has no practical correlate for most religious Jews—the function of the demand to sovereignty instead is to deny the Muslims the power to control access to their own holy site. So it was a totally provocative and arrogant act for Ariel Sharon, accompanied by hundreds of policemen, to go to the Temple Mount and proclaim that this would always remain in Israel. Some people have asked why Palestinians should riot when a Jew comes to visit our ancient Temple spot. But Sharon was not acting as an individual interested in connecting to Jewish history but as the new leader of the political party which never accepted the legitimacy of the Oslo Accord and supported expansion of West Bank settlements. Acting as the leader of a political party that insisted that it would never allow the Palestinians to have unimpeded access to their own holy site, and accompanied by massive police power, Sharon's visit was not that of a Jew seeking to renew connection to a holy site, but of an ultra-reactionary activist seeking to dramatize Palestinian powerlessness.

Predictably, the visit set off Palestinian rioting and stone throwing. And the stone throwing was met by Israeli guns and the death of rioters, and thus began Intifada II. The riots spread throughout the West Bank and Gaza as young men picked up rocks, and in turn were met with bullets. And this pattern continued for several months, with the result that many Palestinian teenagers were killed and far fewer Israelis.

There were two very important incidents which further froze both sides into anger and despair. In the early weeks of Intifada II, some Israeli Arabs protested the shootings of their co-religionists in Palestine, and some young Israeli Arabs threw rocks and set up blockades. These were citizens of Israel, and their behavior was not significantly more threatening than the behavior of, say, American college students during militant anti-war demonstrations in the 1960s. But they were met with overwhelming force from Israeli police, and then in what Arabs described as a pogrom, Israelis swept through their villages and attacked the homes and workplaces of their fellow citizens, without any attempt on the part of the Israeli police or army to stop them. Several Israeli Arabs were killed and many more were wounded. But more deeply wounded was the sense of unity that these Arabs, and many Jewish-Arab dialogue groups, had sought to create for many years.

It was in the aftermath of what was perceived by Arabs as a general assault that went far beyond the national struggle, and that now had taken a racial turn (because from the standpoint of Israeli Arabs, they were normal citizens of the State and their homes should be protected, rather than treated as enemy targets), that another ugly incident occurred. Two Israeli soldiers wandered into a West Bank town in early

October and were grabbed by an angry mob and murdered, their bodies mutilated and dragged through the streets to the cheers of angry Palestinians. This lynching struck a deep chord of fear in the Israeli population, who felt that the sheer brutality and dishonoring of the dead shown by this Palestinian mob revealed "the true desires" of the Palestinian people and therefore showed that Barak's interpretation of the failure of Camp David was correct: that there was no one to talk to because the Palestinian people didn't really want a solution—they only wanted the destruction and murder of the Israeli people.

Barak may have believed that this anger at Palestinians would exonerate him for having failed to produce the magic he had promised at Camp David. But his advisors quickly realized that Barak had set in motion an electoral fiasco for the Labor Party. If Israelis accepted Barak's account of the Palestinians, then why not respond to the hard Right's solutions: abandon the peace process altogether and return to the iron fist? So his advisors convinced Barak to reopen negotiations with Arafat, who had never intended to close them. The negotiations were resumed at Taba, and the negotiator of Oslo, Yossi Beilin, became the prominent force moving those conversations forward. By January 2001, the Taba negotiations were close to an agreement, with terms far more favorable to the Palestinian people than had been offered at Camp David.

Yossi Beilin believes that had those negotiations been allowed to proceed, a final resolution of the conflict could have been concluded in a few more weeks. However, it is not clear that Beilin's concessions to the Palestinian people ever had the active support of Prime Minister Barak. Barak had been following a two-pronged approach to the elections of February 2001. On the one hand, he was continuing negotiations; on the other hand, he was proudly boasting to the electorate that unlike Netanyahu, who had made concessions at Wye, the Labor Party in power had not given up an inch of land and had not restricted the settlers in any way from expanding their settlements. Like Bill Clinton, Barak did not understand that the attempts by liberals to appropriate the discourse of the Right might provide short-term benefits, but ultimately strengthened the Right and made more likely their electoral triumph. So, it was only Barak who was surprised when Arab voters refused to vote, peace-oriented voters felt little enthusiasm to support their candidate, and Ariel Sharon was swept to victory in February 2001.

ARIEL SHARON

The election of Ariel Sharon dramatically accelerated Palestinian despair about the possibility of peace and reconciliation. Sharon had been removed from his Cabinet position as Defense Minister after an independent inquiry had concluded that he bore indirect but significant responsibility for the Phalangist massacre of over 300 Palestinian civilians in the Sabra and Shatilla refugee camps of Lebanon. Those with a longer memory knew that Sharon had been a major figure in the slaughter of Palestinian civilians in the early years of the State. Some Jewish peace forces had called for Sharon to be tried as a war criminal and human rights abuser. Now he was the leader of the State of Israel.

Sharon proved to be every bit as hard-nosed as had been anticipated. He escalated the military struggle against the Palestinian people, and they in turn responded by moving from rocks to using the weapons that they had been allowed to import under the Oslo Accord. Of course, there could be no equivalence in military might—the Israeli army is the most powerful military force in the region, and the Palestinians had no army at all, but only small police units with light arms.

In the first year of Sharon's prime ministership, the Palestinians retained control over their cities while Israel imposed blockades and began sieges from the outside which cut off food and water for various periods in response to terror attacks against Israeli targets. In addition, Sharon relied upon targeted assassinations of Palestinian leaders who were accused of being militants or terrorists.

Since then, a pattern has developed in which Hamas or another anti-Palestinian Authority group, Islamic Jihad, makes a terror attack against an Israeli target, and then, "in retaliation against terror," the Israeli army strikes against Palestinian Authority targets, though the Palestinian Authority has not been involved in the terror attack and usually condemns it. From the standpoint of some observers, it can appear as if Ariel Sharon and Hamas are involved in a de facto alliance against the Palestinian Authority. Both wish to see it overthrown.

From the standpoint of the Islamic fundamentalists, peace with Israel is impossible, an illusion that had allowed the secular Palestinian leadership to receive majority support. The Islamicists believe that secular Palestinians are selling out the struggle in order to achieve a peace that would cede to Israel a part of the Muslim world which should remain Islamic. They expect that the struggle for Palestine may go on for many more decades. During that time one of their goals is to overthrow the secular leadership so that when a Palestinian state finally emerges it will do so under Islamic leadership. So every time there seems to be a possibility of a lull in the struggle, or a possible advance toward peace, they will attempt a suicide bombing of Israeli civilians to increase despair and encourage Ariel Sharon to use that moment to strike at the secular Palestinians of the Palestinian Authority.

Sharon, on the other hand, has been faced with international pressure to deal with the Palestinian Authority and return to the process of withdrawal, a process he has always opposed. In Sharon's view, articulated clearly in 2002, the settlements least likely to be justifiable in terms of military security (namely, those in the Gaza Strip) are as indispensable as Tel Aviv itself, because the issue is not solely defense but the goal of holding on to as much of the Land of Israel as possible. The stumbling block for Sharon has been that the international community keeps pointing to the fact that the Palestinian Authority is denouncing these terror attacks and calling for a resumption of negotiations based on the Taba advances, aimed at establishing a politically and economically viable Palestinian state. The one thing that has made it politically possible for Sharon to resist that pressure has been his ability to point to the terror attacks by Hamas and Islamic Jihad and to blame them on the Palestinian Authority. And though this game has been transparent to others, it appears not to be transparent to many Israeli citizens who, partly out of desperation, have supported Sharon's escalations.

The price has been paid by people on both sides, as the violence has brought huge amounts of suffering on both sides. Morally outrageous acts of violence by Islamic Jihad and Hamas have been met, not with attacks on Hamas and Jihad, but rather on the entire Palestinian people. IDF troops have rolled into West Bank cities, causing devastation, arresting thousands of people (typically rounding up any male from ages 15 to 45, later releasing some after brutal treatment, keeping others without charges and without the normal human rights promised to prisoners of war), bulldozing buildings, destroying the electricity and water systems for urban populations, and engaging in acts of vandalism and terror that have provoked an international cry for impartial observers to investigate (a process thwarted by Israel).

Kibbutz Metzer, known for its support for peace and cooperation with Palestinians, mourns five of its members (including two children) slain by the Al Aqsa Martyr's Brigade, November, 2002.   Brennan Linsley/AP Wide World Photos

On the other hand, a stream of terror attacks, starting with one at a Passover seder held in a vacation resort hotel and moving to the murders of civilians in buses and cafes, have created widespread fear among Israelis and widespread despair that anything could change for the better.

Relatives mourn the death of a Palestinian man shot by Israeli soldiers at a roadblock East of Hebron, 1998.   Rick Bowmer/AP Wide World Photos

Here, too, both sides are right to be outraged at the behavior of the other, and both sides are wrong to hide from themselves their own culpability.

In fact, Palestinian leaders like Hanan Ashrawi and Said Nusseibeh have issued public condemnations of the violence. But no one in the Islamic Palestinian leadership has been ready to organize demonstrations against the violence—or to advocate a consistent, principled nonviolent stance that would on principle reject violence and insist on restraining or even jailing those who do participate in or give aid to those who participate in violence. On the Israeli side, voices like those of Peace Now, Gush Shalom, Yossi Sarid, and the Meretz party have been increasingly marginalized by the electronic media and by the most widely circulated newspapers, which increasingly reflect the fear and anger of the rest of the population.

The coalition government between Ariel Sharon and the Labor Party fell apart in November 2002, but only after two years in which Labor had significantly reduced its moral standing among the Israeli people by providing collaboration and political legitimacy to Ariel Sharon's policies. Having failed to use its power and influence to build a worldview that could counter the right-wing drift in Israeli politics, it seemed unlikely that Labor would be able to win a future election, or if it could win, unlikely that Labor would be able to muster the courage to take the kind of steps necessary for real reconciliation.

In that context, Israelis and peace-oriented Jews in the Diaspora who really believed in reconciliation with the Palestinian people had moved away from the institutions of the Labor party and had begun to form a network of independent organizations to break through the dominant anti-Palestinian discourse which pervaded much of Israeli society and Jewish life in the Diaspora. In Israel, groups like Gush Shalom, Bat Shalom, Women in Black, and Rabbis for Human Rights played an important role in the dark days of Intifada II in showing that not all Israelis would support the brutality of the then Sharon-Peres alliance. The organization of Bereaved Parents brought together parents of Israeli and Palestinian children who had been killed in the conflict—to argue for a peaceful reconciliation. A group of "internationals" from around the globe came to help rebuild Palestinian homes bulldozed by the Israeli army. And over 500 Israeli Reservists, people who had been called upon to serve In the West Bank and Gaza, signed a statement of Seruv— refusal to serve In the West Bank and Gaza though they simultaneously affirmed their commitment to Israeli survival and remained active in the Reserves as long as they were serving inside Israel itself.

Unfortunately, in the early years of the twenty-first century these voices remained a small minority. The cycle of violence had shattered the lives of so many people on both sides of the struggle that there was little willingness to think in terms of the steps it would take to convince the other side that peace remained a possibility. Palestinians viewed the Israeli army offensives which leveled apartment buildings and buried people alive under the wreckage in Jenin, and which at times imposed week-long curfews on the Palestinian people, as further proof that Israel had lost all moral compass. In such circumstances, the combination of outrage and powerlessness made suicide bombings a plausible (though fundamentally morally unacceptable) path. In turn, the suicide bombings lent some plausibility (though not moral validity) to the growing call of some on the Israeli Right to use this moment to exile Arafat and to begin the process of transfer of Palestinians.

In the midst of these escalations came an Arab summit in the Spring of 2002 which promised that those states would finally grant full recognition and normalization of relations to Israel if Israel would return to the pre-67 borders of Israel and would allow the return of refugees to their homes. This offer was almost entirely ignored by Israel, which under Ariel Sharon no longer believed or trusted any Arab voices.

Continuing fear on the part of Israelis was not purely irrational. Palestinian schools continued to teach hate of Jews. Egyptian television aired a series in which the old European Anti-Semitic calumnies against the Jews were revived and applied to the Middle East. In this circumstance, an Israeli who at one point was a supporter of the religious peace movement, described to TIKKUN in November 2002 his own and other Israelis' perceptions this way:

> a) Surrounded by Arab dictatorships that are both attempting to get and use weapons of mass destruction and by a Palestinian authority who has approved of the murder of Israeli civilians, as many as possible, as their prime political technique.
>
> b) Surrounded by the widespread anti-Semitic campaign that has been going on in the Arab-Islamic world since the 1950's, using the same lies and documents that led to the Holocaust.
>
> c) Surrounded by a world that spends more ink and airwaves talking about Israeli massacres that did not occur than about real massacres that do occur (such as Rwanda, for which Egypt and France have a great measure of responsibility) ... Jews have every right to feel paranoid and hated.

Without agreeing to this as a "right," and while insisting that this Israeli and many like him remain blind to the superior power that Israel has as it occupies Palestinian towns and brutalizes a population under its rule, I do want to insist that this way of perceiving the world is an understandable consequence of a long history of oppression in which Jews have not been able to retain a perception of themselves as the powerful force they actually are in the State of Israel. It would be easy to dismiss these feelings as nothing but the ideological cover of the powerful giving themselves permission to ignore the feelings of the powerless. But when we are talking about a people which has itself been the subject of genocide far more murderous than anything they have done to others, we need to be much more nuanced, much more able to recognize that if Israelis and Jews around the world cannot acknowledge their own power it is because they have been so brutalized that they can't actually have the experience of their power, and only experience their danger and fear and powerlessness. What is called for, then, is not a raging anger but a strategy for healing the hurts of the Israeli people.

And similarly those who rage against Palestinians for not being able to see that they could have the power to change the entire political reality if they merely followed the paths of Martin Luther King Jr. and Nelson Mandela must also acknowledge that this inability to see the power they could have through non-violence is a product of a historical experience in which the Palestinian people have been brutalized by British colonization, expulsion from their homes, and have been living as refugees or under occupation.

In short, we are looking at two peoples who have come to a moment of despair and mutual hurt and cruelty. I do not claim that these sides are equal in power. Israel is the force with an army and is occupying the Palestinian people. Yet as Amnesty International made clear in its report in the summer of 2002, some Palestinian militants have engaged in attacks on Israeli civilians that can only be described as crimes against humanity. The deliberate targeting of innocent civilians is not and cannot be justified and is unacceptable in any civilized society. In the Fall of 2002 Amnesty International issued a new report pointing to war crimes committed by Israeli troops in Jenin and Nablus during the Spring of 2002, including the unlawful killing of Palestinians, blocking medical care, using people as human shields, and bulldozing houses with residents inside.

It is certainly appropriate to find fault with both sides. Both sides have acted in ways that violate international standards of decency.

It is true that the systematic destruction by Ariel Sharon of the infrastructure of the Palestinian Authority through two years of savage assaults, targeted assassination of militants (without trial, or any way of defending themselves against the charge of being dangerous), and destruction of the Arafat compound and of most of the police stations of the Palestinian Authority, may have rendered Arafat so powerless that there would be no possible way that he could have ended acts of terror by people nominally associated with his own movement, Fatah. The Al Aska Brigade was composed of just about anyone with a gun who wanted to describe themselves as that—and it seems particularly unlikely that there was any real possibility of senior leaders in the PA or

PLO to exercise any real control over them. Moreover, in the context of an Occupation that was getting ever more brutal, it would have been extremely difficult to exercise moral authority over them. Many of the people who had witnessed their friends or family being wounded, permanently handicapped, or killed by Israeli occupation forces would be hard to talk out of acts of terror, or to convince that there was anything left to do but strike back in the face of extreme acts of repression from the Ariel Sharon/Benjamin Netanyahu government.

Yet this does not excuse Arafat and the rest of the Palestinian leadership from their failure to mount a sustained campaign of non-violence in which, among other things, they explained to their own people why these acts are so destructive to the morality and political viability of the Palestinian movement. Take, for example, the terrible murder of a woman and her two children at a kibbutz inside the pre-67 borders which took place in November of 2002. What was particularly striking about this terror attack was the fact that this kibbutz was famous for its dovish attitudes and its cooperation with a neighboring Palestinians village. Had Arafat used this occasion to launch a campaign against all violence, had he insisted on describing those who participated in these kinds of acts as thugs and murderers who are undermining the Palestinian movement, had he made this the center of a turn in direction for his movement, he would still have been able to have salvaged the Palestinian national movement.It is this kind of transcendent consciousness which is lacking on both sides.

But it is also easy to see how much it looks like double standards for the friends of Israel to cry about the two children killed by the terrorists while totally ignoring the fact that that same day two young Palestinian children were killed by Israeli troops enforcing the occupation.

"But we didn't target them—the IDF killed them in the course of its duties, not for the purpose of killing them." Well, that may be true (though often the details of the killings seem to reveal a wanton disregard for human life on the part of the occupying forces). But it wears thin after a while. How much difference would it make to you if the police in your area started shooting civilians but told you that they were really after suspected terrorists? Would you feel comforted, or feel that they were on a morally higher plane, because they hadn't targeted the children in your area if, day after day, they were killing the children?

Yes, there are differences. The terrorists, it might be argued, should not be hiding out in civilian areas. But that's the point about an occupation—it turns ordinary civilians into terrorists, and that then provides the supposed license to kill in civilian areas. Israelis sometimes complain that the terrorists don't wear uniforms, and thereby they endanger the rest of the civilian population. But that is always the nature of civilian resistance to an unwanted ruler—the civilians use the tools of resistance, and the rulers use the tools of an army against civilians, and eventually the rulers or occupiers are worn down and leave. So why be surprised if you go into a civilian population and occupy its cities against their will, violate their basic human rights, use them as hostages and human shields, torture their young men, and impose twenty-four hour curfews at the risk of death on the entire population, yes, you will find yourself fighting against ordinary civilians, because that's who you are oppressing.

My point is that the blame game makes no sense. Both sides have a story to tell that makes sense. The Occupation did not start this struggle—that you've seen by the whole tale of the past 120 years. The Occupation makes it far worse, but only a deep confrontation with the refugees and their plight will ever end this struggle. And that will require a breakthrough in consciousness on both sides, a breakthrough which can seem more and more remote as the hurtful acts on both sides increase.

But we can respond with compassion for both sides, as well as a certain amount of anger that each side continues to do things that are immoral and self-destructive and wildly insensitive to the humanity of the other. Yet it is also appropriate to respond with a deep sorrow. And prayers that the hopeful energy will reemerge soon, that people on both sides will realize that the path they are on is destructive and cannot ever work to give them what the actually legitimately want, that a new spirit of generosity and kindness is the only hope.

The story is not over. True, it seems unlikely that the political configuration of leaders and the range of likely challengers to that leadership will produce an alignment likely to take the courageous steps necessary to make a powerful breakthrough. Even if Arafat and Sharon/Netanyahu were replaced with a Labor or Labor/Meretz alliance in Israel and by a peace oriented leadership in Palestine, neither side has laid the foundations for real compromise on the issue of Palestinian refugees that would be necessary to finally end this conflict. Yet whenever they are asked in a way designed to elicit their real, underlying desires, most Israelis and most Palestinians recognize that their future depends on the kind of peace and reconciliation that seems hard to imagine as this book goes to press at the end of 2002. Even as angers flair and despair mounts, and those who have been most committed to peace are unsure of which path might lead to that peace, there is a growing recognition on both sides that their very survival depends on finding a way out of this conflict.

What we in the Tikkun Community have tried to do by presenting this narrative to you is to show you that there is a way to understand this history which avoids the blaming of one side or the other. In the next section of the book, I give specific strategic suggestions for how to move from understanding to an actual strategy to bring peace. Then I move back to Q&A and the centrality of overcoming the blame game—because that is a first step in the long march to peace. But let me suggest that before you go to that, you read and reread this narrative till you can tell the story in a way that acknowledges the validity on both sides, and that counters those on either side who are committed to a narrative that makes one side good (or innocent victims) and the other side evil. Then share the story with others. You will find that most people have never heard an account which sees the blame as shared and the motivations of both sides as being decent and understandable.

It is my firm belief that lasting peace and reconciliation are not only possible but likely to be achieved in the next twenty years, and possibly sooner. The hunger for a world of caring and kindness is a more powerful force than the desire to hold onto anger and nurse old pains. True, it will take the courage to forget—to not focus attention on all the wounds and all the disgraceful actions of the other (and there are enough such on both sides to give adequate ammunition for those who wish to perpetuate conflict for the next hundred years). It will take the discipline and hard work of a generation of healers (medical, psychological, and spiritual) and it will take a sustained challenge to the ethos of cynicism that pervades the media, intellectual life, and all too many religious institutions. But it will happen, and when it does, a new generation will look back on this period and say, "What could those people have been thinking?"

I'm writing this book at least in part to let our own generation and future generations know that there are many people who are thinking, even in the darkest of moments, that love and kindness and generosity will prevail, and that we will testify to that possibility even when doing so earns us the scorn of the "savvy," the anger of the partisans, and the disdain of the powerful. And that is what it means in practical terms to believe in Spirit or God or Highest Power or however you feel comfortable referring to the Force of Healing and Transformation—the belief that there is a Force in the universe that makes possible the transformation from that which is to that which can and should be. That power is in each of us (or as the religious tradition puts it, we are created in the image of God), and if we can overcome our egos enough to find ways to work together effectively, if we can withstand the anger that gets directed at us when we believe in the possibility of a world based on love and justice and peace, then we will be able to make a real contribution, right now, in this time and place, to the process by which the world will be healed.

Chapter Six:

STRATEGIES FOR HEALING AND TRANSFORMATION

Peace, justice and reconciliation for Israel and Palestine is possible.

This is the statement of strategy currently guiding the Tikkun Community and it is offered here as a strategy and general principles that others might wish to adopt to guide their Middle East peace work. There are many other groups working for Middle East peace, some of which are listed at the end of this book, and I do not mean this book to be used only by those who wish to be associated with the Tikkun Community, but by anyone who shares our fundamental commitment to peace and reconciliation.

Our central goals in the early years of the twenty-first century:

1. Ending the oppression of the Palestinian people.

2. Ensuring Israel's survival and security and eliminating terror as a daily reality of life in Israel.

3. Recrediting Judaism and the Jewish tradition in the eyes of Jews and of non-Jews who wrongly identify insensitive or immoral Israeli policies with Judaism (an identification made likely because so many Jewish institutions foster that equation), and recrediting Islam in the eyes of people around the world who wrongly identify Islam with a small group of Islamic extremists who have hijacked the loving and

compassionate attitudes of Islam and allowed it to be associated with the murderous and hate-filled activities of suicide bombers.

4. Protecting the Jewish people from the growing global anger and anti-Semitism that is being fanned by Israel's treatment of Palestinians.

5. Developing an ability on both sides to recognize the legitimacy of the other's story and the other's perceptions, and learn how to see the world through the other's eyes as well as one's own. This in turn creates the precondition for the possibility of an approach to reconciliation based on generosity, kindness, open-heartedness and a genuine desire to make the world feel safe and fulfilling to both the Israel and Palestinian people—thus defeating the impulse to terror, suicide, murder or obliteration of the other.

6. Re-crediting the global hopes for a world of peace and justice—which are undermined by views that see this particular struggle as an example of the intractable nature of antagonisms which supposedly proves the futility of trying to heal or change the world.

These goals lead us to the following statement, which is part of the Core Vision of the Tikkun Community:

We are committed to full and complete reconciliation between Israel and the Palestinian people within the context of social justice for the Palestinians and security for Israel. We call upon Israel to end the Occupation, to return settlers to the pre-1967 borders of Israel (providing them with decent housing), and to take major (though not total) responsibility for Palestinian refugees.

We oppose Israel's violations of Palestinian human rights and we insist that Israel adopt a strategy based on open-heartedness toward the Palestinians, repentance for past misdeeds, reparation, and genuine acknowledgement of the ways that we were oppressive, murderous, and oblivious to the legitimate needs of the Palestinian people. We call for an end to the teachings in Jewish and Israeli schools and media which demean or demonize the Palestinian people; instead we seek to replace those with teachings that emphasize the humanity and goodness of the Palestinian people, Arabs and Muslims. Although we affirm Israel as a Jewish state side by side with Palestine, we believe that all non-Jews in Israel, including most importantly Arab or Palestinian citizens of Israel, should have full civil rights in Israel and equal economic entitlements to any Israeli who has served in the army.

We call upon the Palestinian people to acknowledge the right of Jews to maintain their own homeland in the pre-1967 borders of the state of Israel, with Jewish control over the Jewish section of Jerusalem (including French Hill and Mt. Scopus and the Jewish Quarter of the Old City) and the Western Wall, unimpeded access to the cemetery on the Mount of Olives, and other slight border changes mutually agreed upon.

We call upon the Palestinian people to stop acts of terror against Israel and to listen and heed the growing number of Palestinian voices that are calling for a strategy of nonviolent civil disobedience. We call upon Palestinians to end all teachings in their schools and media which demean or demonize the Jewish people or Israel and to replace those with teachings that emphasize the humanity and goodness of the Jewish people.

We recognize that some Palestinians will respond by pointing out the structural violence inherent in the presence of the Israeli Occupation and the settlements. We agree with these points, but still believe that the breakthrough necessary to free Palestinians from Occupation will only come when the Israeli people feel enough safety to contemplate arrangements based on trust. Just as Israelis must demonstrate that they see Palestinians as created in the image of God and deserving of full respect, so the Palestinians must demonstrate that they see Israelis as created in the image of God and deserving of full respect.

Both sides need to recognize a need for repentance for past deeds that were hurtful and oppressive. Jews must understand why Palestinians were fearful that the more highly organized and politically sophisticated Zionist movement that began to emerge in the period between 1920-1948 might lead to the disenfranchisement of Palestinians, and why Palestinians today feel that "the right to return" to their homes is no different from the right of return that was at the basis of Zionism. On the other hand, Palestinians need to acknowledge their own role in helping create the conflict by their armed resistance to Jewish immigration to Palestine in the years when Jews were being annihilated or when Jews were crawling out of the death camps and crematoria of Europe. This is just a sample of the stories we must learn from each other so that we can build reconciliation of the heart, based on genuine compassion for each other.

Political arrangements cannot be trusted until there is a serious commitment on both sides to compassionate listening to each other. It is only when both sides can tell the other side's story with compassion and conviction, and both sides recognize that in some important respects both sides are wrong and both sides are right, that we can hope to move to a real reconciliation of the heart. All the fancy agreements and all the political maneuvering is secondary to developing an open-heartedness and generosity in both peoples to the legitimate needs of the other. We have told the story that way in this book. We want Israelis and Palestinians to learn how to tell the other side's story with compassion and real openness to the legitimacy of both sides.

We call upon the United States and other world powers to intervene with all their influence and economic power both to stop the cycle of violence and to achieve the creation of a demilitarized Palestinian state in all of the West Bank and Gaza (with slight border adjustments mutually agreed upon), an end to the Occupation, and an end to acts of terror. We will support efforts to convince the United States to condition aid to Israel on the end of the Occupation.

We call upon the peoples of the world to come to Israel and Palestine and actively interpose ourselves between the warring sides to provide protection to civilians on both sides. And we call for all parties to adopt the nonviolent philosophies and strategies of Martin Luther King Jr. and Mahatma Gandhi.

Although we do not support any form of nationalism as an ultimate good, we understand why, in this historical moment, the Jewish people need a state of our own. With memories of the murder and genocide of our people still fresh and the perception that we would have been far less vulnerable had we had a state and an army—with the persistence of virulent anti-Semitism in the world today—the Jewish people cannot be asked to be the first to voluntarily eliminate the protections of the nation state. That is why, at this point in time, the Tikkun Community is supporting a two-state rather than a bi-national solution to the Israel-Palestinian crisis, even though some members of our community believe that such a bi-national state is the only way to achieve social justice for Palestinians. After what Jews have been through, it is not reasonable to expect them to be the first to give up the protections of an armed state.

On the other hand, we see nationalism as a perverting influence in Jewish life—and one that must be overcome. So we do hope Israel will become one of the first 20 percent of countries of the world to over-come the trappings of national chauvinism, militarism, and excessive focus on boundaries—say, for example, after the United States, Russia, China, Japan, Iraq, Iran, Syria, India, Pakistan, England, France, Germany, Italy, Egypt, Poland, Argentina, Chile, Indonesia, Phillipines, Saudi Arabia, Algeria, Nigeria, Ethiopia, Uganda, and South Africa have pioneered that path by abolishing borders and accomplishing full dis-armament. Until then, the Jewish people have a right to their own state, which we hope will eventually move in the direction of confederation with Palestine and Jordan for economic and political cooperation.

A state with many Jews in it is not a Jewish state unless it embodies an ethos of love and justice and becomes a living proof that healing and transformation is possible. Israel is not yet a Jewish state in this sense, so we will support the forces that will help it evolve in that direction.

To make it possible for Jewish values of love, justice, and peace to tri-umph inside its own society, and to open the possibility that Israelis could rediscover the deep spiritual truths of Judaism, Israel will have to eliminate all forms of religious control of the state, end all religious coercion, and allow people to find their own religious and spiritual path, giving equal rights and treatment to non-Jews.

We oppose all attempts by some sectors of the Orthodox world to use the Israeli government as a vehicle to impose their own particular perspective on Judaism, including who is "really" Jewish, what counts as a legitimate wedding, divorce or conversion, etc. We support, instead, the fostering of a climate of mutual tolerance and respect among all sectors of the Jewish people. We reject all practices which lead to unequal treatment of Palestinians or other non-Jewish minorities within the State of Israel. So, when we affirm preserving "the Jewish character" of Israel, we do not mean merely a demographically Jewish state but a state which lives up to the highest Jewish values of "love the neighbor," "love the stranger," and "justice, justice shalt thou pursue."

In the short term, the greatest obstacle to the creation of a state liv-ing up to the values of an ethically and spiritually renewed Judaism are the Occupation, the settlements, and the "Settler Judaism" mentality.

Settler Judaism sees the world as always against the Jews, always ready to hurt us—and hence rejects universal ethical standards and equates "good" with "what's good for the Jews." Similarly, settler Judaism assumes that Jewish interests can be achieved through the use of power and coercion, the obliteration of those with whom we disagree, and believes that Jews have some special right to the Land of Israel that allows them to be insensitive to others who live there. Yet in the long-term, the greatest obstacle to Jewish values in Israel as in the United States lies in the triumph of the ethos of selfishness and materialism. For that reason, we reject the vision of an Israel which finds its ultimate mission in becoming "the globalization miracle and new technology and finance headquarters of the Middle East." Rather, we support those who favor a genuinely Jewish society built on principles of love, justice, peace, and caring for others, including non-Jewish others. And the path requires rejecting those themes and currents within our Jewish tradition or our interpretations of history which tend to bring out chauvinism or a narrow focus on the well being of Jews to the exclusion of others, and instead renewing Judaism to focus on those parts of our tradition and our history that bring out in us greater empathy for others, and develop our capacities as loving, generous, open-hearted and compassionate human beings. And it is this same kind of renewal that we support in every other religious and spiritual tradition.

THE TIKKUN INITIATIVE FOR MIDDLE EAST PEACE

After years in which the common wisdom was that the parties themselves would have to arrive at an agreement on their own, with the United States acting as an "honest broker," we in the Tikkun Community learned the following:

a. The U.S. political system, particularly the Congress (which is responsive to the political and economic clout of groups like the American Israel Political Action Committee—AIPAC—as well as to the new found pro-Sharonism of some fundamentalist Christians, and the right wing of the Republican party) is not capable of playing the role of honest broker, but is increasingly pulled to give a blank check to the most hawkish programs of the Israeli government.

b. The two parties are unable to arrive at an agreement which they are capable of implementing on their own, at least until there has been a total transformation of consciousness in both peoples, a rejection of violence and terror on both sides, and a new attitude of repentance replacing the certainty that both sides currently have that the other side is solely responsible for the current mess.

Given a and b, we've concluded that what is necessary is the following:

To call upon the American government to get the UN, NATO or some ad hoc international body to intervene to separate and protect each side from the other, and to convene an international conference to impose a settlement with terms that could actually end the conflict, terms that neither party is likely to voluntarily accept. So we call upon the American government and the American people, to take the next steps towards peace:

• Create an international peace-keeping force, with significant US participation, to separate the two sides and provide protection for each of them.

• Offer Israel (and once it is created, the new state of Palestine) membership in NATO or a mutual defense treaty that commits U.S. troops and the full weight of US military to defend Israel from any attack of surrounding states—thus eliminating their fear that a Palestinian state would endanger Israel's future existence.

• Create an international peace conference based on the Saudi proposals of 2002 (full recognition of Israel by all Arab states in exchange for an Israeli return to the pre-67 borders) and explicitly committed to:

1. End the occupation of the West Bank and Gaza. Israel must return to the pre-67 borders with minor changes, mutually agreed-on. Evacuate the settlements and provide funding to resettle Israeli settlers within the pre-67 borders of Israel.

2. End the settlements in the West Bank and Gaza. Provide monies for settlers to be resettled inside Israel. Give the settlements to the new State of Palestine, but allow those settlers who wish to remain in their homes to do so with the following provisos: first, the settlements can no longer be Jewish-only housing that discriminates against non-Jews in housing and schools; second, those Jews remaining become full citizens of a Palestinian state and do not retain their Israeli citizenship or vote in Israeli elections; third, Israel must make it clear that at least some Jews who remain inside Palestine are likely to be tried under Palestinian law for illegal land seizures, violence against Palestinians, etc. (crimes for which they would have already been prosecuted had they not been protected by the Israeli army and the Israeli legal system with its double

standards for people living in the Occupied Territories). Israel will clearly warn these Jews that Israel will not interfere with this internal matter of a Palestinian state, or interfere with such prosecutions, or claim any jurisdiction over the activities of settlers who remain in Palestine, just as Palestine will not intervene to stop prosecutions of Israeli Arabs when they violate Israeli law.

3. Create an international fund to provide reparations to the Palestinian refugees sufficient to enable them to live at a standard of living roughly comparable to that of the median standard of living in Israel— and that fund will also be used for reparations for Jews who fled from Arab lands sufficient to enable them to live at a standard of living roughly comparable to the that of the median standard for living in Israel.

4. Create an economically and politically viable Palestinian state, provide it with aid sufficient not only to repair all the damage done by the Occupation but also to enable it to function as an economically successful state. Treat the Palestinian state with respect and dignity as it enters the family of nations. Provide arrangements for both Arab states and Israel to equitably share water rights, and create a regional ecological plan and a regional plan for sharing water from Turkey to Israel and Egypt to Syria, Jordan, Iraq, Iran and Saudi Arabia.

5. Provide support for forces seeking democracy and civil liberties within a Palestinian state and ensure that democratic processes prevail.

6. End all terror attacks against Israeli civilians, and end all violence against Palestinian civilians. While the first goal is to create mechanisms of protection for both peoples against terror in ways that do not violate basic principles of civil liberties and human rights, that goal can best be accomplished when it is possible to mobilize the Palestinians and Israelis themselves because they clearly see the terror as both morally repugnant and undermining the future of Palestinian national self-determination. This cannot happen as long as Palestinians feel that their fundamental rights are being denied.

7. Provide support for those seeking democratic and civil rights for Israeli Palestinians and those seeking democratic and civil rights for Palestinians within their own Palestinian society.

8. Normalize relations between Israel and its Arab neighbors based on the right of Jews to have their own state in the Middle East. Insist that Arab countries do their share to help finance the infrastructure of a Palestinian state.

We call on Jews in Israel and around the world to:

1. Support a two-state settlement based on withdrawal of Israel from the Occupied Territories and dismantlement of settlements.

2. Renounce military force as a solution and support the hundreds of Israeli Army reservists who refuse to sanction the Occupation and now refuse to serve in the West Bank and Gaza.

3. Reach out to Palestinians by helping repair the damage gratuitously caused by the Israeli Army in its invasion of Palestinian cities and towns.

4. Donate generously to organizations working for reconstruction of Palestinian civil society. And to groups working for Jewish-Arab reconciliation.

5. Work inside Jewish organizations, synagogue organizations, and other institutions of Jewish life to educate them to the balanced perspective articulated here, and change their policies. Ask them to use this book and others that tell a balanced story, so that American Jews can be exposed to a different perspective than those that have been presented as the "sole truth." Insist that they remain open to the new possibilities. Do not let them marginalize those who are critical of Israeli policy. Fight against the tendencies to identify "pro-Israel" with the policies of any particular government of Israel.

6. Recognize that the only victory possible for Israel in the current circumstance is the victory of reclaiming and reasserting the greatest asset the Jewish people have developed throughout our history: the moral legitimacy of a people who are committed to valuing love and justice and compassion above coercive power, violence and domination. Unequivocally reject violence as a way to deal with the Palestinian movement for national liberation. Commit to a totally nonviolent solution to your problems.

7. Adopt a stance of open-hearted repentance for the unnecessary pain Israel has inflicted on the Palestinian people—and support an ethos of generosity and compassion toward them, treating them with respect and helping them create a state in which they can live with dignity and economic well-being. End the teaching of hatred toward Arabs, and the teaching of one-sided accounts of how Israel was created and how we got to the current situation, both in Israeli and in Diaspora Jewish schools and particularly in institutions responsive to the agenda of the American Jewish community.

We call upon the Palestinian people in the West Bank and Gaza and around the world to:

1. Unequivocally recognize the State of Israel not only as an existing reality but as a state that has a right to exist. Accept Israel not only formally but in your hearts.

2. Renounce military force, terror and violence. Commit yourselves to a totally nonviolent solution to your problems. Meet the violence of Occupation with the morally superior non-violence that can become the battering ram with which to undermine the Occupation.

3. Convey to the Israeli people your commitment to reconciliation of the heart, and acknowledge the parts of your history in which you have not treated Jews with adequate sensitivity and compassion.

4. Take all necessary actions to restrain and prevent suicide bombers. Teach that these people are the most destructive elements, that their actions undermine the moral legitimacy of the Palestinian movement, and that they are in violation of the highest principles of the Palestinian movement for national liberation.

5. End the teaching of hatred in your schools and mosques and churches, and teach Palestinian children about Israel in ways that foster their openness to reconciliation of the heart. Actively combat and critique the teaching of anti-Semitism and its associated ideas in the Arab media.

6. Send financial support to institutions that openly support the peace process and stop sending monies to organizations that do not unequivocally reject the war and hate-of-Israelis agenda in the Arab world.

7. Teach, preach, and articulate a stance of open-hearted repentance for the unnecessary pain Palestinians have inflicted on the Israeli people.

Strategies can't be fully developed in the abstract—they require that critical intelligence be applied to the specific moment. For that purpose we have TIKKUN magazine and the Tikkun Community—where these issues are thought through, debated, and new directions are tried as the current realities evolve. In the next section I try to answer some of the common objections that arise in response to the strategic principles I've outlined here.

Chapter Seven:

ANSWERS TO THE
HARD QUESTIONS

1 *"The Palestinians rejected a good deal offered them in 1947 by the United Nations. Doesn't that show that they have lost all legitimacy to complain about what has happened after they adopted the belligerent path that led to the many wars between Israel and the surrounding Arab states?"*

a. Some Palestinians question the "right" of the United Nations to make this decision in 1947. They may have had the power, but not the authority to make the decision. The United Nations, they say, was only ratifying a previous cutting up of the Middle East by colonial powers. If this answer is taken seriously, however, then it makes no sense to rely on subsequent UN resolutions as the basis for Palestinian claims. Either the UN has the moral authority to determine what should happen in Palestine or it doesn't—you can't have it both ways.

b. Others who argue that the partition plan was legitimate and that Palestinians had a moral obligation to accept the division of their land ordained by the United Nations are usually inconsistent when it comes to their own obligation to live by subsequent resolutions of the United Nations. Those resolutions have called upon Israel to withdraw from the West Bank and Gaza, and have condemned Israeli violence and human rights violations. Either the UN has the moral authority or it doesn't.

c. Was it a good deal? Many Palestinians point out that the1947 deal divided the land in ways that favored the Zionist enterprise at the expense of the people who had been living there before. What is rarely understood in the West is that the Arab states had another plan.The Palestinians asked for a democratic vote of the population (and at the time, they would have had a majority). Some Zionists point out that democracy in that case would have thwarted the right of the Jewish people to national self-determination, and that only partition would have been substantively democratic.

d. Who actually rejected the 1947 UN partition plan? It was not "the Palestinian people," most of whom were illiterate at the time, relied on Muslim religious leaders for their information, and had no process through which they could select their leadership. The leadership was a self-appointed group whose decisions cannot be blamed on the entire people. On the other hand, there is no reason to believe that, given the perceptions Palestinians had at the time of the threat to their lands posed by the Zionists, they would have disagreed with their leaders.

e. The Palestinian's rejection of the 1947 UN partition was in fact a serious mistake for which the Palestinian people have been paying for a long time. Though some Palestinians point to writings by Zionist leaders which give grounds for the belief that Israel might have sought to expand anyway (Israel has never been willing to define what its boundaries are), the political reality is that Israel would have had a much tougher time justifying war against Palestinians and surrounding Arab states had the Palestinian people and the Arab states embraced the boundaries of 1947 and welcomed the new state into existence.

f. Most Palestinians living in refugee camps in some of the worst circumstances facing any human beings on the planet were born in those refugee camps, or were under the age of fifteen when the 1947 partition plan was rejected. They have no moral culpability for the actions of those who took that decision in 1947, however disastrous it proved to be. There is no reason why the decisions taken by a previous generation should legitimate a notion that current generations of Palestinians deserve to suffer, nor any reason why they should accept arrangements with regard to their own national self-determination which are less than those of other national groups on the planet.

2   *"Zionists came to Palestine and took the land of another people."*
    As we've shown in this book, this is not an accurate summary of what actually happened, for the following reasons:

a. There is considerable evidence that the amount of land actually purchased by Zionists before 1948 has been vastly overestimated, giving the impression that the Zionists simply bought their way into a Jewish state. This whole argument may be moot if we consider that by 1947, Jews only owned 1,734,000 dunums or 1,734 square km. of land—only 6.6% of pre-1948 Palestine.

b. Most Jews coming to Palestine in the last 120 years came as refugees escaping oppression. Until 1948, the Palestinian leadership did everything it could to keep them from coming. This meant keeping Jews who were trying to escape the Holocaust from having a place to which to escape. This was morally outrageous behavior, made no whit less morally outrageous by the fact that most other peoples acted in exactly the same way, or that much of the world today still closes its doors and shuts its ears to the cries of despair of refugees seeking asylum.

c. The land was held by Arab Muslims whose ancestors won it through conquest from the descendents of the people who had collaborated with the Romans in throwing the Jews out of that land by force. Roman imperialism was responsible for the Jews leaving the land. Jews, in turn, were the descendents of Israelites who had won the land through armed conquest from still others, who had won the land by armed conquest. There is no "we are the ones who originally owned the land" claim that can be historically validated. If we are in the discourse of moral right, then no one has a high moral right to the land except under the claim that a longer period went by from the time that my ancestors conquered this land than from the time that yours did.

d. It is not unreasonable to refuse to allow more people into your home than it can fit. If five billion of the world's people were to apply for refugee status in the United States, it would not be unreasonable for the United States to set restrictions based on the number that could reasonably be fit into the land and the economy without destroying it, and this number is not simply a "scientific fact" but a judgment call. But it was not legitimate when the United States used ethnicity as the basis for deciding which refugees could come and which could not. Using this same logic, we can say that Palestinians should not have been asked to accommodate more people than the land could hold. Today we know that the land can hold all the Jews who have come there, plus all the Palestinians, and still produce enough food and have a viable economy—so it was not reasonable on grounds of "not enough room" to keep Jews out in the pre-1948 period. Nor were Palestinian leaders seeking to similarly exclude Arabs from settling in the land—it was directed specifically at Jews as Jews. Palestinians who opposed Jewish immigration did not, for example, make a distinction between Jews who supported the Zionist movement and Jews who were ultra-orthodox and did not believe in Zionism, but simply needed a place of refuge—all Jews were equally unacceptable to the Palestinian national movement.

   e. The creation of the State of Israel was the first instance of affirmative action or restorative justice, practiced on an international scale. It set the precedent for all future affirmative action programs.

Most instances of affirmative action have the same downside: they disadvantage, at least temporarily, some other group of people who are not themselves directly the perpetrators of the wrong for which affirmative action is the solution. For example, it is often the case that when African Americans or women get certain advantages through affirmative action, those most likely to suffer in the short run are not the most powerful whites and the most powerful men, but working class whites and men who have faced class oppression in the past. Is it justifiable then, for these working class men to take up arms against African Americans? However, it's imperative that we rectify some of the egregious injustices that were perpetrated on the Palestinians by the clumsy and insensitive way in which this first attempt at affirmative action for the world's Jews was implemented (just as we should also find ways to rectify some of the injustices that were done to whites and men in the course of implementing affirmative action). But there is nothing fundamentally unjust about the attempt to create a state whose primary goal is to rectify past injustices.

On the other hand, there are great dangers in this affirmative action approach, particularly when you create an entire state with a military that intends to use its power to rectify past errors, even while disadvantaging others. How do you create checks and balances so that the state doesn't overstep its affirmative action mandate and begin to oppress or unnecessarily disadvantage other people? This is part of the problem faced by Arabs living inside Israel as citizens—they often find that their legitimate needs are not being addressed by the Israeli state, and that is justified by reference to past oppression of the Jewish people, even though that past no longer needs so much rectification for people who have been living in their own state for the past fifty-five years. The evidence of discrimination against Israeli Arabs is incontrovertible, and goes far beyond anything that would be necessary to rectify past injustices against Jews.

In light of that, one might argue, isn't it time to eliminate all such special advantages and make Israel a binational state with no special legal advantages to Jews, a state of all its current inhabitants rather than a state with a special set of advantages for Jews? On this question, very decent people on both sides of the issue have compelling arguments. On the one hand, the binationalists argue that the current distortions in Israeli policy toward Palestinians are not a matter of accidental errors, but are inevitable as long as a state is defined not as the state of all of its citizens, but as a state with a particular ethnicity or religious group getting particular benefits. That will never be legitimate, they argue, and will always lead people to defend their unequal rights in oppressive ways. On the other hand, those who believe that a specifically Jewish state is still needed make two arguments: first, there already is such a state, it is a democracy (Arabs and other minorities get full democratic rights to run parties for the Knesset, etc.), and that state has democratically chosen to remain a Jewish state; second, eliminating an affirmative action state would make sense when anti-Semitism in the world has been eliminated as a factor in shaping the behavior of other countries so that the Jewish people, victims of genocide just sixty years ago, are no longer in danger in the world and hence no longer needed a special state to protect them and give them special rights (for example, the Right to Return).

Unfortunately, we have not arrived at that moment in which anti-Semitism is no longer a factor. Indeed, it is possible to argue that the barrage of criticism facing Israel today is at least in part a product of the legacy of anti-Semitism.

Now how could we, people who are ourselves sometimes accused of being anti-Semitic by the Israel-is-not-to-be-criticized folk, claim that criticism of Israel is an indication of anti-Semitism? Well, criticism as such does not indicate anti-Semitism. But when the criticism is out of proportion to the offense, and when the criticism of the Jewish state gets far more attention than criticisms of the activities of other states in the world that are far worse in their denial of human rights, suppression of democracy of minorities, and oppressive behavior to enforce occupation or domination of one group by another (as in the case of the genocide in Rwanda, or the treatment of citizens in Iraq, Syria, Saudi Arabia, Egypt, Chechnya, etc.), then that kind of criticism is anti-Semitic. In a similar vein, the American media could be charged with racism for giving a great deal more attention to "black crime" than to the huge amount of white collar crime or systemic crime that the United States perpetrates in other parts of the world in service of its unbridled consumption. (I am referring to worldwide hunger and degradation to the environment that the globalization of capital has wrought upon the third world—a crime that creates millions of victims each year but which is simply not visible to those of us living at the top of the food chain.)

On the other hand, one might argue that the charge of anti-Semitism when people are critiquing Israel is just a way of protecting Israel from the normal scrutiny that every country faces in the world. By tossing around the word "anti-Semitism," those who wish to defend current Israeli policies manage to intimidate everyone who has a criticism of Israel, and this is actually immoral.

There is much to be said for this objection. Most of us who are involved in building a movement that seeks to change Israeli policy have found ourselves labeled this way. Many many Jews have been labeled "self-hating Jews" just because they raise legitimate moral critiques about Israel. And many non-Jews have been intimidated into silence out of fear of being labeled anti-Semitic. This use of the labels is unfair, destructive, immoral, and has zero legitimacy. But it doesn't follow from that that there are no real anti-Semites using criticism of Israel as a cover for their deeper agenda.

What makes this subject all the more difficult is this: at least some of the anger at the Jewish people is based on the contemporary behavior of the State of Israel, and *not* on the legacy of past anti-Semitic attitudes and canards. There are people all over the world who view Israel as an immoral state based on its current behavior, and their judgments are not a transference from previous negative attitudes, because they never heard any stories about Jews until they started to witness what Israel was actually doing to the Palestinian people. If, in light of that actual behavior they get angry at those Jews around the world whose public institutions are raising money to support Israel even as it oppresses the Palestinian people, and who use their political power (such as it is, and not to be exaggerated) to convince the states in which they live to give backing to Israeli policies that are repressive, then that anger cannot be labeled anti-Semitic.

f. Land doesn't "belong" to anyone—except God. Human beings have an obligation to take care of the earth, to protect it, and to use it in ways that are ecologically sustainable and which reflect generosity, love, open-heartedness, and recognition of the spirit of God in every human being.

3 *"You are using Western concepts and experiences and applying them to a different (Arab/Muslim) culture which has different cultural assumptions than you have. You think they want peace, but actually they want the destruction of Western influence in their world, and hence they will never ever accept the existence of Israel."*

This is likely to be true in some respects and not in other respects. We don't expect Arabs to share all our customs. But any generalizations about a people should be treated with deep suspicion—particularly by those of us who are Jews and who have been the subject of a long line of cultural calumnies (accused of being materialistic, greedy, selfish, vulgar, too emotional, too rational, communistic, capitalistic, naturally inclined to crime, naturally inclined to self-righteousness, stiff-necked, more interested in justice than in love, etc.) It has been typically true of Western societies that they use the notion of cultural differences to assign to "native peoples" various forms of pathology which they see as intrinsic to these people's "nature"—and that doing so then provides a justification for Western colonial expansion, domination and "re-education" of the native populations.

This tendency has gained particular ferocity whenever the other population has resisted domination in some way. The very acts of resistance are used as further proof of the demented and distorted consciousness of the natives. So it is no surprise that in the period after Arab states started to use their control of oil as a counter-force to Western colonial expansion, that hatred of Arabs and Muslims became prevalent in Western societies. In Western Europe, the tendency to demean Arabs was intensified because Arabs were arriving as refugees and were sometimes pitted against Europeans for scarce jobs and social/economic resources. In the United States, the use of anti-communism as the major way to deflect attention from domestic problems and injustices declined with the demise of the Soviet Union, and Anti-Arab and anti-Muslim sentiments served as a convenient replacement. They became the "Other" upon whom to dump societal anger and frustrations, and a reason to continue huge expenditures of hundreds of billions of dollars to sustain a military/industrial complex and tax Americans for "Defense." These dynamics were already in place in the early 1990s, well before terrorist attacks on the World Trade Center and other U.S. targets.

In this context, it is most reasonable to be very suspicious of any generalization made about Arabs or Muslims or the societies they have created. Of course there will always be people like bin Laden who do indeed want the destruction of Western influence in their world, but these people do not represent Arabs or Muslims any more than Timothy McVeigh, the bomber of the Federal Building in Oklahoma City, represents the American people. These are not the people we are seeking to "make peace with" anymore than we are seeking to dialogue or make peace with Hamas. Rather, we are trying to isolate and take power away from terrorists, like those in Hamas, by dealing with the valid humanitarian concerns at hand in Palestine.

4 *"Palestinians really want to destroy the State of Israel, and nothing less will ever satisfy them. So isn't an end to violence simply impossible?"*

a. This has been true for some Palestinians and not for others. The percentage of Palestinians who feel this way varies with the historical moment. In general, when it has appeared to Palestinians that the Jewish people were willing to grant Palestinians the fundamental rights they claim for themselves, the percentage of Palestinians supporting the destruction of Israel has declined dramatically, and when it has appeared to Palestinians that the Jewish people are supporting escalations of repression, that percentage has increased dramatically.

b. There have always been some Zionists who have claimed that the full aspirations of the Jewish people could not be accomplished without ridding Palestine of its Arabs. The percentage of Jews who have responded to that extremist picture has decreased whenever it appeared

Palestinian women walk past the rubble of destroyed houses at the Jenin refugee camp in the West Bank, April, 2002.

Greg Baker/AP Wide World Photos

as if Palestinians were ready to live without violence toward Israel, and it has increased dramatically in periods like the current Intifada II, when many Israelis became convinced that Palestinians want to destroy them. Polls in 2002 indicated that over 45 percent of Israelis responded favorably to the notion of "transfer" (a euphemism for ethnic cleansing) of West Bank Palestinians to another country, and 25 percent responded favorably to the notion of transfer of Israeli citizens of Arab ethnicity. The desire to destroy the other side is a characteristic of people on both sides of this struggle, and percentages vary with circumstances. The attempt to label one side as the one that has ideological convictions that will prevent a rational solution are racist, because the evidence is that such ideological convictions exist on both sides and their popularity varies inversely with the level of hope.

c. The desire to destroy "the other" may remain in the fantasies of both sides for a long time. We are concerned with a different question: not what maximalist fantasies people have, but what they are willing to settle for. There is considerable evidence that people on both sides could settle for an arrangement comparable to the one being proposed by the Tikkun Community (see Chapter 6) if it were implemented with a spirit of generosity, open-heartedness, compassion, and mutual repentance.

On the other hand, maximalist fantasies will grow in popularity in direct proportion to despair on each side.

d. Some Islamic fundamentalists are committed to the full destruction of Israel. But not all. There are many Islamic scholars and teachers whose writings explicitly condemn the use of violence and who support a more tolerant attitude toward Israel. Why haven't you heard of them? Because the media in the Western world has little interest in amplifying their voice. If you depended on the media, you probably wouldn't know about the existence of a strong voice in the Jewish world calling for an end to the Occupation and reparations for Palestinian refugees, so if you were in favor of those things you might be thinking that the entire Jewish world had the opposite perspective, and you'd be wrong.

On the other hand, there *are* some Palestinians and some Muslims who will never settle for anything less than the full destruction of Israel. These people, currently organized in Hamas and Islamic Jihad, have increased their base because they have spent a great deal of time and energy providing for basic social services, including health care, food, and employment for Palestinian refugees who would otherwise be in deep need. Those same needs could be met by a democratic Palestinian state that is set up with a sufficient economic base to succeed. A state that is set up without adequate funding would not be able to meet these needs, and would then still be faced with a powerful Islamic movement that could counterpose itself to, for example, the secular democratic vision of the Palestinian Authority. Islamic fundamentalists have also grown in support as the level of despair about life has grown among Palestinians faced with a slow destruction of their society by the Israeli Occupation. They will decline in support as more Palestinians get a sense that their own needs can be met in the Palestinian state that emerges.

When that happens, and most Palestinians find themselves in a state of their own, well-funded and thriving, and under conditions in which there has been a serious and sustained effort by Israel to achieve real reconciliation, the Palestinian people themselves will wish to stop Islamic fundamentalists from jeopardizing all this in acts of terror—so it will be the Palestinian people who will create a climate hostile to these activities, and will treat as criminals those who continue with violence. We have seen such a transition in the South of the United States, where people who engaged in acts of violence against African Americans were at one point treated as heroes, and today are treated as criminals.

Only a spirit of generosity on the part of Israel toward Palestinians and the new Palestinian state will make much of a difference in reducing the credibility and popularity of an Islamic movement.

5 *"Israelis are acting like Nazis, so how can Palestinians be expected to think that peace with them will ever be possible? And why do Jews think they have the right to tell others to not make Nazi comparisons?"*

Although the policies of recent Israeli governments has been oppressive to the Palestinian people, the Nazi analogy is false and misleading for the following reasons:

a. The Nazis were engaged in systematic genocide of every Jew that they could find. They even deflected men and material away from the Russian front so that they could be more effective in killing as many Jews as possible. There is nothing even vaguely comparable going on in the West Bank and Gaza or in Israel itself. There is no systematic attempt to murder every possible Palestinian. There are no gas chambers. There are no roundups of Palestinians who are then systematically murdered by the Israelis. People who say that Israel is acting like the Nazis simply know nothing of who the Nazis were and what they did, or know nothing of what Israel is doing. Or else they blindly hate the Jewish people and are attempting to spread their hate to others.

b. In the period leading up to the actual genocide, Nazis passed a series of laws that singled out Jews for discriminatory treatment. Today, Palestinians living in the occupied territories do face laws that discriminate against them and in favor of the Jews living in the Occupied Territories, but this is not the case for Palestinians or Arabs living in Israel. Palestinians and Arabs who live in Israel are citizens of the State of Israel, and they have the same voting rights, employment rights, etc., as everyone else. There is defacto discrimination, but it is not dejure— it is not part of the legal system, and hence is more comparable to the racism toward African Americans that exists in the United States than to anything done by the Nazis. There are some uncanny similarities in the discourse that faced Jews in some sections of German society in the period 1933-1935 and the discourse facing Palestinians in some sections of Israeli society (particularly in the settlements), and there are some Israelis who would like to see the entire Palestinian people "transferred" (ethnically cleansing Israel), but in terms of the laws of the State of Israel there is nothing comparable to the laws that were developed against the Jewish people in the pre-war Nazi period.

c. To make the Nazi comparison is not only false, but anti-Semitic. It attempts to compare Israel's behavior with that of the worst genocidal maniacs in recent history. Yet the actual number of people killed by the Israeli Occupation is dwarfed by the much more significant crimes by other nation states in the past fifty years: the killing of some three million Vietnamese by the United States, the killing of millions of Cambodians by the Khmer Rouge, the killings of hundreds of thousands of Hutu and Tutsi by each other, the invasion and domination of Tibet by China, the invasion and domination of Chechnya by Russia, and you can probably add your own list here. So Jews rightly ask, "Why are the Jewish people being singled out for special attention, and even falsely accused of doing what the Nazis did, when there are so many other nation states engaged in crimes of far greater proportion?" The answer is that the Jews are being singled out because of the unconscious but real anti-Jewish racism that continues to play a role in political thinking in the world today. We at the Tikkun Community unequivocally condemn this kind of thinking—and while we are dedicated to ending the Occupation and the oppression of Palestinians by Israel, and will critique Israeli behavior until there is real reconciliation between the two peoples, we will also ferociously critique those who engage in anti-Semitic critiques of Israel or Jews.

d. There are real ways in which Israeli policies are brutalizing the Palestinian people. But to make the analogies with the Nazis allows the most right-wing forces in Israel to dismiss these criticisms as little more than anti-Semitic. What Israel is doing is often morally outrageous— and by making false comparisons to the even worse morally outrageous behavior of other states and movements, the critic actually lets Israel off the hook and diverts the argument to grounds on which Israel will be vindicated because it is *not* engaged in genocide. Similarly, those in the Jewish camp who call Arafat or the Palestinian people Nazis are allowing Palestinians off the moral hook, because they can quickly prove that they are not interested in genocide against the Jewish people, and in pushing the discussion to that issue it focuses away from the morally outrageous behavior of suicide bombers who target Israeli civilians as their way to protest the Occupation.

Jerusalem bus bombing, June, 2002.   Zoom 77/AP Wide World Photos

e.There are some people in the world, particularly in Europe, who are quick to jump to Nazi analogies because in so doing they can stop feeling bad about the Holocaust and the criminal behavior of their own society (and possibly their parents or grandparents) at that time. If the Jews are as bad as the Nazis, then they no longer have to question how it could have happened that their own families and people were so screwed up.

6 *"It is people like you who thought peaceful resistance could stop Hitler and look what happened. What's to keep that from happening again? Don't you know that the Arabs want to drive Jews into the Sea? You are naïve if you think you can stop these Nazis with compassion and nonviolence."*

As I mention below, seeing the world as though Hitler was still here and ready to hurt us is a trauma from which the Jewish people needs help to recover. On the factual level, the claim is absurd. Hitler was the head of one of the most powerful economic and military forces in the world, capable of conquering other major powers. The Palestinians are a tiny people without an army, and though the surrounding Arab states are very large in number, they also have no seriously military capacities to challenge the power of Israel. Israel is one of the most powerful military forces in the world. It is not the Palestinians who are occupying Tel Aviv and Haifa but the Israelis who occupy Jenin and Hebron. Moreover, many military authorities in Israel and the Israeli army have long argued that a Palestinian state, even one with arms, would be no serious threat militarily to Israel, whereas the continued Occupation does present a serious threat because it demoralizes the Jewish people and its army and weakens its ties with potential allies around the world.

Nor do the Arab states seek the destruction of all Jews in a way analogous to Hitler. The reality is that there are Jews who continue to live in Bagdad, Damascus, and Cairo—and while there have at times been outbursts of anti-Semitism that should not be tolerated, there is no policy of systematically exterminating them or putting them into concentration camps. To the extent that they prove loyal to the regimes in which they live, they have been allowed to continue to do business and live in peace. Don't get me wrong—these are not models of human-rights respecting societies, and I wouldn't feel safe living there, neither as a Jew nor as a politically progressive thinking individual. But that's different from claiming an analogy with Hitler, who sought the destruction of Jews based on their racial origins, not on the basis of their politics. It's easy to hear this as "apology" for those states—but that is not what I intend. I find them to be oppressive dictatorships and were I living there I'd be part of a revolutionary movement seeking (in nonviolent ways) to overthrow them. In fact, were Israel to change its policies in the directions I've been suggesting in this book, that overthrow of oppressive regimes would become easier, less easily diverted into anti-Semitism which certainly does exist in these states.

I don't blame Jews for not liking these states. But that is different from believing that we have no choice but to live in a state of war with them.

What is naïve is to believe that a Jewish state can exist among 100 million Arabs in a constant state of war and be seen as oppressive to nearby Arabs, and hope to continue for the next centuries. Only an Israel that has manifested a whole new attitude can possibly hope to provide for its own safety. The naiveté of relying on power is far greater than the supposed naiveté of relying on good relations and kindness and generosity.

7   *"Israel needs to be strong to defend itself against possible attacks from surrounding Arab states, so why weaken it by giving up land on that is in any event a tiny area compared to its Arab enemies?"*

a. Israel is not strengthened but militarily weakened when it has to spend its time and resources on repressing three million Palestinians who reject Israeli rule. These Palestinians do not have an army and cannot constitute a military threat to Israel's existence. But they do have the capacity to wear down Israel's military and to terrorize Israeli civilians. The lessons of Vietnam, Chechnya, and other struggles have been learned by many former generals in the Israeli army who advocate, for military/strategic reasons, that Israel withdraw to the pre-'67 boundaries and abandon the settlements in the West Bank and Gaza.

It was this understanding that was at the heart of proposals made by Yitzhak Rabin and other military men whose patriotism and military experience were not being compromised when they decided to end the Occupation.

b. The Iraq war of 1991 led to the bombing of Tel Aviv with SCUD missiles. It was that circumstance which demonstrated that holding a few miles this way or that in the Occupied Territories was largely irrelevant to the instruments of modern warfare that Israel is likely to face in any serious encounter with Arab states. The SCUDS and other instruments of war can travel over the West Bank with ease regardless of whether the territory is being held by Palestinians or by the Israeli army.

c. The likelihood of war with surrounding Arab states would be significantly diminished were Israel to be perceived as having rectified past oppression of the Palestinian people. There are some Muslims who will never accept the existence of a Jewish state in the Middle East. They have much greater support at a time when Palestinians are perceived by fellow Muslims as suffering unbearable pain than they will have after Israel has acted in a generous and repentant way. Surrounding Arab states offered Israel in the Spring of 2002 a peace accord and normal relations, but Israel scorned the offer because it was based on Israel returning to the pre-67 borders. Yet peace with Arab states would deliver far more security than the few miles of territory they get by holding on to the West Bank. And that makes it hard to argue that Israel is just waiting for a good opportunity to make peace, when that peace has already been offered.

8 *"But how can we bargain with these people when they are still fighting us? Does that show that they want peace?"*

Well, the United States bargained with the Vietnamese while the Vietnamese were still fighting a war of terror against South Vietnam and a full scale military struggle with the U.S. Army. That didn't keep us from negotiating and getting out. So why should Israel act as though doing that is somehow beneath its dignity or a betrayal of common sense? If the United States had followed Israel's logic, we would still be fighting the war in Vietnam. Yet once we made peace, the Vietnamese became less ferociously ideological and opened their gates to American economic and intellectual cooperation.

9 *"Is a political settlement really possible—won't these people always be hating each other and fighting?"*

a. Yes and no. A political settlement really is not possible without a spiritual and psychological transformation as well. Until both sides can treat each other with a spirit of generosity and open-heartedness, there will be some on both sides who nurture their own hatreds and desire for revenge. This kind of change of heart is very unlikely as long as Israelis are occupying the West Bank and Gaza and Palestinians are murdering Israeli civilians in terror attacks.

b. However, these people have often lived in peace in the past, and they can live in peace together in the future. There is nothing inevitable about this conflict persisting. There were people who made the same argument about France and Germany after the Second World War— these were two countries who had murdered each other in three major wars killing a far greater percentage of each other's populations than Israel and Palestine have done. Yet changed circumstances have created a reality in which these two bitter former enemies now cooperate and are strategically and economically aligned.

c. We can achieve a different reality—described above in the section *Strategies for Peace*. First, the sides must be physically separated and protected from each other by international intervention. Second, a political solution must be imposed since it will not be arrived at through negotiations, or if it is, it will be a solution which favors the stronger parties rather than a solution that will satisfy the legitimate needs of both sides. Once a political solution has been imposed, then we get to the absolutely most important step: changes in the hearts of both peoples.

d. The changes at the heart level must begin with Israeli repentance. Both sides have done terrible and unjustifiable acts toward the other, and both sides must repent and atone. But given the vast asymmetry of power between the two sides at this historical moment, it must be the more powerful, Israel, that takes the most forceful first steps toward repentance and atonement. If the Jewish people worldwide, and the Israeli people society-wide, were to truly acknowledge the terrible things we have done in our name, the ways that we have been deeply insensitive, and were we to take steps that clearly communicated a generosity of heart aimed at providing a good life for Palestinians (where "good life" would mean—as good as the lives we want for ourselves) and clearly communicated a spirit of contrition based on a new understanding of what had happened (the kind of balanced perspective articulated in this book), then we would, within twenty to thirty years, thaw the icy hearts of those who have been most damaged by our actions. That, in turn, would lead to repentance on the part of the Palestinian people, whose acts of violence and terror are equally a cause for repentance and atonement. It is these processes that will be the only guarantor of a successful and lasting political solution to the problem. And my call for Israel to take the first step is not based on saying that Israel is worse or more evil, but only that the dynamics of having more power require that we also have more humility and more willingness to take the first steps and more.

It was precisely the willingness of the whites in South Africa to agree to a Truth and Reconciliation Commission which thawed the anger of the Black people who had previously been suppressed. When we are willing to acknowledge what we've done, and only then, we will create the conditions in which the oppressed group is also able to acknowledge how terrible were many of the acts of violence that they perpetrated.

There are no political parties in Israel or Palestine who are willing to call for this kind of repentance and open-heartedness toward the other in the first decade of the twenty-first century. Nor do many of the peace forces in the United States talk in this kind of language. The peace forces believe that they would be deemed "unrealistic," "foolish," or "utopian" to talk as though the Palestinian people (or whoever we are talking about) were really human beings who could respond to a serious change of heart on our parts. The peace forces think they would become a laughingstock were they to talk as though they seriously believed in the humanity and decency of the Palestinian people. But if they don't talk in this language, then many other people will rightly suspect that the Left shares with the Right the assumption that "really" the Palestinians lack common decency, that they are all the killers and terrorists whose abhorrent acts have become the central focus of public attention. That message, conveyed explicitly by the Right, and implicitly by the peace forces by their unwillingness to talk about the Palestinian people in terms that affirm their humanity and goodness, lead most of the electorate to feel that both the Left and Right distrust Palestinians. "So then who is best equipped to deal with people we can't trust? Probably the Right." This strategy on the part of the peace forces actually fails to build an alternative to the Right, and so the Right always wins, either by winning an election with their own Right-wing parties, or in effect winning by getting the Left and peace forces to select as their candidates somebody who is going to show that they too can be "tough" and "hard-nosed" with the Palestinians (e.g., Barak, Ben Eliezer, or other militarists who are chosen "because they can win"—even though their instincts are toward repression rather than toward generosity).

Amram Mitzna of the Labor party, Yessi Sarid of Meretz, and the peace forces would be far more effective if they were willing to lose an election or two (which they are going to do anyway) by taking an explicitly humane attitude toward the Palestinian people, challenging chauvensim and anti-Arab sentiments, and educating Israelis to the importance of that perspective.

Moreover, that is the kind of signal that would give Palestinians some reason to hope that they are going to face something besides endless Occupation. If what they see instead is a Labor Party that talks about peace but continues to demean the Palestinian people and refuses to challenge anti-Arab sentiments, they are not going to feel the least bit inclined to risk their lives to challenge the terrorists amongst them.

It is precisely this language of generosity, kindness, open-heartedness and affirmation of the Spirit of God in the Other which is indispensable for creating the climate within which genuine reconciliation could take place. Without this focus, we are likely to see new political agreements which in turn will fail and which will only create new avenues for continuation of the struggle and deepening of cynicism about the possibility of peace. Until a spirit of open-heartedness, generosity, recognition of the sanctity of the lives of the other, and genuine repentance guide the policies of both sides, there is no hope for long-term reconciliation and peace.

10 *"In your public statements as well as in your strategy described in Chapter Six of this book you call for Palestinian non-violence. But how can you, an American Jew living in comfort, call for Palestinians living under conditions of extreme oppression and the constant violence of the occupying IDF forces to adopt non-violence?"*

a. The call for non-violence is made upon both sides. We call for Israel to adopt the path of non-violence as well as the Palestinians. The first step in that process is the immediate withdrawal of Israel from the West Bank and Gaza (with minor border modifications so that the sections of Jerusalem which had a Jewish majority at the time of the signing of the Oslo Accords should still be part of Israel, and some settlements on the border should be incorporated into Israel).

b. The call for non-violence is a matter of principle, based on our commitment to the sanctity of every human being on the planet.

c. The call for Palestinian non-violence is also based on our understanding that one of the major obstacles to any oppressor giving up its position of power is the fear that once it does so it will make itself vulnerable to the retaliatory anger of those who it had been oppressing. While in this book I've done my best to show that the issues are far more complex than that, and that use of the term "oppressor" to describe one side and "oppressed" to describe the other misses the complexities and intricacies of this struggle (which has seen a reversal in power roles over the course of the past 120 years, without a corresponding reversal in the self-perceptions of the parties to the conflict), I do believe that at least some of this fear of retaliation is relevant to the present moment. The most effective way to deal with that fear is to reassure those with power that their fears are not justified, and that the powerless already see them as created in the image of God and deserving of better treatment than the powerless have themselves received from them. This was the brilliance in the strategy of Martin Luther King Jr. and Nelson Mandela. They were able to convince their opponents that once the powerless became powerful they would not use their power in a hurtful way. And it is that idea which created the psychic space for the powerful to then rethink their social order and agree to reduce their own power. This is what is needed today in Israel. Any policy that tends to reassure Israelis that they will be safe when Palestinians have their own state is a policy that is pro-Palestinian, and any policy that tends to undermine Israeli beliefs that they can be safe with Palestine is a policy that is anti-Palestinian. In this sense, the strategies of the Hamas and the Islamic Jihad are really against the best interests of the Palestinian people, as are the policies of the Palestinian Authority which on the one hand denounce the violence while on the other hand seem to give free rein to the violent. It is precisely because we care about the Palestinian people that we call for non-violence, because this is what is objectively the most effective policy for creating an Israeli change of heart.

d. It would be immoral to see what was most likely to help bring peace to the region, and then keep quiet about it for fear that people on one side or the other would accuse you of not living there and hence not sharing the risks and hence not having a right to your views. When that argument comes from right-wing Jews, our answer as Americans is clear: those of us who are Jews have a strong stake in any state that claims to be the State of the Jewish people and puts itself forward as such; those of us who are not Jews point to the fact that Israel continually asks for and receives our tax monies, and as long as it is the largest recipient of American aid it is totally appropriate for Americans to voice their criticisms of how Israel is conducting itself. But on a deeper level, our caring about other people around the world leads us to feel we have a right to criticize the behavior of China in Tibet, of Russia in Chechnya, of the former Soviet Union when it had anti-Semitic policies, and of many other states, so why should Israel or Palestine be exempt from this? Our criticisms (in this case of Palestinians, in other cases of Israelis) comes from our commitment to their well-being. You can disagree with the content of criticisms and argue against them, but it is not appropriate to argue that we don't have the right to make the criticisms because of who we are.

The best thing we can do for the Palestinians is to separate them from the forces of violence, to show the world that the majority of Palestinians are not terrorists out to destroy Israel, but people like you and me. For that reason it is imperative to support voices of nonviolence in the Palestinian world and not to be afraid to criticize those who justify Palestinian violence. People who walk around justifying Palestinian violence are doing no favor to the Palestinian people.

11 *"If Palestinians don't want to destroy Israel, where are the voices of moderate Palestinians—and why don't we ever hear them?*

a. You don't hear them for the same reason that most Americans don't hear the voices of the many American Jews who oppose Ariel Sharon's policies, and the reason why the media doesn't cover voices like that of the Tikkun Community when the media is presenting the "American response" to events in the Middle East. The official media of the American Jewish community ignores these voices totally. Mainstream American press and media tends to either ignore these voices or to relegate them to the back pages where they are rarely noticed. If you want to challenge this tendency, go to www.tikkun.org to the section on the Tikkun Community, and then to Media Critique and join the Rapid Response team.

b. Here is a statement by Palestinian leaders in response to terror in June 2002, condemning a suicide bombing. By the time you read this there will be more such statements, just as there have been before this. This appeal was published in Palestinian newspapers in Arabic (which accounts for some of the clumsiness in the translation). Please note that the people signing this statement on the Palestinian side represent mainstream Palestinians. On the Israeli and American Jewish side, however, there are few people with comparable institutional power who have condemned Israeli acts of violence against Palestinians.

Urgent Appeal to Stop Suicide Bombings

We the undersigned feel that it is our national responsibility to issue this appeal in light of the dangerous situation engulfing the Palestinian people. We call upon the parties behind military operations targeting civilians in Israel to reconsider their policies and stop driving our young men to carry out these operations. Suicide bombings deepen the hatred and widen the gap between the Palestinian and Israeli people. Also, they destroy the possibilities of peaceful co-existence between them in two neighboring states.

We see that these bombings do not contribute towards achieving our national project that calls for freedom and independence. On the contrary, they strengthen the enemies of peace on the Israeli side and give Israel's aggressive government under Sharon the excuse to continue its harsh war against our people. This war targets our children, elderly, villages, cities, and our national hopes and achievements.

Military action cannot be assessed as positive or negative out of the l context and situation. They are assessed based on whether they fulfill political ends. Therefore, there is a need to re-evaluate these acts considering that pushing the area towards an existential war between the two people living on the holy land will lead to destruction for the whole region. We do not find any logical, humane, or political justification for this end result.

Signatories: Below are some of the Palestinian intellectuals and public figures who have signed the petition:

—Dr. Sari Nuseiba Dr. Hanan Ashrawi Saleh Ra'fat Salah Zuheika Mamdouh Nofal Hanna Sineora Dr. Mohammad Ishtiya Ibrahim Kandalaft Dr. Eyad El-Sarraj Dr. Moussa El-Budeiri Huda El-Imam Dr. Marwan Abu El-Zuluf Saman Khoury Dr. Said Zidani Dr. Omayya Khammash Dr. Jad Is'haq Dr. Manuel Hassasian Salah Abdel Shafi Shaher Sa'ad Dr. Mohammad Dajani Imad Awad Fadel Tahboub Majed Kaswani Taysir El-Zibri Dr. Ahmad Majdalani Dr. Taleb Awad Khader Sh'kirat Zahi Khouri Majed Abu Qubo' Ehab Boulous Dr. Isam Nassar Dr. Salim Tamari Dr. Suad El-Ameri Dr. Adam Abu Sh'rar Dr. Riema Hamami Subhi El-Z'beidi Dr. Munther El-Dajani Osama Daher Simone Cupa Jeana Abu El-Zuluf Yousef Daher Jamal Zaqout Dr. Saleh Abdel Jawwad Dr. Nathmi El-Ju'ba Dr. Jamil Hilal Dr. Arafat El-Hadmi Dr. Leila Faydi Dr. Zakaria El-Qaq Amna Badran Dr. Ali Q'leibo Marwan Tarazi Dr. Raja'I El-Dajani Issa Q'seisiya Hani El-Masri Dr. Jumana Odeh Lucy Nuseiba Abdel Qader El-Husseini Zahra El-Khaldi

12 *"Aren't there real power imbalances between Israel and Palestine, and doesn't your attempt to develop a discourse of compassion and not blaming cover up the fact that one people came to another people's land and dislocated them, and is maintaining their expropriation through force and violence? In this case, the language of compassion is a moral dodge."*

The discourse of compassion and transcending blame will be difficult for those people who can only get motivated to do political work when they have a simplistic picture of the world that includes totally good guys and totally bad guys. For them, the complex picture being drawn here will be disappointing and will be dismissed as "too" something, whether that is "too pro-Arab" (as seen by the Israel-is-always-right crowd) or "too pro-Israel" as seen by the "Israel-is-fundamentally-evil" crowd. But for those who actually wish to end the Occupation, it is precisely the kind of balance sought in this book which has the only remote chance of breaking through so that both sides can come to understand each other.

This is not to deny that there are power imbalances. For that reason, even with the compassionate analysis we advocate, we still support making demands on the Israeli government to end the Occupation immediately. But we also know that it is only when the Israeli people feel safe that they will do that, and for that reason, among others, we demand that the Palestinian people stop their acts of terror immediately. In this sense, it is a mistake to talk of one side as having all the power. The Palestinian people do not have the power to overthrow Israeli rule, but they do have the (self-defeating) power to keep Israelis scared. And as long as Israelis are scared, they are more likely to fight to the death rather than put themselves into a position of vulnerability.

Here it is important to acknowledge the trauma of the Holocaust which has never been healed. Israelis feel themselves more threatened than they actually are. This is the cost of the world (including but not only the Arabs) having turned their backs and closed their ears when the Jews were being murdered. Now we have a traumatized people, with a huge weapons supply including nuclear and chemical weaponry, and we have to recognize that they are not going to be pushed into submission by a world that shows no compassion for their fears. And since their fears have a real basis and are restimulated daily by acts of barbarity from some elements (not most elements, just some) in the Palestiinian world, the only sensible strategy is one based on compassion together with firmness, or "tough love." On the one hand, that means pressuring Israel to end the Occupation, but on the other hand it means simultaneously resisting all efforts to discredit Israel's right to exist or to undermine its ability to defend itself against real enemies. It is this balanced approach which has the possibility to eventually create the sense of safety that Israelis need to change.

13   *"What are the appropriate tactics to use in this struggle?"* Tactics are always to be evaluated in terms of their likely short-term impact (as opposed to principles, which should be evaluated by moral criteria). So tactics that might make sense in 2003 or

2004 might be inappropriate in 2005, and those that should not be used in 2003 might be very relevant for 2005. We always need to keep an open mind about tactics, and to make careful analysis of what are likely to be their impact in terms of generating the conditions in which peace, reconciliation, social justice, security, and an ethos of kindness and generosity can be established.

It's very important in building a movement for peace, justice, reconciliation and open-heartedness to not turn differences about tactics into principles. In my experience in progressive social change movements, it is very easy to get people to fight with each other about tactics, and to have an organization become bogged down in those kinds of internal debates (often because the people in the movements feel more comfortable having debates internally than they do talking to strangers and doing public education about the core issues of their movements). It behooves us to not allow that kind of divisiveness to keep us from building unity among all those who really do want a world of peace and justice for both Israel and Palestine. You can be part of the discussion of strategy and tactics in the Tikkun Community. Join the Tikkun Community at www.tikkun.org and then participate in our internal discussions (if you agree with the worldview articulated at that website in the location called Core Vision).

14 *"I agree with a lot of what you say, but I can't stand getting involved in politics because people in the movement spend so much time acting out, going on ego trips, being insensitive to others, speaking in superficial ways, or not reflecting the ethos of caring and love which is what made me interested in getting involved in the first place."*

Yes. This is a familiar problem to many of us. Being involved in building a social movement can often be frustrating, and some of the people we meet will inevitably make us feel uncomfortable and wish we were at home with our friends and family, rather than trying to create something at a time when things look so difficult.

The problem is this: nothing will ever be changed if we wait to find the group of people to do it with who are not in some ways screwed up, psychologically or spiritually damaged, or in some other way untogether, lazy, irresponsible, scared, posturing, impulsive, too head-tripping, too emotional or too wounded. Because there is nothing on this planet but people who are wounded in some way or other—that's all there is. So the

appropriate attitude towards screwed up people we meet in social movements is compassion, just as we hope that they too will have compassion
toward us and our own limitations as human beings. If we can maintain
that compassionate attitude toward each other, we may have a chance to
help foster the same kind of compassion in the larger world, and it is that
compassion which is the indispensable condition for the possibility of
peace and reconciliation between Israelis and Palestinians.

15 *"Israel is building a wall between itself and Palestine. Won't
that be a better solution than bringing in an international
force to separate the two sides?"*

If the wall were being built on "the Green Line" (the pre-1967 border of Israel) that might be acceptable. But in fact, the wall is being built
to incorporate more of the West Bank into Israel, and that will not be
acceptable to the Palestinians or to the world community which has
insisted on principle in the years since 1945 that countries not expand
their borders through conquest. Israel claims its legal basis from the
1947 UN resolution authorizing its existence. But if UN resolutions
confer legitimacy, then Israel needs to abide by subsequent resolutions
that call upon it to return territories won by conquest in 1967.

16 *"You call for an international force to separate and provide
safety for both sides. But defacto that means pushing the IDF
out of the territories, while on the Palestinian side there is no reason to
believe that such a force would be any more effective than the IDF has
been in preventing suicide bombers. So how does this provide protection for Israel?"*

The only security that Israel can ever have is the security gained
through good relations with her neighbors. To imagine Israel trying to
exist as a state perceived as hostile to the interests of her 100 million
Arab neighbors is to condemn Israelis to a life of insecurity, terror, and
possible ultimate destruction (as weapons of mass destruction become
more easy to deliver and more accessible to terrorists in the next fifty
years). The only way that Israel can get those good relations with her
neighbors is to end the Occupation and then to develop an attitude of
humility to replace the perceived arrogance of Israeli military power, an
attitude of repentance to acknowledge the hurt and pain that has been
caused to the Palestinian people (though we also call for a spirit of

repentance from the Palestinian people, we realize that it is the more powerful force that must take the first dramatic steps of a generous spirit toward those over whom it has ruled for the past thirty-five years), an attitude that replaces discrimination against Israeli Arabs with a commitment to sharing Israel's internal resources equally with its own Arab citizens, and an attitude of respect toward the legitimate needs of the Palestinian people for the same dignity and well being that Israel has achieved for itself. There is simply no other path to Israeli security.

A first step in this process is for the Palestinian people to feel that they are no longer under the boot of Israeli power. It would be preferable if that could be achieved by Israel taking a unilateral step and withdrawing to the pre-67 borders (with minor border adjustments which I've mentioned above). I do not mean partial withdrawal, but a full withdrawal including a withdrawal from the settlements. But that seems unlikely under any political configuration that can be envisioned as I write this. That's why it becomes necessary for the peoples of the world to intervene and separate the two sides.

As the actual pressure of daily life lifts, and Palestinians become less desperate about their own family survival from Israeli occupying forces, and feel much more secure because of the presence of an international force separating them from Israel, they will be much more amenable to proposals for reconciliation with Israel—proposals that they cannot be expected to take seriously as long as the Occupation continues (which is why they found it difficult to take seriously the Camp David discussions in 2000, seven years into a process which was supposed to lead to Israeli withdrawal from the West Bank, but which instead had seen a dramatic increase in Israeli settlers).

In the circumstance of the negotiations that then become possible for the creation of a Palestinian state and the funding of an international plan of reparations for Palestinian refugees, the Palestinian people will come to feel that they have something real to gain in working out reconciliation with Israel. Under those circumstances, they are far less likely to provide the sea of support for terror that makes the terrorists feel that they are legitimate expressions of the needs of their own people.

It is, however, unlikely that this or any other method will fully eliminate the anger and fanaticism that produces at least some acts of terror. Just as the widespread support for the government of the United States could not prevent right-wing conspirators from blowing up the Federal

Building in Oklahoma City, and just as the growing police forces in the United States cannot protect Americans from a level of violence that we now simply define as "crime," so it will not be possible to ever guarantee that Israel will be free of some strikes against it by some fanatics. However, the meaning of those acts of violence will be very different when they are no longer perceived by the Palestinian people as anything but the acts of crazies who are in fact destroying rather than representing the best interests of Palestinian liberation. Understood as "crime" by both peoples, rather than as acts of aggression by one people against another, these acts of terror will decrease in number and be greeted with universal denunciations not only in the West but in Arab lands as well.

We cannot demand of a strategy that it produce a higher level of security for Israelis in their daily life than we have been able to obtain for ourselves in our own society.

There will, of course, be those who respond by saying, "You are naïve to think Israel will achieve security by creating good relations with Arabs. These people will settle for nothing less than the destruction of all Jews." I understand the sources of that kind of fearfulness, but for reasons already discussed in the questions above, I do not think that this is more than an inability to get beyond the traumas of the past and face the possibilities of the present.

One thing seems certain to me: the strategy of occupation and repression already tried by Ariel Sharon's government has not produced security. The number of deaths of Israelis during the period of Sharon's government was much higher than the number of deaths during the period in which Israel appeared to the Arab world to be moving toward disengagement on the West Bank. The Right's strategy has been tried, and it does not work. The strategy of imposing our will has been tried, and it does not work. Now it is time to give an opportunity for a very different strategy to work: the strategy of generosity, openheartedness, repentance, and sharing our resources and know how to create a viable Palestinian state.

17 *"But won't the Palestinians insist on 'the Right of Return' and wouldn't that mean in effect the end of the Jewish state?"*
There is no possibility that Israelis would agree to a Right of Return in the context of Israeli insecurities and fears. As long as there is in fact a climate of hostility and mutual suspicion it makes no sense to raise this

issue, except for those whose secret agenda (conscious or unconscious) is to derail the possibility of any serious reconciliation. There are, for example, some people on the Left who wish to push this demand to the center of the discussion because they want to be able to prove that Israel's very existence is incompatible with Palestinian rights, and some Palestinians living in exile who are as uncompromising in their demands for those who live in Palestine as are some Jews living in the United States uncompromising in their demands for the militancy of Israelis. On both sides there are exiles who are willing to have the people living in the area fight on endlessly and suffer endlessly. But for those who actually want to end the struggle, this demand is a non-starter.

On the other hand, if the other parts of our strategy are actually implemented, and with the spirit of generosity, kindness and repentance at the center of how it is done, it will then be possible to work out a plan for a limited but real right of return in a context that no longer seems so frightening. While that cannot be expected to be part of the original deal between Israel and Palestine (and therefore we emphasize a plan for reparations), it will become possible once peace and security have become part of the daily life experience of both peoples, to reraise this issue and to work out a reasonable compromise.

I believe that such a compromise might take the following form: Israel allows something like 15,000 refugees to return to Israel each year for the next thirty years. These numbers are small enough that the returnees could not constitute a demographic threat to the possibility of a Jewish majority unless Israelis stop having children. On the other hand, it is a number large enough to ensure that refugees who have no capacity to accept life away from their places of birth could return to them.

Most countries in the world have immigration quotas, and this kind of quota would assure Palestinian families of the possibility of being reunited. Israelis, on the other hand, would rightly want to have methods to ensure that the people they were bringing back came with pacific intent, understood fully that the homes that they wished to go back to no longer exist, and that the lands which they once worked are now owned by others who were born after 1948 and who cannot be expected to give up the land into which they were born. This kind of "understanding" is not conceivable in circumstances of struggle and anger as they exist at this moment, but it is very conceivable in a larger context in which there is a genuine change of heart and attitude by the Israeli government and the Israeli people, a change that is reflected in the actual life experience of the Palestinian people. It is only when those changes have been absorbed into the consciousness of Palestinians that it will be possible for both sides to work out an arrangement for Return that will provide for Israeli security and still recognize the legitimate desire of refugees to return to the land of their birth. But until those changes in consciousness happen, the demand for a Right to Return will rightly be seen as a way to derail a peace agreement, and for that reason it is not part of the Tikkun Community's set of positions, and what I say here reflects my own personal views. The Tikkun Community has no official position on The Right of Return, and focuses instead on something more realizable: substantial reparations sufficient to create economic well-being for the entire Palestinian people.

18 *"Why bother with all the attempts to build a movement around Middle East peace in the United States when you know that what really counts is the electoral outcomes in Israel. If we can just get the Labor party and Meretz party back into power, all this will be worked out."*

Unfortunately, that is not true. The Labor party and Meretz have both shown remarkably little capacity to empathize with the Palestinian people and their needs, and remarkably little capacity to address the importance of open-heartedness, generosity of spirit, and repentance which are, in my view, the absolute prerequisites for making a peace agreement work. We saw in the years after the signing of the Oslo accord how any agreement can break down if there is no spirit of generosity behind them. Yet both Labor and Meretz are filled with politicians who think that these "spiritual" issues are irrelevant to politics, and have no real place, and that if they were to be part of what was being talked about, the Israeli macho consciousness would simply ridicule them out of existence.

Not that Labor and Meretz are wrong about the current state of Israeli consciousness. But a political leadership that wants to bring peace is going to have to challenge that macho attitude and explain why it is precisely the issues around kindness, generosity, open-heartedness, and repentance that are the keys to political breakthrough when dealing with a population over which you have exercised domination and oppression. It is these spiritual issues which are central, not peripheral, and only a political force that understands the psychodynamic and spiritual dimension to this conflict could possibly come up with a plan sufficient to actually reach the hearts of the Palestinian people and thus provide them with the incentive they need to isolate rather than revere the "martyrs" who are actually self-destructive murderers and children who have lost their moral compass.

Understanding the spiritual and psychological dimension of this struggle is part of what I've been trying to do in this book, and it is the key element in building a successful and lasting peace and reconciliation. It is that which the Tikkun Community has to offer the peace movement and the peoples of the Middle East.

19 *"Shouldn't we be hopeful now that Amram Mitzna is the head of the Labor Party? After all, Mitzna is a dove, has called for an immediate end to settlements in the Gaza strip, an immediate return to negotiations with Palestinians based on where they got to at Taba in January of 2001, and he seems to represent a new spirit for the peace forces."*

Yes, Mitzna is a huge advance on the phony peace people in Labor like Barak and Peres, both of whom gave cover to the Ariel Sharon government as it pursued harsh and insensitive policies. Those of us who support peace will certainly welcome any advances that Mitzna can make toward that goal.

But even if Mitzna were able to agree to ending the Occupation and dismantling the settlements, that would not end the struggle. Until the fate of the three million Palestinian refugees has been sensitively addressed, this struggle will continue—and there will be many right-wing and centrist Israelis who will say, "See, even when you give them everything, they will not be satisfied with less than the full destruction of the State of Israel."

There is a way to deal with this situation, and Mitzna is unlikely to take it. That way is for Israel to take three key steps:

1. Acknowledge that it would be willing to take back a symbolic number of refugees (I've suggested above something like 15,000 a year for the next thirty years).

2. Implement immediately the full Tikkun plan (in the strategy section above) including reparations for Palestinian refugees.

3. Seek to do public acts of repentance and atonement for the oppression caused to the Palestinian people. For example, a Labor government

could encourage hundreds of thousands of Israelis to personally participate in rebuilding Palestinian homes and buildings damaged during the
Occupation and in building new housing for Palestinian refugees. It
could publicly teach the Israeli people that their obligation as patriots is
to personally befriend Palestinians and help humanize Israelis in their
eyes. And it could enthusiastically sponsor a Truth and Reconciliation
Commission designed to expose the realities of the pain of the Occupation to both Israelis and to Palestinians (in the latter case, to insist that
they also hear about the pain that some Palestinians inflicted on the lives
of innocent Israelis).

Everything depends on the spirit with which these actions are done.
In Arab culture, it is often the graciousness and respect shown, not the
actual details of the agreement, that is critical. That doesn't mean that
one can be mean-spirited in the contents of the offer but put a big smile
on it. The content has to be open-hearted and generous. But even the
most generous offer from Israel, if offered or implemented in a
begrudging style, will not offset the psychic wounding that has been
happening to the Palestinian people for the past decades.

Spirit Matters. It matters that you treat people as though they are
embodiments of the sacred, and not just instruments for your own ends.

That, of course, is the spiritual message of Tikkun. But it's also the
central truth of practical politics, and the key to bringing lasting peace
to the Middle East. Act in a way that shows that we care about the
Palestinian people and they will respond. Act as though we don't, and
they will respond to that also and in a way that perpetuates the struggle.

And this is why the resolution of the Israeli/Palestinian struggle is so
central to the well-being of the entire planet. On an unconscious level
everyone on the planet knows that the Jews, Christians, and Muslims
have a common religious heritage whose central message is that people
are created in the image of God and deserve to be treated as such—and
that the calls for justice, peace, love, generosity, and sharing that per-
meate these religions are outgrowths of this central idea. In *Spirit
Matters: Global Healing and the Wisdom of the Soul*, I show why the
application of this spiritual ideal (through what I call "the globalization
of Spirit") is the most effective alternative to the globalization of capital, and the most likely way to build a mass constituency for a new kind
of politics that can demand that we stop destroying the planet and recognize our shared responsibility as stewards for the environment and as

people who must take care of each other. But if the very peoples who articulated these ideals cannot implement them in the Middle East, many people reason, they will never be possible on a global scale. That is one reason why the world is so invested in the outcome of this particular struggle.

Because the Jewish people are more powerful militarily, economically and politically, it is our responsibility to take the first many steps, to act in a way filled with generosity and repentance, and not expect that our new mood will be immediately reciprocated by Palestinians. A courageous leader would explain this to the people of Israel, and would be willing to take the political costs of doing so. Such a leader would have to be willing to face and argue against all the "realists" who think that showing weakness is going to encourage Arabs to be less willing to compromise. The leader that Israel really needs would be one who could respond to these criticisms by helping his own country understand that the greatest strength is shown when one does not rely on strength, that the greatest courage that the Jewish people could have would be to allow ourselves to trust in the humanity of the Other. Given all that we've been through, I don't blame anyone who can't take this step. But it's the necessary step.

That's the kind of path that would have to be followed by an Israeli leader who would not just talk peace, but deliver it. And nothing I've heard about Amram Mitzna (or, for that matter, any of the other "doves" be they in Labor, Meretz, Peace Now, or in the party of religious doves that was called Meymad) leads me to believe that he or they are close to having the internal strength and wisdom that it would take to follow this path.

So, while I'm going to celebrate any victories that happen should Labor or Meretz or other peace parties actually come to power, I'm not going to expect that Healing Israel/Palestine is actually going to occur until this ancient spiritual insight can be lived. Or to put it another way, until the Jewish people is ready to take seriously its most revolutionary Torah mitzvah (command): "Thou shalt love the stranger."

Until we've tried that, anyone arguing that "we've tried everything and nothing works" has been stuck in the arena of "practical politics," and the deep teaching of the Jewish Renewal movement of which I am part is that "practical politics" doesn't work—all that works is to throw one's lot in with a path of justice, generosity, love, peace, patience, compassion, and forgiveness. In short, *Tikkun*—healing and transformation of a severely wounded world. All the rest is commentary.

20 *"Still, aren't you very unrealistic to hope for peace and reconciliation, to talk about Spirit (particularly to an Israeli society that is so deeply angry at religious people for the role that they play in public life), and to think you can preach love and kindness to a Jewish people who have been traumatized by hate and evil?"*

The current reality of anger, violence and hate has been brought to us by the "realists" who have been trying one strategy after another, none of which have worked. It may be more realistic to forget about "realism" as narrowly defined by the pundits, politicos and depressed former idealists, and instead give love and kindness a real chance. I don't mean let Israel disarm itself and throw flowers. I do mean, let Israel get out of the West Bank and Gaza while retaining its military power to defend itself, but then engage in a serious campaign for the next decades to provide adequate reparations and to make public repentance for our side (even while acknowledging that both sides have been the problem). If we act in good faith, acknowledging our side of the responsibility, and atoning for that part, and do so consistently and with an unmistakable spirit of generosity, we can make a breakthrough for peace that the realists have been unable to deliver.

Of course, there will still be acts of violence. I know some racists in the United States who say, "see, the level of Black crime and violence against whites shows that the capitulation to them by voting for Civil Rights did not work to bring social peace." And I'm sure that there will be some level of violence that continues against the Jewish people for many decades. But it will be isolated and unsupported by most Palestinians, and can be treated as crime.

I believe that the path of love and generosity, not the path of violence, is the only path to security. As someone who loves the Jewish people, and as someone who cares about all people, I believe that it is time for the Jews to take this path, the ancient path recommended in our holy books. I hope the Palestinians can also take this path, but I think the Jews have more power and must take the leap first. Let it be said in our generation that "From Zion went forth the spirit of Torah, and the word of the Lord was being taken seriously in Jerusalem." To secure the Jewish future, the Jews must become known as the force of idealism, generosity and love, not the voice of selfishness, racism, tribalism, violence and fear. And if not now, when?

21 *"Isn't the real problem the lack of democracy and corruption inside the Palestinian Authority?"*

There is no question that that is a real problem. Friends of the Palestinian people should be doing every nonviolent action we can do to support an end to the tyrannical regime of Yassir Arafat in favor of the creation of a truly free and democratic society for the Palestinian people. We should reject all those arguments that tell us that this has no history among Arab peoples (democratic processes did not have much of a history among Jewish people living in Eastern Europe or in North Africa some hundred years ago) and that this would be a Western cultural imposition. There are many Palestinians who would be speaking up and calling for a nonviolent path today if they were not fearful of violent reprisals or imprisonment from Arafat's regime or from some of the criminals who use the excuse of a national liberation struggle to impose their tyranny in some parts of Palestinian society. Any ways that we can find to support and amplify the voices calling for democratic reform should be pursued.

At the same time, it is important to differentiate that concern from those who are using the issue of democracy as yet another club to beat down the Palestinian people or to argue that they do not deserve the same rights and freedom from occupation as other peoples. When the Israeli Occupation forces call for a greater democratic process, they are cynically manipulating our commitment to democratic values, and they do that to perpetuate their own power. So this is an issue analogous to the way that corporate interests have called for democratic controls over the union movement in the United States. On the one hand, any time we can throw out of the unions those who are tyrannizing working people, we should rejoice. Corruption of unions has been no service to the needs of working people and has discouraged many of them from participation. But corporate demands are almost always tied to "union reform" that actually attempts to weaken the unions and make them less capable of fighting against overwhelming corporate power.

So, we both support the call for reform and also want to be sure that it is not imposed by those who have a very different and venal agenda. We will support democratization and liberalization movements inside

Palestine, but we will not allow these issues to be used as an excuse for continued Occupation.

22 *"Don't the continuing brutal acts of Palestinian violence against Israelis show that they are morally underdeveloped as a people?"*

I abhor the acts of violence on the part of some who claim to represent the Palestinian people. But there is no reason to believe that their actions are representative of the entire Palestinian people. I remember how difficult it was for those of us who protested against the war in Vietnam to have any way to stop the violent actions of a very few people in our movement whose rocks through windows and bombs were used by the media and the Right to portray us all as having abandoned our moral integrity.

I also abhor the acts of violence done by Israelis. I ahbor the long history of violent land seizures, the destruction of Palestinian villages, the forced expulsion of Palestinians from their homes in 1948, the refusal of Israel to allow them back into their homes, the destruction of their homes or their appropriation by the Israeli government. I abhor the acts of violence of Israelis who grabbed land from Palestinians to build settlements, and I abhor the acts of violence perpetrated daily by the Israeli army as it enforces Occupation.

I do not mean to create any kind of "moral equivalence" between one act of violence and another. Every act of violence is hurtful and evil, and each is a unique and dreadful violation of the Spirit of God in each human being.

Much of this book has been meant to show the context of this violence, to help us understand that it doesn't flow from the evil or demented nature of either people. But the book is not meant to leave you without moral judgments. I have such: both sides have acted in morally reprehensible ways, both have inflicted unnecessary violence and cruelty on the other, and both need to repent.

I do find it particularly distasteful to hear some Westerners trying to adopt supposedly scientific theories of psychological development or spiritual development and using them as a club against the Palestinian people. The evidence usually provided for lower levels of development among Palestinians could be equally provided for many Israelis that I have known in the time that I have spent living in Israel.

The teaching of hate in Palestinian schools, while terrible, matches the teaching of hate I have heard with my own ears in various synagogues on Shabbat in Israel, and what I've witnessed being taught to children in the settlements who, by age five, often already embody hateful attitudes toward Arabs. The truth is that these developmental claims and claims about indoctrination are usually one-sided and represent cultural biases rather than a seriously compassionate ability to hear the pain on both sides and to recognize the distortions on both sides.

Let me take as an example the particularly upsetting acts of violence that were perpetrated recently against Metzar, an Israeli kibbutz famous for its support for the peace movement. I sent out to the Tikkun Community email lists an unequivocal condemnation of the violence, pointing out that nothing could possibly justify the acts of killing a mother and her two children—that this was cold-blooded murder, and that no "context" could make it OK. I believe that Uri Avnery, a leader of the Israeli peace movement, fully shares that judgment. Yet he insists, and I agree, that although understanding the context is not an excuse or a pardon, context is nevertheless important for those who start rushing in to make sweeping judgments about the moral inferiority of one side or the other. For that reason, I'd like to quote his response to the acts at Kibbutz Metzar, which could equally have been said of many other past acts which we do not condone or accept or mitigate, but which we do need to understand, just as, I insist, we need to understand the legacy of the Holocaust and its distorting impact on Israelis, even though in understanding that we ought not mitigate, condone, or accept current acts of cruelty and violence against the Palestinian people.

Revenge of a Child
by Uri Avnery   November 16, 2002

Since last Sunday, a question has been running around in my head and troubling my sleep: What induced the young Palestinian, who broke into Kibbutz Metzer, to aim his weapon at a mother and her two little children and kill them?

In war one does not kill children. That is a fundamental human instinct, common to all peoples and all cultures. Even a Palestinian who wants to take revenge for the hundreds of children killed by the Israeli army should not take revenge on children. No moral commandment says "a child for a child."

The persons who do these things are not known as crazy killers, blood-thirsty from birth. In almost all interviews with relatives and neighbors they are described as quite ordinary, nonviolent individuals. Many of them are not religious fanatics. Indeed, Sirkhan Sirkhan, the man who committed the deed in Metzer, belonged to Fatah, a secular movement.

These persons belong to all social classes; some come from poor families who have reached the threshold of hunger, but others come from middle class families, university students, educated people. Their genes are not different from ours.

So what makes them do these things? What makes other Palestinians justify them?

In order to cope, one has to understand, and that does not mean to justify. Nothing in the world can justify a Palestinian who shoots at a child in his mother's embrace, just as nothing can justify an Israeli who drops a bomb on a house in which a child is sleeping in his bed. As the Hebrew poet Bialik wrote a hundred years ago, after the Kishinev pogrom: "Even Satan has not yet invented the revenge for the blood of a little child."

But without understanding, it is impossible to cope. The chiefs of the IDF have a simple solution: hit, hit, hit. Kill the attackers. Kill their commanders. Kill the leaders of their organizations. Demolish the homes of their families and exile their relatives. But, wonder of wonders, these methods achieve the opposite. After the huge IDF bulldozer flattens the "terrorist infrastructure," destroying-killing-uprooting everything on its way, within days a new "infrastructure" comes into being. According to the announcements of the IDF itself, since operation "Protective Shield" there have been some fifty warnings of imminent attacks every day.

The reason for this can be summed up in one word: rage.

Terrible rage, that fills the soul of a human being, leaving no space for anything else. Rage that dominates the person's whole life, making life itself unimportant. Rage that wipes out all limitations, eclipses all values, breaks the chains of family and responsibility. Rage that a person wakes up with in the morning, goes to sleep with in the evening, dreams about at night. Rage that tells a person: get up, take a weapon or an explosive belt, go to their homes and kill, kill, kill, no matter what the consequences.

An ordinary Israeli, who has never been in the Palestinian territories, cannot even imagine the reasons for this rage. Our media totally ignore the events there, or describe them in small, sweetened doses. The average Israeli knows somehow that the Palestinians suffer (it's their own fault, of course), but he has no idea what's really happening there. It doesn't concern him, anyhow.

Homes are demolished. A merchant, lawyer, ordinary craftsman, respected in his community, turns overnight into a "homeless," he and his children and grandchildren. Each one of them a potential suicide bomber.

Fruit-trees are being uprooted in their thousands. For the officer, it's just a tree, an obstacle. For the owners, it's the blood of his heart, the heritage of his forefathers, years of toil, the livelihood of his family. Each one of them a potential suicide bomber.

On a hill between the villages a gang of thugs has put up an "outpost." The army arrives to defend them. When the villagers come to till their fields, they are shot at. They are forbidden to work in all fields and groves within a one or two kilometers' range, so that the security of the outpost will not be endangered. The peasants see from afar, with longing eyes, how their fruit is rotting on the trees, how their fields are being covered by thorns and thistles waist high, while their children have nothing to eat. Each one of them a potential suicide bomber.

People are killed. Their torn bodies lie in the streets, for everyone to see. Some of them are "martyrs" who chose their lot. But many others—men, women, children—are killed "by mistake," "accidentally," "trying to escape," "were close to the source of fire"—and all the hundred-and-one pretexts of professional spokesmen. The IDF does not apologize, officers and soldiers are never convicted, because "that's how things are in war." But each of the people killed has parents, brothers, sons, cousins. Each one of them a potential suicide bomber.

Beyond these are the families living on the fringes of hunger, suffering from severe malnutrition. Fathers who cannot bring food to their children feel despair. Each one of them a potential suicide bomber.

Hundreds of thousands are kept under curfew for weeks and months on end, eight persons cooped up in two or three rooms, a living hell difficult to imagine, while outside the settlers have a ball, protected by the soldiers. A vicious circle: yesterday's bombers caused the curfew, the curfew creates the bombers of tomorrow.

And beyond all these, the total humiliation which every Palestinian, without distinction of age, gender or social standing, experiences every moment of his life. Not an abstract humiliation, but an altogether concrete one. To be dependent for life and death on the whim of an 18-year-old boy in the street and at one of the innumerable checkpoints that a Palestinian has to pass wherever he goes, while gangs of settlers pass freely and "visit" their villages, damage property, pick the olives in their groves, set fire to the trees.

An Israeli who has not seen it cannot imagine such a life, a situation of "every bastard a king" and "the slave who has becomes master," a situation of curses and pushes at best, threats with weapons in many cases, actual shooting in some. Not to mention the sick on the way to dialysis, the pregnant women on the way to hospitals, students who don't get to their classes, children who can't reach their schools. The youngsters who see their venerable grandfather publicly humiliated by some boy in uniform with a runny nose. Each one of them a potential suicide bomber.

A normal Israeli cannot imagine all this. After all, the soldiers are nice boys, the sons of all of us, only yesterday they were schoolboys. But when one takes these nice boys and puts them in uniforms, pushes them through the military machine and puts them into a situation of occupation, something happens to them. Many try to keep their human face in impossible circumstances, many others become order-fulfilling robots. And always, in every company, there are some disturbed people who flourish in this situation and do repulsive things, knowing that their officers will turn a blind eye or wink approvingly.

All this does not justify the killing of children in the arms of their mother. But it helps to grasp why this is happening, and why this will go on happening as long as the occupation lasts.

23   *"You call for American support for an end to the Occupation. What kind of changes would it take in America for that to happen?"*

Many Americans understand that there is something deeply wrong with the Israeli Occupation of the Palestinian people. But they are reluctant to get involved because of the particular way that elements in the organized Jewish community have defended Israel. That way is to charge that anyone disagreeing with the current policies of the State of Israel (whatever they happen to be) is anti-Semitic or, if Jewish, a "self-hating Jew."

These charges are particularly powerful because the most morally sensitive Americans remember the long history of anti-Semitism, recognize that the Christian world was responsible for much of this, correctly suspect that not enough has been done to atone for these past crimes, and so feel particularly unwilling to take actions which Jews are calling anti-Semitic. Thus, the most right-wing governments in Israel are able to manipulate the moral decency of ordinary Americans.

But these non-Jews are doing no favor to the Jewish people by allowing themselves to be manipulated in this way. The people doing this manipulation are themselves decent people who are, in my view, deeply mistaken about what serves the best interests of the Jewish people. In my view, the best interests of the Jewish people, and the only plausible long-term survival path for the State of Israel, lies in reconciliation and peace with the Palestinian people and with all other states in the region; the path of war and eternal struggle is the path of suicide for the Jews. There will come a time when the technology of weapons of mass destruction is such that even a crazy individual is able to deliver it to a population center and hurt many many people. There will be no effective defense. The only real path to defense is to build decent relationships with others.

Once you realize this, you realize that the real objectively "pro-Israel" forces are those who are calling for an End to the Occuaption, an end to violence on both sides, and the beginning of a process of reconciliation and atonement. And those who are quick to label as anti-Semitic or self-hating or anti-Israel everyone who critiques Israeli policy are doing a grave disservice to the Jewish people.

Getting out this message to the American public is complicated in part by the fact that the forces in the Jewish world who have used this kind of manipulation to intimidate both non-Jews and Jews who are critical of Israeli policy have a great deal of money and political power. Organized as effective political lobbies, they have been able to convince many politicians and others in public life (college presidents, journalists, editorialists, magazine editors, television and movie producers) that their own personal futures will be put at risk if they provide a voice for those who are critical of Israeli policy.

As a result of all this, it is very difficult to get a hearing for our peace perspective in the American media. And when the voices of opposition are heard in the media, they often select as spokespeople those with the least nuanced perspectives. Those of us who are both pro-Israel and pro-Palestine, who truly believe in the validity of the State of Israel and truly believe in the decency of the vast majority of the Palestinian people, and who will not accept the crude distortions that go for analysis in American media and politics (e.g., that the Palestinians were offered a great deal by Barak, or that the Palestinian people will settle for nothing less than the full destruction of Israel), are systematically excluded when the media represents the sides of the conflict.

So we need to engage in a very serious and prolonged campaign to educate the American public to a more complex view of what is happening in Israel/Palestine, and this book can be one part of that process. The Tikkun Community is a new national organization for people who want to be part of what we call a "progressive middle path," that is, a path that will not accept that the only way to be pro-Israel is to go along with the Occupation, and that the only way to be pro-Palestine is to accept the demeaning of Israel or the weakening of its ability to defend itself against real enemies. We try to signal this by saying that we are both pro-Israel and pro-Palestine: our point is that the best interests of Israeli safety and security lie in a reconciliation of the heart with the Palestinian people, that the best interests of the Palestinian people lie in a reconciliation of the heart with the Israeli people, and that the road to this reconciliation lies in being able to tell the story in a way that recognizes the validity of both sides, and then to move toward repentance and atonement for all the unnecessary pain both sides have inflicted on the other. If this approach makes sense to you, you are invited to join us.

You might, as step one, go to our website, www.tikkun.org and read the *Core Vision* of our community. Then, you can join on line, or you can call our office at 415-575-1200 or email us at magazine@tikkun.org to find out our annual membership fee and to get assistance in creating a local Tikkun Community. Please send us your email address so that we can stay in touch with you.

The Tikkun Community is organizing groups in communities to do outreach and education, teach-ins, present visiting speakers, show movies, create public events, and house parties (can you invite some friends and neighbors or people with whom you study, work, pray, or play to come to your house and spend an evening talking about these issues, studying this text or watching a video that we can provide for you to help you start this education process in your own circle?). We are organizing education on a national level as well. We are providing training sessions for organizers and educators (please attend one). We have created a media Rapid Response Team to challenge distortions in the media. We have created a national organization called the Tikkun Campus Network for people on college campuses who share our approach. We are developing local initiatives which people can put on the ballot as measures calling for an End to the Occupation. We are organizing groups to engage in nonviolent demonstrations to get our message heard. We are encouraging artists to create pro-peace art, musicians to create pro-peace songs and music, television and movie producers and directors to use their talents to produce shows and films that get our perspective heard. We are encouraging professionals in every sphere to help us bring this message to their colleagues. We are creatng a national presence for a different way of thinking about these issues.

And we are not alone. There are many other fine organizations doing work to educate the public about these issues. They include Rabbis for Human Rights, Americans for Peace Now, Brit Tzedek v'Shalom, and many of the social justice arms of various Protestant denominations.

I especially want to call to your attention the work of the Association of Bereaved Parents, headed by Yitzhak Frankenthal, which brings together Israeli and Palestinian parents of victims of the violence, parents who in their sorrow have come to realize that peace is the only way to prevent more senseless loss of life.

An indispensable source of information about the violation of human rights in the West Bank and Gaza is supplied by B'tselem, the Israeli Human Rights Organization. Their reports have provided the documentation that proves the reality of Israeli torture of Palestinians, and many other abuses that are part of the daily realities of the Occupation.

Getting this information widely disseminated is only one part of the strategy of The Tikkun Community. I hope that you'll join us and work for peace. Or join one of the other organizations working in this direction. There is no "one correct path," and each of the groups makes important contributions. Which are the ones that deserve support? Well, one criterion is this: are they willing to publicly endorse the strategy calling for an end to the Occupation, reparations for the Palestinian people, security for both Israel and Palestine, etc., outlined in an earlier section of this book? Here is another criterion: any group that takes this book, distributes it widely, uses it as a basis for study groups, and agrees with its basic approach (though I'm sure that there are errors in details, and that others will come forward and make even better analyses and more persuasive arguments), is probably on the right track, and any group which does not is probably too sectarian or has some principled objection to validating the truths of both sides—in which case I wouldn't wholeheartedly support that group. By the way, there are many groups doing good work in Israel or Palestine that are not really peace groups: e.g., The New Israel Fund. NIF does support non-profits in Israel doing education for tolerance. But they will not fund any specifically peace-oriented political movements, so don't think you are funding the peace activities when you support NIF (though there are a lot of other good reasons to support their important work).

If you are a member of a church or synagogue, ask them to officially endorse our proposal to end the Occupation, etc., and to affiliate with The Tikkun Community. Or ask them to invite a Tikkun Community speaker and find a way to support other ways to fund and give public support to the peace movement. Our synagogue in San Francisco, Beyt Tikkun, is a separate organization from the Tikkun Community (which is not just for Jews and is not committed to any particular spiritual path) has also done something else that is worth considering: we've decided to financially support both an organization in Israel that does work in providing emergency medical assistance to victims of terror and also an organization of refuseniks (Israeli soldiers who refuse to enforce the Occupation).

The Tikkun Community is planning to send volunteers to Palestine to help rebuild homes destroyed by the Occupation, and to provide aid and medical care to those still living under Occupation, as well as to Israel to assist families who have been harmed by the violence.

And the Tikkun Community is creating a national voice for those who wish to have this perspective heard in the public arena. Help us shape that strategy—join and become active in building the Tikkun Community. Come to our leadership trainings. Come to our national conferences. Create something real in your community. And encourage people to study this book so that they can feel empowered to be representatives of a perspective that affirms healing and transformation.

The Tikkun Community is not a political organization. We are part of a 501c(3) non-profit, and contributions are tax-deductible. We do not engage in campaigns to support any candidate for office. What we do is public education. Eventually, there will need to be political parties that have the wisdom to articulate this progressive middle path. In the meantime, our task is to build a strong movement of people who are ready to share these ideas with others and to challenge the distorted way Israel-Palestine is dealt with in political life.

24 *"Aren't you afraid that you may unwittingly be generating anti-Semitism?"*

Actually, the main danger for anti-Semitism comes from those who are suppressing debate about Israel. Israeli policies are destructive and hurtful, not only to the Palestinian people, but also to the moral integrity of the Jewish people. If Judaism and the Jewish people are seen as nothing but cheerleaders for the policy of a particular nation-state, they become tainted by all the compromises and distortions that are inevitably part of any political order, and all the more so when that political order is oppressing two million people who wish their own national self-determination.

For Jews who have suffered abuse and hatred for so long, the notion that there could be such a thing as anger at Jews for policies that we support seems incomprehensible. Isn't all anger at Jews simply irrational anti-Semitism? It's not anti-Semitic to be angry at those Jews who support Israeli policies that are oppressive. It is anti-Semitic when the anger gets directed at all Jews, or gets articulated in anti-Jewish language, because not all Jews do support the policies of Occupation or oppression of Palestinians, and talking as though all Jews are responsible for the distortions of some Jews is a classic case of racism.

But the biggest and most explosive source of anti-Semitism is the way that non-Jews are being treated by the American Jewish establishment today. When non-Jews are told that it is anti-Semitic to criticize Israel, they may be effectively silenced. But at some point in the future, when American global interests may not seem so well served by the current state of Israel, the media and American political leaders may not be so willing to support Israel or the American Jewish establishment. At that point, there is likely to be an explosion of anger against Israel and Jews by many people who have been silenced today and who unconsciously resent that fact. I watched this kind of thing happen when the Right in American politics was able to exploit the unconscious anger that many whites and many men felt at the way they had been disrespected and silenced in the process of women and African Americans getting their rights. It was that silencing, even more than disagreements about the actual policies of these civil rights groups, that was the basis for a huge explosion of anger against what was then called "PC" or political correctness.

Today, many Americans are experiencing the full pressure of a Jewish political correctness being pushed upon them by major elements in the organized sectors of the American Jewish community. I worry that it is this, more than anything, that will form the basis for a future explosion of anger against Jews. That's one of many reasons why as a Jew I believe that the most effective way to undermine anti-Semitism is to counter this kind of Jewish "PC" by putting out a counter message: it is NOT anti-Semitic to publicly question or criticize the policies of the State of Israel.

Of course, there are some anti-Semites who will use those criticisms to advance their own hateful agendas. All the more reason why we need to carefully distinguish between legitimate criticisms of the State and illegitimate criticisms of the entire Jewish people. Moreover, we need to insist that the criticisms of Israel be proportional to its crimes (not, for example, making it seem as if they rival the far worse crimes being perpetrated by many other nation states), that they be balanced (acknowledging and giving appropriate energy to critique of the crimes of some of those who speak on behalf of the Palestinian movement and the crimes of Arab states), and that they be accompanied with the kind of compassionate understanding with which we should view all of human activity at this moment in the evolution of consciousness. Without this balance, proportionality, and compassion, we can begin to suspect that there is real anti-Semitism being expressed and that we should fight against it.

25 *"So how do you manage to keep your hope when the obstacles are so great, when you yourself receive death threats frequently for saying what you say, when you find your views being distorted in the media and in public discourse, and when you find that you have neither the funding nor the political clout to make the changes you are fighting for?"*

It is true that this is not an easy moment or an easy position. There are people who are pro-Palestine who say that the Tikkun perspective is nothing but a carefully construed pro-Israel perspective, and there are people who are pro-Israel who say that the Tikkun perspective is nothing but a carefully construed pro-Palestine perspective. I get hate mail from both sides, although the death threats come mostly from fellow Jews who say that I am betraying the Jewish people, a traitor, "worse than Hitler," and many other hurtful and hateful things. It is particularly disturbing to me when I hear people saying that they "know" that I or Tikkun stand for things we simply do not stand for! I hope that you'll be able to help us a little on that point once you have absorbed the perspective articulated here, which is central to the vision of the Tikkun Community: a world of love is possible, but it can be built only if all of us acknowledge our own distortions and develop a path that involves both inner spiritual growth and healing, and outer social transformation to a world of peace and justice. It is this two-fold path, working both on ourselves as individuals and on the economic and political arrangements of the world, that is what we mean when we talk about having a spiritual orientation in the Tikkun Community.

I sustain a commitment to that process by strengthening my own inner spiritual practice of Judaism, but I know that there are many other spiritual paths. For me, the nourishment I get from observing Shabbat, doing the commandments, following the path of Jewish tradition, and doing that with a community of fellow Jews, is deeply sustaining. Studying Torah and Prophets, and all the elaborations, debates, midrash, and spiritual meanderings of our people through the past three thousand years provides me with a source of inspiration. Ultimately, it is my own personal connection to God, Spirit, the Power of Healing and Transformation, and knowing how that energy has manifested through history in the past, and witnessing it manifest in many loving beings whom I encounter and with whom I build community, that continues to provide me with a foundation for hope.

Our world can be healed. When we overcome all the cynical realism taught us by the shapers of public opinion, when we allow ourselves to be compassionate toward each other, when we refuse to allow the powerful to define for us the limits of the possible, when we learn to support each other in a spirit of generosity, we can build a world that corresponds to our highest ideals. Many blessings will come to you if you dedicate your life to building a world of peace, justice, generosity, and love. Let's do it together!

—Rabbi Michael Lerner
December 2, 2002

Appendix:

RESOURCES FOR PEACE

RECOMMENDED READING

Roane Carey and Jonathan Shann, *The Other Israel: Voices of Refusal and Dissent,* The New Press, 2002

Stanley Cohen, *States of Denial: Knowing About Atrocities and Suffering,* Polity Press, 2001

Abba Eban, *An Autobiography,* Random House, 1977

Abraham J. Edelheit, *History of Zionism,* Westview Press, 2000

Samih K. Farsoun, *Palestine and the Palestinians,* Westview Press, 1997

Hanan Hever, *Producing the Modern Hebrew Canon,* New York University Press, 2002

Arthur Hertzberg, *The Zionist Idea,* Jewish Publication Society, 1960

Rahsid Khalidi, *Palestinian Identity: The Construction of Modern National Consciousness,* Columbia University Press, 1997

Michael Lerner, *The Socialism of Fools: Anti-Semitism on the Left,* Tikkun Books, 1992

—*Jewish Renewal,* HarperPerennial, 1995

—*Spirit Matters: Global Healing and the Wisdom of the Soul,* Hampton Roads, 2000

Benny Morris, *The Birth of the Palestinian Refugee Problem, 1947–1949,* Cambridge University Press, 1988

—*Righteous Victims,* Alfred A. Knopf, 1999

Eugene L. Rogan and Avi Shlaim, eds. *The War for Palestine,* Cambridge University Press, 2001

Avi Shlaim, *The Politics of Partition,* Oxford University Press, 1998

—*The Iron Wall: Israel and the Arab World,* W.W. Norton & Co., 1999.

Zeev Sternhell, *The Founding Myths of Isael: Nationalism, Socialism and the Making of the Jewish State,* Princeton University, 1998

GETTING INVOLVED:
THE TIKKUN COMMUNITY

The Tikkun Community is an international organization of Jews, Christians, Muslims, Hindus, Buddhists, and many secular humanists who are committed to social healing and transformation, including bringing healing and reconciliation to Israel and Palestine.

Our national co-chairs are: Rabbi Michael Lerner, editor of TIKKUN Magazine, Cornel West, professor of divinity at Princeton University and author of *Race Matters,* and Susannah Heschel, chair of Jewish studies at Dartmouth.

The Tikkun Community operates on three levels:

a. An organization of local Tikkun Communities, each of which is composed of people who agree with the *Core Vision* (check it out at www.tikkun.org) and who have joined the national organization. The local communities work on many of the national projects, as well as their own projects.

b. A national organization that presents a national voice for all those who want to end the Occupation and bring peace and justice to the Middle East, and who have a compassionate attitude toward both sides along the lines reflected in this book. We have several national task forces and people in local Tikkun Communities are encouraged to be involved in one of them.

c. A national support network for people in a wide variety of social change movements who do not specifically work on Tikkun Community projects but who support the *Core Vision* and who get nurturance from participating in our activities.

Because we are under-funded, we are always in need of volunteers in our national office. Unpaid interns can work either for the year (and some of them in the past have eventually been hired when that was possible and appropriate) or for a three-month stint. Needless to say, we are also badly in need of financial support and fundraisers. Feel free to organize a benefit for us at any time and in any way that you choose.

Among the Task Forces of the Tikkun Community:

• **Media Critique:** Rapid Response

This group is meant to challenge the media and to insist on balanced and fair coverage of Israel/Palestine, Iraq, and the spiritual dimension of American political and social reality. We are seeking volunteers who will regularly call people both in the local and national media and challenge them to be more honest and to provide the public with information that is normally excluded from mainstream media—information based on the assumption that the pain and suffering of everyone on this planet is equally important, and that social justice and peace are equally necessary for everyone. Some members of this group read articles or listen to broadcasts and then write critiques of what they've heard, which are then posted on our website. Other members of this group actually call or write to the media and, using the critiques as background, proceed to challenge the journalists and editors to produce a fairer and more balanced perspective on contemporary political and social realities. Our current focus is on the way that Israel/Palestine news has a "spin" that casts one side as all-good and the other as all-bad. Part of the task of this task force is to encourage people to "partner" with specific media people, to develop a relationship with journalists and broadcasters so that they will be open to hearing our ideas. media@tikkun.org

• **Education**

This task force focuses on the immediate need to educate people about a "progressive middle path" in relation to the Middle East. Here are some of the spheres in which the Education Task Force will operate:

* Public Sphere:
  – Outreach to unions, churches, synagogues, mosques, ashrams, community organizations, non-profits, business leaders, professional organizations—finding ways to raise our issues in these contexts.
  – Teach-ins, conferences, lectures, weekend retreats.

- Leafletting, bringing information, and tabling at public events.
- Recruiting people into the Tikkun Community. Individuals within the committee are encouraged to hold house parties (or find Community members who can) where they invite a bunch of folks, show the Tikkun video, talk about Tikkun, have structured dialogue and bonding activities, in order to invite people into the community.
- Develop booklets, video tapes, audio tapes, movies, and material for our web site.

* Internal
  - Organizing trainings, retreats, and conferences for the Tikkun Community including an annual conference (like our Teach-In to Congress) on the East Coast and an annual retreat to recharge our spiritual and activist batteries and to provide in-depth learning and schmoozing for members of the Tikkun Community.
  - Organizes education for local Tikkun Communities including teaching nonviolent communication, bringing the insights of spiritual and philosophical traditions to focus on contemporary issues, and developing songs for the Tikkun Community.

• **Political Outreach**

Although we are not a political organization, and as a non-profit we are prohibited from endorsing candidates or in spending more than 5 percent of our energies in backing legislation, we are able to use the sphere of politics to accomplish public education. community@tikkun.org

* Legislative: This task force will work on outreach to educate our public officials about our perspective and The Tikkun Initiative for Middle East Peace (described above). It will also work to pass resolutions that articulate our ideals—either in local city councils, state legislatures, or even in the U.S. Congress. While we are not expecting our positions to get passed, we do believe that we can use this sphere to promote a serious public debate about fundamental issues that have been ignored or misrepresented in the public sphere. This task force will work with the Education Task Force in seeking endorsement of our positions by unions, community organizations, etc.

* Action: planning events and actions, NONVIOLENT confrontations with power—direct actions and demonstrations and rallies—trips to the Middle East to assist in nonviolent peace-oriented actions there.

* Bridging—Coalition building and outreach. This is so that we work together on issues whenever alignment is possible (including bringing in Arab/Muslim voices).

• **Tikkun Campus Network (TCN)**
We are creating chapters on college and high school campuses around the United States to educate about our "progressive middle path" of support for both Israel and Palestine. These groups will create teach-ins, seek to have the school governing bodies or student bodies endorse our Tikkun Initiative for Middle East Peace, organize demonstrations and nonviolent direct action in support of peace and justice, challenge anti-Semitism and anti-Palestinian propaganda, and create dialogues to replace angry confrontations. campus@tikkun.org

• **New Bottom Line**
The full idea of a New Bottom Line is presented in *Spirit Matters: Global Healing and the Wisdom of the Soul.* In short, it advocates that institutions should be judged efficient or productive not only to the extent that they maximize money or power, but also to the extent that they maximize people's capacities to be loving and caring, ethically and ecologically sensitive, and capable of responding to the universe with awe and wonder. With this New Bottom Line we can immediately see that the policies of both Israel and Palestine have been inefficient, unproductive, and irrational—as has been much of the foreign policy of the United States. In formulating the Middle East as part of the larger struggle for a world of kindness and generosity, the Tikkun Community sees the specifics of Healing Israel/Palestine as integrally connected with the task of healing and transforming the rest of life on this planet in ways that will encourage social justice, open-heartedness, generosity, and ecological responsibility.

* Organizing professional groups, unions, business people, and workers to create groups aimed at envisioning what their work world and professional orientation would be if there were a New Bottom Line of love and caring to replace the ethos of selfishness and materialism. This provides the larger framework for peace and justice work, by showing that the idea of a world based on caring is not utopian nonsense but rather an immediate and pressing need for everyone on the planet. We have a law group doing this kind of thinking now, but this task force will encourage the development of other such groups in different areas of work and professional life.

* Social Responsibility Amendment to the Constitution and the Social Responsibility Initiative. Requires corporations with incomes of $20 million or more to get a new corporate charter once every ten years which will be granted only to those corporations that can prove a history of social responsibility (as measured by an Ethical Impact Report) to a jury of ordinary citizens.

The Tikkun Community's national office is at 2107 Van Ness Avenue, Suite 302, San Francisco, CA 94109. Phone: 415-575-1200. Email: community@tikkun.org   Website: www.tikkun.org

OTHER ORGANIZATIONS
DOING PEACE AND JUSTICE WORK

There are many organizations doing peace and justice work in the Middle East and in the United States—so many that it would probably be possible to fill a book with the list of all of them. Some people argue that this is one of the problems for peace: the progressive forces cannot find a way to work together.

There is much legitimacy in this complaint. I've found that it is difficult to get the different peace and justice organizations to share information, much less to strategize together. Among the reasons for this: 1. Lack of adequate funding. Because the organizations have to compete for scarce support dollars, they often find it important to be able to stress to potential donors what they are doing that is unique—something that pushes them toward less cooperation with each other. 2. Ideological differences real and imagined. 3. Ego. Organizations and their leaders often develop a sense of their own special-ness. Moreover, the culture of progressives is one that tends to undervalue leadership and give it very little support (financially or emotionally), which gives an incentive for some to start their own little groupsicles where they can get the recognition that they deserve but can't find where the groups' interests merge. 4. Fear of national organization. Americans in particular have a strong tradition of grass roots organizing that mitigates against being part of a national organization. We've found that even local groups that understand that they would be far more effective if they linked and coordinated their activities with a national organization, nevertheless resist for fear that someone will be telling them what they should be doing. They feel more comfortable being relatively powerless but fully self-directing than being more powerful but yielding a certain amount of autonomy so that they could in fact work in concert with others.

There's also an argument in favor of a plurality of groups. Many of these groups work in different ways, appeal to different kinds of people, and hence attract those who might not be attracted to social justice and peace work were there only a few major organizations working in this sphere with homogenized agendas and styles.

Here are some of the organizations worthy of your consideration. In future editions of this book we will list more organizations, particularly those who intend to use this book for study groups and make it available for sale at their public events.

ISRAELI HUMAN RIGHTS GROUPS AND ADVOCATES OF PEACE

The Abraham Fund supports coexistence between Israel's Jewish and Palestinian Arab citizens.
15 Arlozorov Street
Jerusalem 92181 Israel
Phone: 972-2-566-5133
Fax: 972-2-566-5139
tafjer@netvision.net.il

Association for Civil Right in Israel (ACRI) works to protect the civil liberties and human rights of all individuals in both Israel and the Occupied Territories. It focuses on legal action, education, and public outreach.
P.O. Box 35401
Jerusalem 91352 Israel
mail@acri.org.il
www.acri.org.il/english-acri/engine/search.asp

Al-Haq monitors, documents and investigates human rights violations and conducts research pertaining to the rule of law in Occupied Territories to combat specific abuses.

Main St., Ramallah
P.O. Box 1413
West Bank, Palestinian Authority
haq@alhaq.org
www.alhaq.org

Bat Shalom A feminist peace organization of Israeli women. Bat Shalom, together with The Jerusalem Center for Women, a Palestinian women's peace organization, comprise The Jerusalem Link, which works to secure a just peace.

P.O. Box 8083
Jerusalem 91080 Israel
Phone: 972-2-563-1477
Fax: 972-2-561-7983
www.batshalom.org

Bereaved Parents Circle An organziation of Israelis and Palestinians who have lost close relatives as a result of the Israeli-Palestinian conflict, victims of war and terror. They are engaged in a media campaign and educational programs in support of peace in Israel and Palestine.

Yitzhak Frankenthal, General Manager
Ef'al Seminar, HaYasmin Street #1
Ramat Ef'al 52960 Israel
Phone: 972-3-535-5089
Fax: 972-3-635-8367
Frankent@netvision.net.il
www.theparentscircle.com

B'Tselem The Israeli Information Center for Human Rights in the Occupied Territories. B'tselem documents human rights abuses in the Occupied Territories and seeks to change Israeli policy in the Occupied Territories and ensure that its government, which rules the Occupied Territories, protects the human rights of residents there and complies with its obligations under international law. Its reports are printed in Hebrew and English and made available to media.

8 HaTa'asiya St.
Jerusalem 93420 Israel
Phone: 972-2-6735599
mail@btselem.org
www.BTselem.org

Coalition of Women for a Just Peace is an umbrella organization for eight to ten different women's peace organizations including Women in Black, Bat Shalom, NELED, New Profile, NOGA, MachsomWatch, TANDI, the 5th Mother and WILPF. CWJP identifies its principles at the CWJP Website.

www.coalitionofwomen4peace.org/coalitionID/EnglishIDCoalition

Gush Shalom Led by Uri Avneri, this is one of the most courageous parts of the Israeli peace movement. During the darkest days of the Barak and Sharon brainwashing it was sometimes a lone voice of sanity—when Peace Now was remarkably passive and quiet. It is heavily engaged in direct action (breaking the blockade on Palestinian villages and towns, rebuilding demolished homes, helping Palestinians to pick olives in areas threatened by the settlers) while initiating public campaigns (boycott of products of settlements, marking the Green Line, Jerusalem Capital of the Two States, warning IDF of war crimes) and conducting day-to-day peace education.

P.O. Box 3322
Tel-Aviv 61033 Israel
info@gush-Shalom.org

Hamoked (Center for the Defense of the Individual) An Israeli organization founded in 1988 to defend human rights in the Occupied Territories. It has provided assistance to several thousand Palestinian victims of violence, human rights abuses, and bureaucratic harassment. HaMoked registers complaints and follows through on them through administrative and legal channels until the matter is successfully resolved. In addition to its individual assistance, HaMoked advocates for human rights at the policy level.

    www.ariga.com/humanrights/hamoked.htm

Israeli Committee Against House Demolitions (ICAHD) Nonviolent direct-action group established to oppose and resist Israeli demolition of Palestinian homes. Also resists land expropriation, settlement expansion, by-pass road construction, policies of "closure" and "separation," the wholesale uprooting of fruit and olive trees and more. Activities include: rebuilding razed homes and replanting uprooted trees. Members include Israeli peace and human rights organizations who coordinate with local Palestinian organizations. Jeff Halper, coordinator.

Jerusalem Center for Women Palestinian non-governmental women's center in East Jerusalem, created in 1994 as a parallel to the Israeli Bat Shalom group. Activities include monitoring human rights abuses by the Israeli government and the Palestinian Authority. Until the start of the new Intifada conducted joint dialogue and conflict resolution courses with Bat Shalom for Israeli and Palestinian women and joint-run symposiums such as "Sharing Jerusalem: Two Capitals for Two States."

    www.j-c-w.org

Keshet-Mizrahi Group aiming to equalize Israeli society for Sephardim or North African Jews. Members are mainly second generation Mizrahi Jews.

Machsom Watch Organization of about seventy Israeli women who, since the start of the al-Aqsa Intifada, have been keeping watch on Israeli actions at checkpoints in and around the West Bank. (Mark Dow, "Crossing the Threshold", *In These Times,* April 26, 2002, www.inthese
times.com/issue/26/13/feature5.shtml)

New Profile seeks to change the profile of Israeli society from a militarized society of war and might, to an actively peacemaking society in which the rights of all people are respected and promoted equally, and the military occupation of others' lands ends.
    www.newprofile.org

Netivot Shalom – Oz L'Shalom Religious peace group. Oz L'shalom, formed in 1975, was a small group of Orthodox Jews, who describe themselves as the only religious Zionist peace organization. It merged with Neviot Shalom, which uses Jewish law and tradition as a basis to support or oppose political and military activities, trying to unhook right-wing policies from Judaism.
    P.O. Box 4433
    Jerusalem 91043 Israel
    Phone: 02 566 4218

Palestinian Center for Rapprochement PCR is a Palestinian community service center. Dialogues aimed at developing mutual understanding, activating participants to work for peace and justice, educating and training for peace and reconciliation, and the work to increase the public role in building a just and lasting peace in the region, are high on the agenda of PCR. PCR seeks to activate and lead people in a nonviolent resistance against occupation and for human and national rights.
    64 Start Street, Beit Sahour
    P.O.Box 4, Palestine
    www/rapprochement.org

Physicians for Human Rights-Israel promotes and protects the medical human rights of all residents of Israel and the Occupied Terriotires.
30 Levanda St., Tel Aviv 66020 Israel

Public Committee Against Torture in Israel
P.O.B. 4634
Jerusalem 91046 Israel
pcati@netvision.net.il
www.stoptorture.net.il

Rabbis for Human Rights A group of some ninety ordained rabbis and a number of rabbinic students founded in 1988 during the first Intifada that works to counter violations of human rights of West Bank Palestinians and Israeli Arabs. Also deals with issues related to foreign workers, women's rights and Ethiopian Jews, and seeks to give voice to the Jewish tradition of human rights. Members are Israeli citizens. There is no political affiliation or ideology. Co-Directors Rabbi Arik Ascherman and Rabbi Jeremy Milgrom have been involved in direct action on behalf of Paletinian rights in the West Bank.
www.rhr.israel.net/overview.shtml

Ta'ayush Arab-Jewish group that engages in direct actions of solidarity and humanitarian aid to besieged Palestinian towns and villages. Actions are carried out by Palestinian and Jewish citizens of Israel, in coordination with Palestinians in the Occupied Territories. They include bringing convoys of food and medicine to Palestinian villages, protesting, and trying to defy the Israeli siege and closure of Palestinian areas.
http://taayush.tripod.com/taayush.html
http://minerva.tau.ac.il

Yesh Gvul A group of Israeli soldiers and reserve officers who are refusing to serve in the Occupied Territories. Their website stresses the right and the duty of every soldier to scrutinize his/her orders and reject those he/she finds morally and politically repugnant.

  P.O. Box 6953
  Jerusalem 91068 Israel
  Phone: 972 2 6250271
  Fax: 972 2 6434171
  peretz@yesh-gvul.org

Tel Aviv Independent Media Center
  www.indymedia.org.il

U.S. Based Middle East Peace Organizations

Americans for Peace Now The mission of Americans for Peace Now [APN] is to help Israel and the *Shalom Achshav* movement in Israel to achieve a comprehensive political settlement of the Arab-Israeli conflict consistent with Israel's long-term security needs and its Jewish and democratic values.

  1815 H Street, NW, Suite 920
  Washington, DC 20006
  Phone: (202) 728-1893
  apndc@peacenow.org
  www.peacenow.org

Am Kolel is a Judaic Resource and Renewal Center devoted to meeting unmet spiritual needs in the Jewish community and responding to issues in society with a progressive Jewish presence. Their Tikkun Olam Committee is concerned with domestic, Middle East, and global issues. Rabbi David Shneyer is the founder and spiritual leader.

  15 West Montgomery Ave.
  Rockville, MD 20850
  Phone: (301) 309-2310
  am-kolel.org

Brit Tzedek v'Shalom, the Jewish Alliance for Justice and Peace, is a national organization of American Jews deeply committed to Israel's well-being through the achievement of a negotiated settlement to the Israeli-Palestinian conflict. Major focus: to generate greater dialogue within the American Jewish community in order to direct U.S. foreign policy toward the realization of a just peace.

P.O. Box 180175

Chicago, IL 60618-0175

info@btvshalom.org

www.btvshalom.org

Churches for Middle East Peace CMEP, an interdenominational Christian group, advocates peace and justice for Palestinians via a two state solution, a shared Jerusalem, respect for the rights of Palestinian Christians and protection of Christian holy places. Corinne Whitlatch is executive director.

100 Maryland Ave. NE, Suite 313

Washington, DC 20002

Phone: (202) 488-5613

cmepdc@aol.com

www.cmep.org

Christian Peacemaker Teams Christian Peacemaker Teams-Hebron is an initiative among Mennonite and Church of the Brethren congregations and Friends Meetings that supports violence reduction efforts around the world. A small team has gone to live in Hebron and daily communicates to the world the assaults on Palestinians by the IDF and by Israeli settlers in Hebron (but also critiques Palestinian violence).

P.O. Box 6508

Chicago, IL 60680

Phone: (773) 277-0253

cptheb@palnet.com

The Compassionate Listening Project Brings groups to the Middle East to listen to both sides.

P.O. Box 17
Indianola, WA 98342
Phone: (360) 297-2280
Fax: (360) 297-6563
office@mideastdiplomacy.org
www.mideastdiplomacy.org

Foundation for Middle East Peace Dedicated to informing Americans about the Israeli-Palestinian conflict and assisting in a peaceful solution that brings security for both peoples.

1761 N St. NW
Washington, DC 20036
Phone: (202) 835-3650
info@fmep.org or pcwilcox@fmep.org or jeff@fmep.org
www.fmep.org

The Jewish-Palestinian Living Room Dialogue Group An initiative to bring American Palestinians and Jews together for a long-term dialogue to discover common ground and improve the environment for reconciliation here in America.

1448 Cedarwood Drive
San Mateo, CA 94403
Phone: (650) 574-8303
Fax: (650) 573-1217
LTRAUBMAN@igc.org
www.igc.org/traubman/

Jewish Peace Fellowship is a nondenominational Jewish organization committed to active nonviolence as a means of resolving conflict, drawing on Jewish traditional sources and contemporary peacemaking sages.

P.O. Box 271
Nyack, NY 10960
Phone: (914) 348-4601
jpf@forusa.org
www.jewishpeacefellowship.org/Us.htm

A Jewish Voice for Peace is a diverse and democratic community of activists inspired by Jewish tradition to work together for peace, social justice, and human rights. They support the aspirations of Israelis and Palestinians for security and self-determination.

P.O. Box 13286
Berkeley, CA 94712
Phone: (415) 789-8279
info@jewishvoiceforpeace.org
www.jewishvoiceforpeace.org

The Middle East Children's Alliance works for peace and justice in the Middle East, focusing on Palestine, Israel, Lebanon and Iraq. Their programs emphasize the need to educate North Americans about the Middle East and U.S. foreign policy, and seek to insure the human rights of all people in the region, especially the rights of children.

905 Parker Street
Berkeley, California USA 94710
Phone: (510) 548.0542
www.mecaforpeace.org

Open Tent's mission is to promote understanding and appreciation of Middle Eastern cultures and faith traditions, and to engender mutual respect, harmony, cooperation, and a sense of shared heritage among people of Middle Eastern backgrounds.

1033 N. Orlando Avenue
Los Angeles CA 90069-4207
Phone: (323) 650-3157
www.opentent.org
OpenTent@aol.com

Seeds of Peace brings Arab and Israeli teenagers together from across the Middle East to interact and develop leadership and conflict resolution skills "before fear, mistrust and prejudice blind them from seeing the human face of their enemy."

370 Lexington Avenue, Suite 401
New York, NY 10017
Phone: (212) 573-8040
info@seedsofpeace.org
www.seedsofpeace.org

The Shalom Center is a network of American Jews who draw on Jewish tradition and spirituality to seek peace, pursue justice, and heal the earth. It is associated with Aleph: the organization of Jewish Renewal. Director: Arthur Waskow.

  6711 Lincoln Drive
  Philadelphia, PA 19119
  Phone: (215) 844-8494
  Shalomctr@aol.com
  www.shalomctr.org

The Tikkun Community is the international organization for peace, justice and reconciliation that has published this book. For more information, look at the detailed desciption just above this list of organizations.

  2107 Van Ness Ave
  San Francisco, CA 94109
  Phone: (415) 575 1200
  community@tikkun.org
  www.tikkun.org

U.S. Interreligious Committee for Peace is a national organization of American Jews, Christians and Muslims. The Committee carries on programs of dialogue, education and advocacy in support of U.S.policies for comprehensive and lasting peace between Israel, the Palestinians and the Arab states. Director: Ronald Young.

  16020 94th Avenue NW
  Stanwood, WA 98292
  Phone: (360) 652-4285
  USICPME@aol.com.

Rabbi Michael Lerner was mentored by Abraham Joshua Heschel at the Jewish Theological Seminary in New York. He received a Ph.D. in philosophy (ethics and political philosophy) from the University of California, Berkeley in 1972 and a Ph.D. in social/clinical psychology from the Wright Institute in Berkeley in 1977. Since then he served as director of the Institute for Labor and Mental Health, Dean of the Graduate School of Psychology at New College of California, and founder of Beyt Midrash le'Shalom in Jerusalem. He received rabbinic ordination from Rabbi Zalman Schachter-Shalomi and now serves as rabbi of Beyt Tikkun synagogue in San Francisco, California.

He was the co-founder of TIKKUN Magazine and has served as the editor since its inception in 1986. He is the author of *The Socialism of Fools: Anti-Semitism on the Left* (TIKKUN Books, 1992), *Surplus Powerlessness* (Humanities Press, 1992), *Jewish Renewal: A Path to Healing and Transformation* (HarperPerennial, 1995), *The Politics of Meaning* (Addison Wesley, 1996), and *Spirit Matters: Global Healing and the Wisdom of the Soul* (Hampton Roads, 2000).